W9-BRZ-586

SOLZHENITSYN

TWENTIETH CENTURY VIEWS

The aim of this series is to present the best in contemporary critical opinion on major authors, providing a twentieth century perspective on their changing status in an era of profound revaluation.

Maynard Mack, *Series Editor*
Yale University

SOLZHENITSYN

A COLLECTION OF CRITICAL ESSAYS

Edited by
Kathryn Feuer

Prentice-Hall, Inc. *Englewood Cliffs, N.J.*

A SPECTRUM BOOK

Library of Congress Cataloging in Publication Data
MAIN ENTRY UNDER TITLE:

Solzhenitsyn : a collection of critical essays.

    (Twentieth century views) (A Spectrum Book; S-TC-126)
    Bibliography: p.
    CONTENTS: Feuer, K. B. Introduction.
Aucouturier, M.—Solzhenitsyn's art.   Kasack, W.
Epic and dramatic structure in Solzhenitsyn's
work. [etc.]
    1.–Solzhenitsyn, Aleksandr Isaevich, 1918–
—Criticism and interpretation—Addresses, essays,
lectures.   I.–Feuer, Kathryn.
PG3488.04Z886   891.7'8'4409   75–34416
ISBN 0-13-822627-X
ISBN 0-13-822619-6 pbk.

10 9 8 7 6 5 4 3 2 1

PRENTICE-HALL INTERNATIONAL, INC. *(London)*
PRENTICE-HALL OF AUSTRALIA, PTY. LTD. *(Sydney)*
PRENTICE-HALL OF CANADA, LTD. *(Toronto)*
PRENTICE-HALL OF India PRIVATE LIMITED *(New Delhi)*
PRENTICE-HALL OF JAPAN, INC. *(Tokyo)*
PRENTICE-HALL OF SOUTHEAST ASIA PTE. LTD. *(Singapore)*

To the memory

of

JULIAN GRIGOR'EVICH OKSMAN (1894–1970)

eminent Russian literary scholar,
survivor of ten years in Soviet labor camps
and further years of exile,
who, like Solzhenitsyn, after his "rehabilitation"
chose the courageous course of thinking,
living, and writing as a free man,
and who then, like Solzhenitsyn,
expelled from the Union of Soviet Writers
and thus deprived of the means of earning his living,
refused to recant
but rather continued his work
for the freedom of Russia and of Russian literature,
work which will endure
when the names of his persecutors
are buried by history—or by infamy

Contents

On Reading *The Gulag Archipelago*

Solzhenitsyn in English: An Evaluation

Solzhenitsyn and Autonomy

Acknowledgments

Quotations from *The Gulag Archipelago, 1918–1956, An Experiment in Literary Invvestigation* by Aleksandr I. Solzhenitsyn, translated from the Russian by Thomas P. Whitney, are used by kind permission of Harper & Row, Publishers, Inc. and William Collins Sons & Co., Ltd. Copyright © 1973 by Aleksandr I. Solzhenitsyn. English language translation Copyright © 1973, 1974 by Harper & Row, Publishers, Inc.

Quotations from *The First Circle* by Aleksandr I. Solzhenitsyn, translated from the Russian by Thomas P. Whitney, are used by kind permission of Harper & Row, Publishers, Inc. and William Collins Sons & Co., Ltd. Copyright © 1968 by Harper & Row, Publishers, Inc. English translation Copyright © 1968 by Harper & Row, Publishers, Inc.

Quotations from *Cancer Ward* by Aleksandr I. Solzhenitsyn, translated by Nicholas Bethell and David Burg, are used by kind permission of Farrar, Straus & Giroux, Inc. and The Bodley Head Ltd. Copyright © 1968, 1969 by The Bodley Head Ltd.

Quotations from "Nobel Lecture" by Aleksandr I. Solzhenitsyn, translated by Alexis Klimoff, from *Aleksandr Solzhenitsyn: Critical Essays and Documentary Materials,* J. Dunlop, R. Haugh, and A. Klimoff, editors, are used by kind permission of Nordland Publishing Company.

Quotations from *"August 1914:* Solzhenitsyn and Tolstoy" by Kathryn B. Feuer are used by kind permission of Nordland Publishing Company.

Quotations from "Solzhenitsyn and the Legacy of Tolstoy" by Kathryn B. Feuer, originally published by the University of California Press, are reprinted by permission of The Regents of the University of California.

An excerpt from A. Solzhenitsyn's reply to George Meany's letter of February 25, 1974, is used by permission of the AFL-CIO.

The map of the Soviet secret prison (Gulag) system is used by kind permission of Isaac Don Levine and the AFL-CIO. Copyright © 1951 by Isaac Don Levine.

LOCATION OF FORCED LABOR CAMPS IN THE SOVIET UNION

This is an adaptation of a map compiled by Isaac Don Levine in 1951 and published by the Free Trade Union Committee of the American Federation of Labor. The size and scope of the forced labor camp network in the Soviet Union was originally verified through thousands of release certificates. These stated the location of the particular camp in which the prisoner was confined and bore the seal of the NKVD.

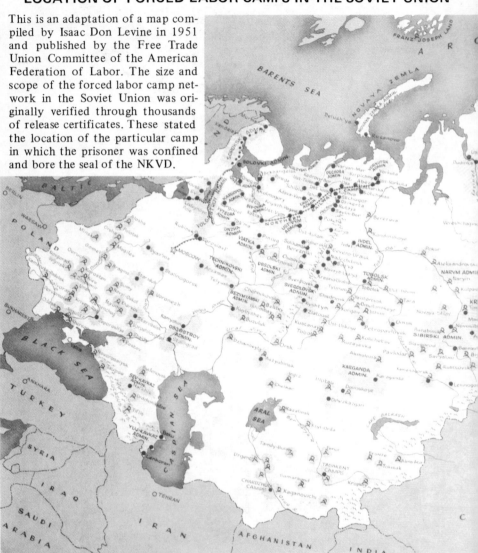

Areas in gray indicate groups of camps under the central GULAG control system. Hammer and sickle symbols indicate individual camps under control of local authorities

SOLZHENITSYN

Introduction

by Kathryn B. Feuer

Solzhenitsyn is now so much a part of our consciousness that it is hard to realize that his first work, *One Day in the Life of Ivan Denisovich*, was published barely a dozen years ago, in November 1962, and that his first novels appeared only in 1968. The reader will not then expect to find here articles in which a great writer's works are recollected in tranquillity. Yet he will find, I think, that despite their different approaches the critics are in remarkable agreement as to the essential features of Solzhenitsyn's art.[1] That Solzhenitsyn's work has already evoked so many studies of high quality is eloquent testimony to his artistic power, and eloquent refutation—should such be needed—of the view that his reputation rests more on his political fate than on his talent.

Many of these essential features are adumbrated in Michel Aucouturier's fine appreciative essay. Solzhenitsyn is a realist whose works, without being designedly "symbolist," achieve the symbolic realm of all true art. Robert Louis Jackson specifies this view in his meticulous demonstration of how the story "Matryona's Home" translates words into a Russian icon, while Georges Nivat discovers much illuminating use of symbol in the novels. Another point of agreement is that Solzhenitsyn is—in our aesthetically fastidious age—unashamedly a moralist. Art and morality: their conjunction is only one sign of what Mary McCarthy has called "The Tolstoy Connection" and a sign too of Solzhenitsyn's talent for irony and anger which, sometimes in a phrase, sometimes in a series of chapters, transforms polemic into high art. Although Solzhenitsyn markedly departs from the Tolstoyan novel in his extreme compression of time-span, his gift for the delicate prolongation of the moment is very much in the Tolstoyan pattern as is his preference for works *de longue*

---

[1] This impression will be confirmed by the essays in the superb collection, *Aleksandr Solzhenitsyn: Critical Essays and Documentary Materials*, listed in the Bibliography of this volume. The collection was edited by John B. Dunlop, Richard Haugh, and Alexis Klimoff; it will be cited henceforth as Dunlop *et al.*, eds., *Aleksandr Solzhenitsyn*.

haleine (as Tolstoy described *War and Peace*), that is, works open-ended or epic in scope. Wolfgang Kasack goes far beyond this generalization in his penetrating study.

Solzhenitsyn's deep religious faith and intense patriotism have been universally noted. These fundamentals of his creed were apparent in *The First Circle* and *Cancer Ward*; their consummate importance became clear, however, in *August 1914*, as Nikita Struve's masterly discussion demonstrates. In his "Afterword" to that work, Solzhenitsyn explains why he has for the first time sent a book abroad: because in the USSR it would be necessary to print the word "God" without a capital G.[2] Russia and Religion are here tightly entwined; only piety could make Solzhenitsyn violate his overriding precept, that he writes for publication in his country and for his fellow countrymen. In this he is linked to many of his great forebears, who wrote for the unhappy many of their nation but whose works have achieved, almost despite their authors' intentions, the universality of all true art.

Solzhenitsyn's "Afterword" and *August 1914* announce another equally important tenet of his thought and art, his belief in History as, along with the wine of Christian faith, the spiritual bread essential for his nation's survival. One could have deduced from his earlier works that Solzhenitsyn was writing history as witness, but it was *August 1914* which made clear his belief in the *necessity* of history. Patricia Blake's essay elucidates the issue with a depth of "Solzhenitsyn scholarship" as well as historical scholarship.

And finally, among the essential features of Solzhenitsyn's art—language. For his Russian readers no aspect of his work has been so stunning. It is as if he is single-handedly trying to restore to Russia not only her history but also her happier heritage, her vivid, ever-creative spoken language, and her subtly expressive written language, which, since the 1930s, have been buried under layers of pompous bureaucratese, clumsy prudishness, cloying Pecksniffian sentimentalism, and falsifying euphemisms—buried and also ossified into reactionary syntactic forms strongly "influenced" by Stalin's literary style, whose pounding effect can best be conveyed by comparison to a verbal migraine headache. Solzhenitsyn said in his "Letter to the Fourth

---

[2] Solzhenitsyn's "Afterword" has, incomprehensibly, been omitted from the English translation of *August 1914*. It can be found, however, in the collection of documents edited by Leopold Labedz, *Solzhenitsyn: A Documentary Record*, cited in the Bibliography of this volume. The reader may be interested to know that in the recent twenty-volume scholarly edition of Tolstoy, the spelling of God has also been changed to the lower case, although Tolstoy's capitals were preserved in the great Soviet Jubilee Edition of his works.

Congress of Soviet "Writers"[3] that creative, innovative Russian literature need not die; his own works demonstrate its survival and also the survival of a richly productive and expressive spoken Russian. Because language is the essential ingredient of literature and the one least accessible to the foreign reader, I am particularly pleased to be able to include here the sensitive study by Alexis Klimoff of Solzhenitsyn's works in English translation. In singling out the translators' successes and failures, Klimoff illuminates for the non-reader of Russian (and for the Russian reader less expert than he) much that is linguistically and stylistically distinctive in Solzhenitsyn's work.[4]

When I began this collection Solzhenitsyn was still in the Soviet Union and my intention was to include only purely literary studies. Since then Solzhenitsyn has begun the publication of *Archipelago GULag*,[5] been arrested, then forcibly exiled. I think that the literary emphasis remains valid, yet it would be scrupulousness gone mad to consider Solzhenitsyn's works in an aesthetic vacuum; to deny their political impact would be as constrictive as to deny their moral nature. It is valuable, especially for readers to whom Stalin is a man who died before they were born, to know that the events described in *Gulag* did indeed happen and that not all the horrors have yet been catalogued. The bracing, incisive review by Robert Conquest, a long-time student of Soviet internal politics, should always be borne in mind by those who might otherwise deduce from Solzhenitsyn's subtitle ("an attempt at artistic investigation") that some kind of "artistic license" has been taken with the facts.

Conquest's review raises another consideration, that many of the facts about the Soviet camp system have been long known in the West but somehow pushed to the outskirts of consciousness. There can be no more striking evidence of this than the map "Location of Forced

---

[3] The text of the Letter may be found in Dunlop *et al., op. cit.,* and also in Labedz, *op. cit.*

[4] See also the fine article by Donald Fanger, "Art and Foreign Matter," in Dunlop *et al., op. cit.,* and also in the same volume articles on Solzhenitsyn's language by Boris Unbegaun and Vera Carpovich. (For those who read Russian the study by T. G. Vinokur, "O yazyke i stile povesti . . . 'Odin den' Ivana Denisovicha'" [*Voprosy kul'tury rechi*, no. 6, 1965] is an essential work. Insights will also be found in the studies by Leonid Rzhevsky.)

[5] Solzhenitsyn's Russian title is "ARKHIPELAG GULag." "GULag" is an acronym, one of many widely used in the USSR; its first three capital letters stand for *C*hief *A*dministration of the *C*amps; its last two letters complete the first syllable of *lager*, camp. Since this spelling is distracting to English readers, I shall write *Gulag* hereafter, except in quotation of the Russian title.

Labor Camps in the Soviet Union" (see p. xiv). On February 25, 1974, on behalf of the AFL-CIO, President George Meany invited Solzhenitsyn to visit the United States and enclosed a copy of the map which, as Mr. Meany remarked in his letter, the American Federation of Labor had published *"a quarter century ago."* (Italics added.) In his reply of March 5 Solzhenitsyn commented:

> And this is a sign of the extent of the great disintegration and lack of information in the world: That I, who for so many years was concerned with problems of Soviet slave labor camps, had no idea of the generous support for our sufferers on the part of the American Federation of Labor nor of the publication by *you* of the GULag map. (I had tried on my own to put one together!)[6]

The map was compiled and copyrighted by the eminent expert on Soviet affairs, Isaac Don Levine, and first published by him in the May 1947 issue of *Plain Talk.*

Further testimony to the accuracy of Solzhenitsyn's facts is offered by Roy Medvedev, another distinguished student of Soviet political history and one who writes from within the Soviet Union, although his works appear there only in *samizdat.*[7] Medvedev's insistence, in his review of *Gulag,* on Solzhenitsyn's factualness is impressive evidence, because he does not accept Solzhenitsyn's fundamental premises: that what we have come to call (or dismiss as) Stalinism was implicit in Leninism and the October Revolution from the outset; that the same principles, only modified in application, reign in the USSR today. I find Solzhenitsyn's case overwhelmingly persuasive, Medvedev's a

---

[6] The complete texts of Mr. Meany's letter and of Solzhenitsyn's reply may be found in "News from the AFL-CIO," March 15, 1974. The invitation was accepted by Solzhenitsyn in the summer of 1975. See the *Chronology of Important Dates* in this volume.

[7] *"Samizdat,"* self-publishing, is the term widely used in the Soviet Union for the practice of copying and circulating typescripts of manuscripts forbidden by the authorities. The story is often told of the mother who pays a typist 500 rubles to make a copy of *War and Peace,* which can be purchased anywhere for less than 5, "because my son won't read anything unless it's in *samizdat.*" The term is an acronym, coined from *"sam,"* self, and the first two syllables of *"izdatel'stvo,"* publishing house; it is also an evident mockery of *"Gosizdat"* the acronym for the State Publishing House. *"Samizdat"* has generated two further additions to the Russian language: *"Tamizdat"* and *"Khamizdat."* *"Tam"* means there; *"kham"* means a semieducated boor. Thus *"tamizdat"* refers to Russian literature published outside the Soviet Union, but smuggled in (such as Solzhenitsyn's novels), while *"khamizdat"* refers to Russian literature or Western works on the USSR secretly printed in small editions restricted to high party and police officials. Such was the publication of Solzhenitsyn's play, *The Feast of the Conquerors,* cited in note 16, p. 9. The possession or distribution of *samizdat* can be a criminal offense.

moving and eloquent testament of faith and courage rather than a convincing refutation. Surely, however, there can be only one opinion—unmitigated gratification—that there *are* open and honorable debates among the Soviet dissenters or "freethinkers," [8] and also unalloyed admiration that the fatal temptation to conceal disagreements and to speak in "one voice" has been resisted.

Solzhenitsyn belongs to the great tradition of Russian writers in having accepted as a patriotic and moral obligation a burden created by Tsarist censorship and perpetuated by the more brutal and adroit Soviet censorship, the notion of the writer's role as spokesman for the conscience of the nation. It is a role which has subjected Russian writers to a peculiar fate: the conviction held by readers that every detail of an artist's private life, social behavior, or political opinions is a proper subject for public praise and blame, advice and admonition. While he was in great physical danger in the Soviet Union Solzhenitsyn was somewhat sheltered from such controversies (just as Dostoevsky was during his ten years in Siberia); now that he and his family are safe, however, one must expect forbearance to be replaced by stormy debate.[9] Though I do not wish to write about Solzhenitsyn

[8] Andrey Sakharov has written that instead of "dissenters" (*inakomyslashchie*—those who think otherwise) he is "fonder of the old Russian word for 'freethinkers,' *volnomyslyashchie*." See his extremely interesting article, "How I Came to Dissent," *The New York Review of Books*, March 21, 1974, pp. 11–12.

[9] Indeed the debates in the Russian intellectual community, inside and outside the USSR, are already stormy, but here I shall comment only on the response of Western observers. Solzhenitsyn's patriotism, his Christianity, his refusal to summon the Russian population to take up their pitchforks against their armed government, his unwillingness to demand nothing less than immediate parliamentary democracy from rulers who have waded to power through corpses, all this has dismayed many Western liberals, as have his trenchant criticisms of the double standard by which Soviet mass atrocities are regarded as less scandalous than democracies' misdemeanors or authoritarian governments' individual atrocities. (See "The Real Solzhenitsyn" by Jeri Laber, *Commentary*, May 1974, pp. 32–35, and also the extensive correspondence about this article, *Commentary*, September 1974, pp. 8–18.)

At the same time, there has been a remarkably thoughtful response from some often associated with the "New Left." To cite only two examples: "Solzhenitsyn: A Footnote to the Book of the Dead," by Joe Esterhas (*Rolling Stone*, August 1, 1974, pp. 42–47) and "The Penal Colony Known as the USSR," by Irving Louis Horowitz (*Transaction*, July–August 1974, pp. 22–26). As to the "Old Left," the French Communist Party has shown the same forthright double-face it manifested at the Soviet invasion of Czechoslovakia, while the Italian Party seems to have been genuinely shaken, both by the invasion and by Solzhenitsyn. The most striking evidence of the problem Solzhenitsyn has posed for Communists loyal to, or unwilling totally to break from, the Soviet regime is found in the study by the late Georg Lukacs, *Solzhenitsyn* (Cambridge, Mass.: M.I.T. Press, 1971). Whether Lukacs was the man (he has made clear his distaste for personal publicity) I think one can predict that the qualities which sustained him when he and his family were in physical jeopardy will continue to support him in exile. These qualities are admirably defined in Walter Kaufmann's discussion of "Solzhenitsyn and Autonomy."

Although publication of *The Gulag Archipelago* was a political event of incalculable importance, the book is above all a work of art which will be read when the brutalities of the first half decade of Soviet power have receded to the footnote status of Holinshed's *Chronicles*. George Gibian and Victor Erlich have undertaken the forbidding task of literary analysis of this unprecedented work. Gibian's association of Solzhenitsyn's method with that of Walter Scott opens up a valuable new dimension for our understanding of the "documentary" strain in all his work. Erlich's deceptively modest title, "On Reading *The Gulag Archipelago*," masks the rich store of philosophic and artistic insights to be found in his article, which, it should be noted, discusses not only Parts I–II but also the recently published Parts III–IV.

---

trying to save Solzhenitsyn (and he did try to save others) by demonstrating that he was, somehow, a writer of "socialist realism" or trying to save "socialist realism" by demonstrating that it had produced a Solzhenitsyn, can be determined only by a master dialectician. This sad book is admirably analyzed by Irving Howe in "Lukacs and Solzhenitsyn," Dunlop *et al.*, eds., *Aleksandr Solzhenitsyn*, pp. 147–55; and see also the review by "e.e." in *Canadian Slavonic Papers* 13, nos. 2–3 (1971): 253–60.

On the other hand, the Old non-Bolshevik Left were among the first to grasp Solzhenitsyn's political significance, in such works as *Rebels and Bureaucrats: Soviet Conflicts as Seen in Solzhenitsyn's "Cancer Ward,"* by George Saunders (Merit Press: New York, 1969) and "Alexander Solzhenitsyn—A New Historic Impulse," by Dora Taylor (*International Socialist Review,* June 1972, pp. 32–39). And it was *Intercontinental Press* which alone (at least in the U.S.) published the full text of Roy Medvedev's review of *Gulag* (in their issue of March 25, 1974) and who have generously made their translation available to me for inclusion in this volume. Mention should perhaps also be made of the response to Solzhenitsyn within the Soviet Union. Between 1962 and 1965, when it was possible to publish favorable or objective accounts of his work, the most notable contributions were made by Alexander Tvardovsky, the editor of *Novyi Mir*, in his introduction to *One Day in the Life of Ivan Denisovich* (included in several English translations of that work) and by V. I. Lakshin, whose articles may be found in Priscilla Johnson, *Khrushchev and the Arts* (Cambridge, Mass.: M.I.T. Press, 1965, pp. 275–88) and in *The Current Digest of the Soviet Press* 16, no. 12 (April 15, 1964): 3–8, and 18, no. 46 (December 7, 1966): 9–12. Since 1965, a great deal has been written about Solzhenitsyn and circulated in *samizdat;* Roy Medvedev's review of *Gulag* is one example, and he has now written a review of the second volume. Lidiya Chukovskaya, the critic and novelist, has also made notable contributions to this literature, which is so voluminous that in 1973 the YMCA Press published, in Russian, an entire volume devoted to *samizdat* articles on *August 1914* alone. While I am not competent to comment on the response to Solzhenitsyn's work in Eastern Europe, I am told that within the limitations of censorship there, it has been lively and enthusiastic.

Michel Aucouturier points out that of *Ivan Denisovich, First Circle*, and *Cancer Ward* Solzhenitsyn has called only the second a "novel." Since then, *August 1914* has appeared; its title page reads "Knot 1," while *The Gulag Archipelago* is subtitled "an attempt at artistic investigation." Despite some of the mildly experimental techniques of *August 1914*, Solzhenitsyn has made it clear that he is not an admirer of the "new novel"; [10] he has been quoted: "What genre do I consider the most interesting? A polyphonic novel with concrete details specifying the time and place of action. A novel without a central hero. . . . Each character becomes central when the action reverts to him." [11]

Innovation *within* the genre; so it has been in Russian fiction from the beginning: *Eugene Onegin*, a "Novel in Verse"; *Dead Souls*, a *"Poema"*; Lermontov's *Hero of Our Time*, a "novel" composed of five tales artfully linked by play with chronology, with narrational modes, and with frames within frames; Goncharov's *Oblomov*, which achieves the unity of a novel only through the presence within it of a previously written étude, "Oblomov's Dream." Turgenev attached great importance to the distinction between his novels and his novellas; Tolstoy and Dostoevsky virtually invented the philosophic novel. Exploratory reshaping of the realistic novel continued through the 1920s and doubtless lives on today, in desk drawers and shoeboxes scattered over the Soviet Union, as it lives in the works of the well-known American writer of Russian descent, Vladimir Nabokov. It was Tolstoy who best defined this phenomenon: *"War and Peace,"* he said, "is not a novel, still less a poem, still less an historical chronicle. *War and Peace* is that which the author wanted to and could express, in the form in which it has *been* expressed." [12] And more generally:

[10] At Solzhenitsyn's meeting with the Secretariat of the Union of Soviet Writers, September 22, 1967, he argued: "In the West they say the novel is dead, and we gesticulate and deliver speeches saying that it is not dead. But rather than make speeches we should publish novels—such novels as would make them blink as if from a brilliant light, and then the 'new novel' would die down and the 'neo–avant-gardists' would disappear." See Labedz, *op. cit.*

[11] Quoted by Ludmila Koehler, "Eternal Themes in Solzhenitsyn's *The Cancer Ward*," *The Russian Review*, January 1969. The quotation is taken from an interview with Solzhenitsyn by Pavel Lichko, published in *Slovacky Zhivot*, March 31, 1967; an English translation appears in Labedz, *op. cit.* Although, as is explained in Labedz' introduction to the article, Lichko seems to have played a dubious role with respect to the unauthorized distribution of Solzhenitsyn's work to Western publishers, I see no reason to doubt the authenticity of this nonpolitical statement. "Polyphonic novel" is a term coined by the Russian critic M. M. Bakhtin to describe the novels of Dostoevsky.

[12] L. N. Tolstoy, *Pol. sobr. soch.* [Complete Collected Works] (Moscow: 1928–58), vol. 16, p. 7 (emphasis added).

The history of Russian literature since Pushkin's time not only presents many examples of deviation . . . from the European form of the novel, but also it offers not even one example of the opposite. . . . Generally speaking, we Russians don't know how to write novels in the sense in which this type of literary work is understood in Europe. . . . The Russian artistic idea cannot be fitted into that frame and seeks for itself something new.[13]

Innovation within the genre is, however, only one of Solzhenitsyn's ties to the Russian literary tradition. Many other linkages are noted in the articles in this volume, and doubtless every reader will make his own observations; here I should like to add a few of mine. Not the lyric but the parodic Pushkin seems to have been a source for some of Solzhenitsyn's most brilliant tours de force,[14] and there are many examples also of Pushkinian irony and of that special Pushkinian wit which is expressed in a single, precisely chosen word. I find no significant influence of Gogol on Solzhenitsyn, though granting that both are undisguised moralists, that both have been accused of "reactionary nationalism," even that both write of "dead souls." There do exist, however, two important parallels: their creative use of the nonliterary language and their talent for the grotesque and the absurd. Donald Fanger, in a lecture which (so far as I know) he has not published, first drew my attention to the existence of these elements in Solzhenitsyn, relating them to the work of contemporary artists of the absurd. If Fanger has not pursued the idea, perhaps it is because so much of the grotesque and absurd which Solzhenitsyn portrays is also documentary representation of everyday life in the USSR.[15]

---

[13] *Ibid.,* vol. 13, p. 54.

[14] As I have written elsewhere, with reference to *The First Circle*: "Potapov's highly stylized narration of 'Buddha's Smile' is a sustained mock epic, brilliantly evocative of both *Graf Nulin* and *Istoriya sela Goryukhina* (after all, Potapov is the camp Pushkinist). . . ." Kathryn B. Feuer, "Solzhenitsyn and the Legacy of Tolstoy," *California Slavic Studies*, 6 (1971): 113–28, reprinted in Dunlop *et al.*, eds., *Aleksandr Solzhenitsyn*, pp. 129–46. The editors of *California Slavic Studies* have generously permitted me to incorporate parts of that article in this introduction; when such quotations are made I shall give page references to both publications; *e.g.,* for this passage, p. 115/132.

[15] For example, in a letter published in the *New York Times*, August 30, 1974, Solzhenitsyn calls attention to the plight of a young Ryazan woman, Svetlana Shramko, committed to a mental hospital for complaining about air pollution. "To be committed to a mental institution for defending the environment," he writes, "may seem an implausible figment of the imagination to the Western reader. But that is exactly, to the last detail, how things are done in the Soviet provinces." (Georges Nivat also makes passing reference to the element of the absurd in Solzhenitsyn's work, mentioning Kafka and Ionesco. The statement appears in one of the passages omitted from the translation of his article in this volume.)

In his article on "Matryona's Home" Jackson suggests subtle links between Turgenev and Solzhenitsyn, and it would be fruitful to explore this relationship further. Matryona bears more than passing resemblance to Lukerya of "The Live Relic," while Solzhenitsyn's "Zachary-the-Pouch" could be part of a twentieth-century *Notes of a Bicyclist*," for the chief features of Turgenev's *Notes of a Hunter* are there: civic concern, love for the Russian countryside and its unsensational beauty, blended in the portrayal of a complex "simple" man of the people. Additionally, the kinship between both writers' poems in prose is self-evident, in that these are works which seem close to the hearts of the authors, have been generally disliked by literary critics, and often deeply loved by unsophisticated readers.[16]

Even more than with Turgenev, I find fundamental ties between Solzhenitsyn and a great, often neglected, older writer, Sergey Aksakov. Both men's writings seem on the surface stolidly prosaic and undramatic; both have been charged with providing merely a dull reproduction of reality. In fact, their works exhibit precisely the opposite qualities: devastating frankness in psychological probing, especially self-probing, and a fearlessly unfashionable acknowledgment of the reality of absolute moral authority. George Gibian underlines a phrase in *Gulag*: *"voda zadumalas'"*—the water bethought itself—which Solzhenitsyn attributes to the Bashkir people. Aksakov, who also spent time among the Bashkirs, noticed and used this very

[16] For a perceptive discussion of these works see John B. Dunlop, "Solzhenitsyn's Sketches," in Dunlop *et al.*, eds., *Aleksandr Solzhenitsyn*, pp. 317–25. The prose poems and sketches are not treated in this collection, and only "Matryona's Home" of the tales, while discussion of Solzhenitsyn's two plays is included only in the article by Wolfgang Kasack. For the most comprehensive critical treatment of the plays to date, the reader should consult the articles by Gleb Zekulin, cited in Kasack's article. The plays suggest another association between Solzhenitsyn and his predecessors. A reading list in Russian nineteenth-century drama will include some works by writers who were primarily dramatists, but also great plays by Pushkin, Gogol, Turgenev, Tolstoy and Chekhov. I don't think that Solzhenitsyn has yet written a great one, but since his productivity is as enormous as his talent, this statement may be outdated by the time this book is in print. (I mention "two plays" because Solzhenitsyn has published only two; we know that he has written at least one more, however, *The Feast of the Conquerors*, which has been "published" thus far only by the KGB, who do not send out catalogues.) Solzhenitsyn renounced this work, as having been "written not by Solzhenitsyn, member of the Writers' Union, but by nameless prisoner Shch–232. . . ." (Meeting of the Secretariat of the Union of Soviet Writers with Solzhenitsyn, September 22, 1967; cited from Labedz, *op. cit.*) Solzhenitsyn is at last in a position to exercise what should be a writer's minimal right, to reject his own work. Because anger and outrage have, however, fueled some of his best writing, I confess to a hope that "Solzhenitsyn"—expelled and exiled former "member of the Writers' Union"—may reconsider and publish the play.

expression in his *Family Chronicle*; it appears in his bravura portrayal of the damming of a river. There is a line of descent in Russian literature which begins, I think, with the "Autobiography" of Archpriest Avvakum, reappears in Aksakov, sometimes in Tolstoy, in the Pasternak of *Doctor Zhivago*, and now in Solzhenitsyn. It is a "minority" stream, yet one which has fed the tradition as valuably as have the Onega and the Pechora (mapped by Boris Eikhenbaum)[17] and which deserves its own cartographer. It worships life but not at any price and it never confuses the innocence of nature with the human capacity for both good and evil; it celebrates builders and doers and—equally—genuine soul-searchers; it is fertile of linguistic innovation. (Nabokov, although he might be elegantly uncomfortable in such robust company, has traveled this river too, I think.)

With respect to language, "Solzhenitsyn has learned from Tolstoy, but he has also incorporated into his style the delicacy of Chekhov's language of nuance and the achievements of the great practitioners of skaz." [18] Simon Karlinsky has remarked on the kinship between Solzhenitsyn's language and that of one of Russia's most original and avant-garde twentieth-century prose stylists, Remizov.[19] In a forth-coming work, Rufus W. Mathewson, Jr., writes of the concern among writers so diverse as Solzhenitsyn, Pasternak, and Andrey Sinyavsky for reestablishing the integrity of language. Contemporary Soviet poets like Bella Akhmadulina and Andrey Voznesensky seem also engaged in this quest. (In speaking of current literature one should add that there are innumerable interpenetrations between Solzhenit-syn's writings and the other truly great works produced [though not published] in the Soviet Union in the past decade, Nadezhda Mandel'stam's two volumes of memoirs, *Hope Against Hope* and *Hope Abandoned*.)

Solzhenitsyn himself has touched on his relationship to Dostoevsky[20] in the Nobel Lecture. He writes of Dostoevsky's prophetic insight:

> It is not even brute force alone that is victorious in the modern world, but also its clamorous justification: . . . Dostoevsky's *Devils*, who had

[17] In arguing that Lermontov intended Pechorin, the hero of *Hero of Our Time*, to be a rehabilitation of the romantic hero Pushkin had criticized in the character of Eugene Onegin, Eikhenbaum noted the existence on the map of Russia of the different but parallel rivers Onega and Pechora. (B. M. Eikhenbaum, *Stat'i o Lermontove* [Moscow-Leningrad, 1961].)

[18] Feuer, *op. cit.*, pp. 118–19/135.

[19] Simon Karlinsky, review of *August 1914*, *The New York Times Book Review*, September 10, 1972. Karlinsky also offers fresh insights on Solzhenitsyn's relationship to Chekhov.

[20] For an important discussion of Solzhenitsyn and Dostoevsky (and of other matters as well) see Czeslaw Milosz, "Questions," Dunlop *et al.*, eds., *Aleksandr Solzhenitsyn*, pp. 447–55.

seemed a part of a provincial, nightmarish fantasy of the last century, are now infesting the world before our eyes, reaching lands where they could not earlier even have been imagined.[21]

And Solzhenitsyn the artist quotes from *The Idiot* Dostoevsky's "enigmatic remark: 'Beauty will save the world.' " In our world of force and violence, he asks, is this utopian nonsense? No; for

> a true work of art carries its verification within itself; artificial and forced concepts do not survive their trial by images; . . . However, works which have drawn on the truth and which have presented it to us in concentrated and vibrant form, seize us, attract us to themselves powerfully, and no one ever—even centuries later—will step forth to deny them.[22]

Except for the notable compression of time-span in their novels, Solzhenitsyn and Dostoevsky employ radically different literary strategies. For example: "In our educated Russian society . . . there are no sacred traditions: at most someone may possibly frame some for himself out of books, or deduce something from old chronicles." [23] Most of us would accept this as a quotation from *The Gulag Archipelago*; in fact it comes from *Crime and Punishment*, and refers to the atheistic and materialistic radicals of the 1860s. Thus far the passage might demonstrate again Dostoevsky's prophetic power which Solzhenitsyn appreciates so well. But—these words are spoken by Svidrigailov, who personifies in the novel the victory of Evil over Good in man's soul. It was one of Dostoevsky's characteristic techniques to put his most cherished ideas into the mouths of his most guilty or buffoonish characters. There is one occasion when Solzhenitsyn does something similar (in a passage to which I shall refer again below) when he allows the Stalinist, Rusanov, to articulate his own doubts about Tolstoy's doctrine of nonresistance to evil, but even there the usage is different, ironic rather than "polyphonic." Clearly, the important ties between Solzhenitsyn and Dostoevsky lie not in literary style and device but elsewhere, in realms crucially important to both: their love for Russia, and their belief in redemptive Christianity. Yet analysis in these areas would also reveal differences. Solzhenitsyn can share Dostoevsky's hope that Beauty will redeem the world, but probably

---

[21] "Nobel Lecture," trans. Alexis Klimoff, *ibid.,* pp. 490–91. The Lecture is one of Solzhenitsyn's finest and most important works. Of the numerous English translations, I recommend those by Klimoff and by Thomas Whitney.

[22] *Ibid.,* p. 482.

[23] Feodor Dostoevsky, *Crime and Punishment,* trans. Jessie Coulson, ed. George Gibian (New York: Norton, 1964), p. 472.

not his messianic belief that Russia can redeem the world. Solzhenitsyn may well have been, as Dostoevsky said of himself, "a child of the age, *a child of nonbelief and doubt*," but the faith expressed in Solzhenitsyn's novels is strong and serene; one does not feel that he would add, as Dostoevsky did, that he would continue to doubt "until my coffin closes." [24]

But surely the relationship between these two writers begins from what biographers would call the common "formative circumstance" in their lives: Dostoevsky's ten and Solzhenitsyn's eleven years in prison camp and exile. It was Mihajlo Mihajlov who first noted, from a comparison of *Notes from the House of the Dead* with *Ivan Denisovich*, that both the mental and physical torments of Soviet prisoners appeared worse than those of Tsarist prisoners.[25] The power of evil not only breaks man's body, it also twists the heart and shrivels the spirit. Occasionally, however, there is the rare individual whom subjection to evil strengthens and ennobles. From starvation and suffering, Dostoevsky and Solzhenitsyn came, not to understand as an intellectual concept, but to *know* that man's selfhood rests on something other than the material conditions of life; persecuted by their own countrymen, in the person of their governments, they emerged with an intensified love of country; deprived of freedom and even of the right ever to be alone, they learned the reality of inner freedom. Shorn of trust in the natural goodness of their fellow men, both came out, nevertheless, with what Alexander Schmemann has called "a lucid, seeing love." [26] This love, however, is like the calm eye of the hurricane: in Dostoevsky the surrounding storm taking the form of a rage to *know*, to probe ideas to their ultimate meaning or absurdity; in Solzhenitsyn taking the form of a rage to *understand*, to comprehend the past as it created and keeps creating the present, and, as part of this enterprise, a fervor to expose. Thus we come full circle, for the aim of Solzhenitsyn's investigations and revelations, like the aim of Dostoevsky's probing, is the moral redemption of Russia.

In each of his long works after *Ivan Denisovich*, Solzhenitsyn has

---

[24] Quoted in Konstantin Mochulsky, *Dostoevsky: His Life and Work*, trans. Michael A. Minihan (Princeton, N.J.: Princeton University Press, 1971), p. 120.

[25] Mihajlo Mihajlov, *Russian Themes*, trans. M. Mihajlova (New York: Farrar, Straus, 1968), pp. 78–118. Mihajlov's *Moscow Summer* (New York: Farrar, Straus, 1965) also contains much interesting material relevant to Solzhenitsyn.

[26] Alexander Schmemann, "A Lucid Love," in Dunlop *et al.*, eds., *Aleksandr Solzhenitsyn*, p. 388. In this profound article Solzhenitsyn's relationship to Tolstoy and Dostoevsky is discussed most interestingly (and quite differently from what I outline here). See also Father Schmemann's other fine essay in the same volume, "On Solzhenitsyn."

made important, explicit references to Tolstoy. Even without these signposts, however, it would be clear that it is Tolstoy who has most influenced him as an artist and most engaged him as a thinker. The literary influence is straightforward, the philosophic one "most interesting where he is powerfully attracted yet not entirely convinced. The life story Nerzhin hears from Spiridon . . . [makes] Nerzhin wonder: 'Did not Spiridon's complicated life . . . somehow correspond to the Tolstoyan teaching that there are no just and no guilty ones in the world? . . .' But Spiridon says no: 'The wolf-hound is right but the cannibal is not' (*First Circle*, chap. 63). . . . However deep his response to the idea that 'God Sees the Truth' but men cannot judge, Solzhenitsyn . . . [cannot] assume so lofty . . . a detachment. And yet he remains aware of the 'circle of wrongs' which can issue from righteous judgment, and of how easily consciousness of just intentions can muffle the conscience. With painful irony he ascribes his own doubts about the Tolstoyan position to Rusanov, Rusanov whose whole life has been a history of non-resistance to evil and active compromise with it: 'He's a namby-pamby, your Tolstoy! . . . Evil must be resisted, my boy, evil must be fought!' " [27]

In *August 1914* Solzhenitsyn argues against Tolstoy's ideas of historical determinism[28] and, by implication, against his pacifism, for the young Tolstoyan hero, Sanya Lazhenitsyn, does join the army: "I feel sorry for Russia." Solzhenitsyn may be trying to suggest that Tolstoy's law of love of one's neighbor can also embrace one's nation,[29] but of course this is a shaky resolution. "There Are No Guilty Ones in the World," Tolstoy proclaimed in *Resurrection* and also in an article with that title. This creed seems to have been a necessary element in Tolstoy's own variety of Christianity, born, I think, not from any fatalistic philosophy, but from an inability to accept (as shown by his inability to portray artistically) the forgivability or expiation of guilt. Solzhenitsyn, a more mainstream Christian, knows that there are guilty ones in the world, and this knowledge has been apparent in all

[27] Feuer, *op. cit.*, pp. 126–27/144–45.

[28] In an article on "The Theme of Fate in Solzhenitsyn's *August 1914*" (*Slavic Review*, June 1972), Kevin Windle attempts to reconcile Tolstoy's and Solzhenitsyn's ideas in this regard, but the reconciliation rests on what seems to me a misunderstanding of Solzhenitsyn's conception of history, as a "vital, illogical force against which man cannot rebel. In this sense the words 'history' and 'fate' are almost synonymous" (p. 401). The whole weight of Solzhenitsyn's work says the opposite; that man *can* take his destiny into his own hands; history is essential because man can shape his destiny only when he understands the forces which have shaped it.

[29] See Kathryn B. Feuer, "*August 1914*: Solzhenitsyn and Tolstoy," in Dunlop *et al.*, eds., *Aleksandr Solzhenitsyn*, pp. 372–81.

his work, before it emerged as a central theme in *The Gulag Archipelago*. "The wolf-hound is right, but the cannibal is not." Or, as Sanya Lazhenitsyn remarks in his interview with Tolstoy: "Lev Nikolaevich, are you sure you're not exaggerating the power of love?" Sanya has observed from his own experience that, at least in his part of the country, "universal mutual goodwill *does not exist,* Lev Nikolaevich, *it does not exist!*" (*August 1914*, chap. 2).

A bond between Tolstoy and Solzhenitsyn which has no ambiguities lies in their publicistic writings, their appeals and open letters (in which both have achieved some of their most impressive artistic effects), in their common understanding that the artist and the citizen are undivorceable. One particularly striking feature of these writings is the subtle matter of tone. Reading Tolstoy's "Letter to the Tsar and His Assistants" one might be reading a draft of Solzhenitsyn's *Letter to the Leaders of the Soviet Government.* Not because so many of the abuses they deplore remain the same or have got worse, though this is depressingly apparent, but because both men, sometimes in anger, sometimes in cajoling reasonableness, write from an un-self-conscious and thus all the more impressive stance of perfect equality with their rulers. I used to consider this tone a natural consequence of Tolstoy's feelings about himself as an hereditary aristocrat and of his belief that the Tsar, at the center of the nexus of power, was subject to all the temptations of ambitious egoism from which the autonomous land-owner had removed himself. And this aristocratic pride was unaltered by Tolstoy's "crisis," after which he sought to give up his title and most of his land, for his view of himself as a man seeking no favors, beholden to no one, remained strong as ever; his new humility was directed to the poor, not the powerful.

Reading Solzhenitsyn's publicistic writings, however, forces modification of this view of Tolstoy's tone; for here it is the tone of a man who grew up in poverty, a victim of reverse social discrimination, of unjust arrest and cruel imprisonment, of exile, work as a village schoolteacher, cancer (an affliction which, like torture, often has the paradoxical effect of creating not healthy anger but shame),[30] brief fame and success, then again, ever-increasing persecution.[31] One could

---

[30] Solzhenitsyn comments on this painful phenomenon: with respect to cancer, in *Cancer Ward*, chaps. 30 and 32; with respect to torture, throughout *Gulag Archipelago*.

[31] History repeats itself in eerie ways. When Solzhenitsyn's international fame made it dangerous for the Soviet government to persecute him openly, his friends became subject to KGB harassment and worse; one, broken by police interrogation, committed suicide. (See the *Chronology of Important Dates* in this volume.) In 1896 "the Minister of Justice . . . told Tolstoy's close friend N. V. Davydov, who relayed it to him, that 'the government is unable to persecute Leo Nikolaevich himself, but that

not invent a series of life experiences and externally inculcated attitudes toward self more different from Tolstoy's. Hence one must suppose that this tone, courteous without blustering or self-abasement, always serenely self-assured, is the tone intrinsic not to the hereditary but to the spiritual aristocrat, whom circumstances shape but do not determine.

I have sought to place Solzhenitsyn's work in the context of the critical response it has evoked and in the context of Russian literary tradition. I should like to turn now to a brief analysis of his achievement, drawing on his first published work, *One Day in the Life of Ivan Denisovich* and one of his most recent, *The Gulag Archipelago*, I–II.

I was not among those who recognized Solzhenitsyn's potential greatness in *Ivan Denisovich*. The work's honesty and restraint and remarkable language made it notable, but to me it seemed chiefly a documentary achievement. (I don't think I'd have guessed *Crime and Punishment* from *Notes from the House of the Dead*, either.) For the astute reader however (and there were many) the essential clues were there. Let us look, not at the entire day, but only its first hours, its first ten pages,[32] from the moment when Ivan Denisovich wakes up to the moment he sets out on his long day of labor.

From the first paragraph it is clear that one is reading from within the consciousness of a particular individual, who thinks his story in his own distinctive language. A few paragraphs later, one learns that Ivan Denisovich Shukhov has also his own distinctive code: he avoids "hanging around" the mess hall because "if there was something left in [other people's] bowls, you couldn't stop yourself, you'd start licking the bowl." An old camp-hand had counseled: "In camp, I'll tell you who's the first to go: the one who licks bowls . . . and the one who goes and squeals to the Chief [Security Officer]." Immediately after, a vein of ironic realism appears: "About squealing to the Chief, of course—he was overdoing it there. The ones who did that knew how to look after themselves." The code is soon revealed to be more than a means of physical survival. An inner sense of justice has survived

---

persecution of people who distribute his works serves as persecution for Leo Nikolaevich.' " Ernest J. Simmons, *Leo Tolstoy* (Boston: Little, Brown, 1946), p. 519.

[32] I speak of the first ten pages of the work as it was originally published in *Novyi Mir*, where it took up a total of 66 pages. In the translation by Ronald Hingley and Max Hayward, *One Day in the Life of Ivan Denisovich* (New York: Praeger, 1963) which I have often followed, and which I recommend to nonreaders of Russian, the tale takes 203 pages; the passages examined here are found on pp. 1–34. For information about the revised Russian edition of this work, published by Solzhenitsyn in Paris in 1973, see the article in this volume by Alexis Klimoff.

massive external injustice; Shukhov is unfairly punished by a warder: "if he'd deserved it, then he wouldn't have felt so upset." And even human trust survives; hungry though his fellow prisoners are, there are those he can rely on to save his breakfast for him.

Among the prisoners there are recognized codes of behavior: rotten fish bones are spat out on the table, spitting them on the floor is considered "bad manners." Even within the group, Ivan Denisovich remains an individual; when he got fish he ate every bit, even "the eyes when they were still in the fish's head, but when they'd come off and floated separately in the bowl—big fish eyes—then he didn't eat them. The other prisoners laughed at him for this." And he has kept his pride. Desperately wanting a puff from a friend's cigarette, he didn't "ask him straight out," but only stood near him and "looked past him." A notorious scavenger, Fetyukov, approaches. Ivan Deniso-vich "went tense all over from waiting and longing. Right now this cigarette butt meant more to him than freedom itself. But he wouldn't lower himself and do like that Fetyukov, and look straight into the guy's mouth."

"The *manners* I speak of," Jane Austen has a character say, "might rather be called conduct, perhaps, the result of good princi-ples. . . ." [33] I find this passage a *locus classicus* for understanding the importance of the moral component in the traditional "novel of manners." One might better have anticipated *First Circle* and *Cancer Ward* had one realized how fully Ivan Denisovich's code, expressed on the level of manners, embodied a system of principles.

Other major themes in Solzhenitsyn's work might also have been perceived by the careful reader of these first pages of *Ivan Denisovich*. His hard-wrought code exemplifies the inner freedom experienced by such later prisoners as Nerzhin, Gerasimovich, and Kostoglotov. Even the idea, important in *First Circle* and *Gulag*, that honest artistic or intellectual work may be carried on only in prison is introduced through the prisoner medical orderly Vdovushkin, who had been a literature student, and for whom a doctor had arranged a "soft" job because "he wanted him to write in prison what they wouldn't let him write in freedom." But the prisoner's freedom cannot be understood outside the context of his constant struggle with the absolute conditions of his enslavement and the precarious nature of his hour-to-hour survival. It is a common fantasy to imagine prison as a place of spiritual rest, of surcease from decisions and choices. (Probably some such notion lay behind Tolstoy's and Stendhal's portrayals of the inner freedom found in prison and that is why the

---

[33] Jane Austen, *Mansfield Park* (London: Everyman's Library, 1963), p. 71.

scenes of Pierre's and Fabrice's imprisonment, masterful as they are, persuade us more intellectually than emotionally.) As he tried to conceal his bread by sewing it into his mattress, "everything in Shukhov was strained to the breaking point . . . and his brain was racing ahead, figuring out what to do next." Throughout his day Ivan Denisovich faces one harrowing decision after another. The choices which Solzhenitsyn's heroes and heroines must make in the novels, and which are described so movingly with respect to himself and all mankind in *Gulag*, begin here. They are as fateful as they are never-ending.

Solzhenitsyn's concern for Russia's history, *for what has been done to her*, also appears in these first pages of his first published work. "There, across the table, a young fellow was crossing himself before he'd even dug in his spoon. Must be a new one, a Western Ukrainian [*i.e.*, a Ukrainian from Polish territory, taken over by the Soviet Union only after 1945]. The Russians—they'd forgotten which hand you cross yourself with." And again: "They just couldn't drill it into the Western Ukrainians; even in camp they talked to you politely." Since the Revolution "the look of our nation has changed," Solzhenitsyn writes in chapter 40 of *August 1914*, "the faces have changed and the camera lens will never find again those trusting bearded countenances, those friendly eyes, those patient, selfless faces."

Solzhenitsyn's use of insistent detail, sometimes massive, sometimes tellingly single, is a feature (a very Tolstoyan one) of *Ivan Denisovich* which has remained a stylistic constant in his subsequent work. So has his fondness for proverbs and folk wisdom; an instance appears in these first pages of *Ivan Denisovich*: "What does the guy who's warm know about the one who's shivering?" Because restraint is the controlling, stylizing device of this first book it could not have prepared us for the eloquent anger of much of his later writing. But perhaps one should have sensed the anger. Ivan Denisovich, scrubbing the floor of the warders' room, hears one of them say a phrase which recurs again and again in Solzhenitsyn's works: "They're not worth the bread we give them. We ought to feed them on shit!" It is a satisfying moment when a few minutes later, on that subfreezing morning, Ivan Denisovich spills "out his pail of water on the path the Chiefs used."

But I return to those floating fish eyes which Shukhov would not eat. They are a detail, but also much more. They prefigure two of Solzhenitsyn's most original techniques. First, his mastery of that "variety of Russian realism which uses the concrete, physical everyday entities of the external world to represent the intangible, spiritual, personal yet universal phenomena of the inner world." A realism in which, at the end of the haunting blood transfusion scene in *Cancer Ward*, a dirty puddle outside is transformed into a mysterious lofty cloud which Oleg sees on the ceiling, and "the puddle not only reflects but *is* the cloud." [34] Second, those fish eyes foretell Solzhenitsyn's gift for endowing material objects with spiritual significance, such as (to cite only a few examples from *Cancer Ward*) Kostoglotov's army belt, the oxygen bag, the blossoming apricot tree. And they even point to a category of meaningful objects which I think Solzhenitsyn invented, "those which are empty or absent or simply not there: the rhesus monkey is not in its cage and is never seen; there is a sliver of moon but no bird in the cage which Ivan the glassblower spins (for the New Year's tree which is barely glimpsed . . .); the spot on the stairs over which Clara cannot walk is invisible; the music which Agniya strives to make Yakonov hear comes after the church bell has ceased to ring, while the bell to whose tolling Nerzhin listens is 'mute'. . . . [These] absent objects signify the nonmaterial reality of such moral entities as freedom, guilt, injustice, truth." [35]

When we turn to *The Gulag Archipelago*, its opening pages again prove instructive.[36] Solzhenitsyn tells of reading in a nature journal about a frozen, prehistoric salamander, "preserved in so fresh a state, the scientific correspondent reported, that those present immediately broke open the ice encasing the specimens and devoured them *with relish* on the spot" (p. ix/6). "With relish"—this one word (in Russian, *[okhotno]*, with great pleasure) is all Solzhenitsyn needs: who but starving forced laborers would eat prehistoric salamanders *with great*

---

[34] Feuer, *op. cit.*, p. 122/140.

[35] *Ibid.*, pp. 121–22/138–39.

[36] Aleksandr I. Solzhenitsyn, *The Gulag Archipelago: 1918–1956*, I–II, trans. Thomas P. Whitney (New York: Harper and Row, 1973–74). All of my quotations from the book are taken from this edition, to which page references are given, followed by references to the Russian publication: A. Solzhenitsyn, *ARKHIPELAG GULag* (Paris: YMCA Press, 1973). An expert evaluation of the translation must await the researches of a Klimoff. I approached it with mixed feelings: admiration for Whitney's other Solzhenitsyn translations and shock at the solecism on its cover, "Aleksandr I."—as if referring to the Tsar. (The second initial in Russian names stands for a patronymic; one should use both initials or both names, or just a first name or initial.) The translation seems to me generally accurate, and it unravels many words and phrases I had not understood. There is some loss of the characteristic vivacity of Solzhenitsyn's language, but this is inevitable. Thus I decided that my own versions would not be better, and would be less accurate without the help Whitney provided. Having said this, I would quibble over two words in the first passage quoted. "With relish" unfortunately suggests the condiment to some readers; and where Whitney writes "scientific" correspondent I prefer "learned" correspondent (the Russian word means both) as better conveying Solzhenitsyn's irony.

pleasure? We see immediately Solzhenitsyn's continuing concern for history and learn explicitly that this concern transcends his personal suffering: "I have absorbed into myself my own eleven years there—not as something shameful nor as a nightmare to be cursed . . ." (p. x/7). Thus he carefully explains that this account is based not just on his own experience, but on all the data he, as historian, has been able to collect. His acknowledgment of sources includes a note reminding us of a theme found in his novels, his scorn for the falsification of reality in Soviet literature: "Material for this book was also provided by *thirty-six* Soviet writers, headed by Maxim Gorky, authors of the disgraceful book on the White Sea Canal, which was the first in Russian literature to glorify slave labor" (p. xii/11).[37] The Preface concludes: "And someday in the future, this Archipelago . . . will be discovered by our descendants like some improbable salamander. . . . So perhaps I shall be able to give some account of the bones and flesh of that salamander—which, incidentally, is still alive" (p. x/7). Here in miniature, before the book proper is even begun, we find many features of Solzhenitsyn's art united, above all his particular genius for converting the simple object—the salamander as mentioned in the nature magazine—into a compelling detail—the eager eating of that repulsive salamander by starving political prisoners—into a dominant image and symbol—the salamander of buried historical truth.

Two sections of *Gulag* which have elicited much comment are better understood if the reader bears in mind that for all his fidelity to the facts, Solzhenitsyn is writing an "artistic investigation" and that for him, art is inextricable from morality. First, there is the harsh portrayal of Bukharin, which has been considered unfair by such sympathetic readers as Victor Erlich, George Kennan, and Roy Medvedev. Bukharin, whom Lenin called "the favorite of the Party," has come down to us as a talented, generous and humane figure; as all the nightmares have unfolded, his presence among the old Bolsheviks has been a talisman of what was positive and idealistic in the October Revolution. But surely it is because of Bukharin's admirable qualities that Solzhenitsyn singles him out; it is precisely the good man who becomes a test case in the question whether personal integrity can survive Ideology. Solzhenitsyn's political struggle with the myth of

---

[37] During the period of the "Social Command" in Russian literature (1929–32) Gorky sponsored and participated in a book celebrating the construction of the "Stalin" White Sea Canal, which was built by forced labor. The book, very influential in its time, gives a falsified picture of men who are well treated, who work joyously, who are rehabilitated.

Leninism is clearly motivated; he addresses those among his fellow freethinkers who see Stalinism as an aberration and who hope to achieve democratic socialism by a return to Leninist Marxism. Lenin, however, who from the first called those who disagreed with him "insects" to be "crushed," could not serve Solzhenitsyn's moral-artistic purpose, to present a protagonist in whom the best human qualities existed—and were destroyed.

Similarly, one should remember the book's artistic shaping in reading the confessional passages which run through it: Solzhenitsyn's account of himself as an arrogant student, strutting in demonstrations; an arrogant officer, believing himself better and justifiably more privileged than the common soldiers; a worshipper of the Revolution and of Lenin to the extent that even in prison he resented another prisoner's being addressed by the sacred name of "Ilyich"; as, above all, once having considered an invitation to become a member of the Secret Police. One must remember that since Augustine the artist has used confession as a hortatory device, he wins the reader to conversion by assuring him that he is no worse, probably better, than the writer. And Solzhenitsyn has a further point to make, one we have seen in all his preceding works—that each of us *keeps on* being confronted with moral choices and decisions, that life swarms with temptations, the most seductive of which is taking for granted one's present righteousness because of a past good act or honorable commitment. Thus we find in *Gulag*, besides the artistically stylized "confession," two passages of self-revelation which, I think, represent unabsorbed, still painful reminders of human frailty: Solzhenitsyn's recollection that as an officer he did not try to stop the torture of a captured Vlasovite who begged for his help, and his recognition that he had known something of the truth for many, many years, denoted by the inclusion in his account of "The Slave Caravans"—without comment, merely as eye-witness information—of two sentences: "And in the twenties, transport on foot was one of the basic methods. I was a small boy, but I remember very well how they drove them down the streets of Rostov-on-Don . . ." (p. 586/578).

Many have observed that in Solzhenitsyn's long novels there is no single hero; in *Gulag*, however, the story of millions told through hundreds, Solzhenitsyn artfully interweaves his own story into the documentary material. This is a transforming artistic device of great power. As the impact of horror on horror becomes so unbearable that one lays the book aside, one soon picks it up again, partly because of its compelling style, but partly because, while it may be impossible to care sufficiently about millions, one does care intensely about the narrator-protagonist who individualizes them. Furthermore, one knows that the narrator-protagonist not only survived but triumphed over the system, which seems to have engaged almost incidentally in destroying bòdies as it set about its primary task of destroying minds and souls. Art here does not palliate by giving us a happy ending; it puts the horrors in a dimension which makes them bearable.

Gulag is full of interpenetrations, thematic and stylistic, with Solzhenitsyn's previous works. The question whether life is worth preserving at any price skeins through *First Circle* and *Cancer Ward*; here Solzhenitsyn makes his statement explicitly, again and again. For example: "Perhaps the passion to save one's life at any cost had *already* come into being" (pp. 333/337-38). Or:

> "The only ones who *survive* in camps, [an old prisoner advised] are those who try at any price not to be put on general . . . work."
>
> "At any price?"
>
> "At any price!"
>
> . . . I [forgot] . . . only to ask him one thing: How do you measure that price? How high do you go? [p. 564/557]

When Solzhenitsyn describes the special poignancy for a prisoner of a conversation with a woman, we recall the loved women of *First Circle* and *Cancer Ward*, separated from their husbands by prison bars or loved because although they are custodians of the men—doctors, MGB officers—they are also women, capable of tenderness, eager for love. We remember the "Screen" scenes of *August 1914* when Solzhenitsyn writes in *Gulag*: ". . . all this is Russia: the prisoners on the tracks . . . , the girl on the other side of the Stolypin partition, the convoy going off to sleep, pears falling out of pockets, buried bombs, and a horse climbing to the second floor." [p. 522/518] When Solzhenitsyn speaks of the bird on the prisoner's windowsill, we are reminded of the bird symbolism in *First Circle* (does it go back to Sterne's caged starling?); when, in the same passage, he says that "the lonely prisoner has to have been purged of every imperfection, of everything . . . that has prevented his muddied waters from settling into transparency" (p. 483/483), we remember the puddle which for Kostoglotov became a shimmering cloud, and also the many passages in the novels in which the existence of the soul is affirmed precisely in terms of hard-won spiritual "transparency." When Solzhenitsyn writes of the inscriptions on prison walls—anguished, angry, or simple signatures of existence—we see again the "absent objects" of the novels; for the inscriptions are not there to be read: "the cell walls . . . had been plastered, whitewashed and painted more than once, [they] gave off nothing of the past" (p. 189/196).

In the end, everything in the book returns to the theme of history.

These inscriptions are suppressed documents, as are the omitted passages in the classics of Russian Marxism; the works of the great Russian émigré scholars and artists are "living" history, concealed from Soviet Russians (pp. 262–63/267–69) as are the great works produced within the country but never published there. All are part of that terrible pyre Solzhenitsyn sees in the Lubyanka prison:

> I was staring . . . at a mound of piled-up manuscripts . . . covering the entire center of the floor in this half-empty room, thirty-six square yards in area . . . like the burial mound of some interred human spirit. . . . And brotherly pity ached in me for the labor of that unknown person who had been arrested the previous night, these spoils from the search of his premises . . . dumped . . . on the parquet floor of the torture chamber at the feet of that thirteen-foot [portrait of] Stalin. I sat there and I wondered: Whose extraordinary life had they brought in for torment, for dismemberment, and then for burning? [p. 137/146]

New strains, however, also appear in *Gulag*. Though Solzhenitsyn's patriotism remains strong, there is evidence of painful conflict. He writes of his own generation in their youth as having been, without realizing it, morally "ransomed by the small change in copper . . . left from the golden coins our great-grandfathers had expended . . . when morality was not considered relative" (p. 161/169).[38] This perhaps goes no farther than the remarks about the Western Ukrainians in *Ivan Denisovich*. But now: "We didn't love freedom enough!" he cries (p. 13, n. 5/p. 27, n. 4). "We are so used to taking pride in our victory over Napoleon that we leave out of account the fact that because of it the emancipation of the serfs did not take place a half century sooner" (p. 272/277). Or: "While one group of Russians sat traitorously dozing behind the Vistula watching the death of Warsaw through

---

[38] This passage may be a key to Solzhenitsyn's ambiguity toward Tolstoy's philosophy of love. Tolstoy was strongly influenced by Rousseau and by the notion that one can ultimately rely, if one listens to it totally, on the voice of conscience. Like most of us, Solzhenitsyn has experienced the truth of this, and he writes of it. But he has also witnessed countless brutalities committed by those who were evidently unrestrained by the voice of conscience. Essentially he is making a Lockean response to Tolstoy's subjectivism, saying that conscience was a reliable governor when the seemingly innate ideas of conscience were (unconsciously) shaped by a fixed moral tradition, "the golden coins" of our great-grandfathers. In *Gulag* he sees those who have inherited only "the small change in copper" or not even that (and in "The Easter Procession" he presents a younger Soviet generation whose heritage seems to include barely a moral kopeck). Thus he suggests that when a formative moral tradition has been disrupted and replaced by Ideology, Ideology can then inscribe any principles at all on the yielding surface of the *tabula rasa*.

their binoculars, other Russians crushed the [Warsaw] uprising [against the Nazis]! Hadn't the Poles had enough Russian villainy to bear in the nineteenth century without having to endure more of it in the twentieth?" (p. 257, n. 10/p. 263, n. 10). Throughout *Gulag*, in many voices, that anguished cry resounds: "We didn't love freedom enough!"

And finally (it is hard to write "finally" in commenting on this endlessly rich work) there is another new strain to be found here, again a courageous and sad one. Implicit in his novels and explicit in his Nobel Speech is Solzhenitsyn's faith in art, in the power of the "free word." There is potent expression of this faith in *Gulag* also, when he writes of his feelings on the publication of *Ivan Denisovich*:

> And I . . . thought: If the first tiny droplet of truth has exploded like a psychological bomb, what then will happen in our country when whole waterfalls of Truth burst forth.
> And they will burst forth. It has to happen. [p. 298/303]

Yet Solzhenitsyn now seems also to experience the fear that perhaps Auden was right when he said that "poetry makes nothing happen. . . ." For immediately after these words he reflects:

> We forget everything. What we remember is not what actually happened, not history, but merely that hackneyed dotted line they have chosen to drive into our memories. . . .
> I do not know whether this is a trait common to all mankind, but it is certainly a trait of our people. . . . It may have its source in goodness, but it is vexing nonetheless. It makes us an easy prey for liars. [p. 299/305]

Can the obedient, lovable nature of the Russia Solzhenitsyn cherishes be reconciled with love of freedom, with knowledge that survival is not worth any cost, the precepts through which he hopes Russia may recover her soul? Only history will tell; and some part of history will be shaped by what Solzhenitsyn has written, is writing now, and will write—the history not only of Russia but of us all.

In compiling this book I have received assistance from many of my colleagues at the University of Toronto, including Harold Bedford, Hans Eichner, Irina Evreinova, Ralph Lindheim, George Luckyj, Richard Marshall, Catherine Naumova, Josef Skvorecky, and Gleb Zekulin. I am grateful also to Harry Goldberg, Isaac Don Levine, William Petersen, Eugene Sosin, and Gleb Struve, and to Dr. Zhores Medvedev for making available to me the authenticated Russian text of his brother's review of *Gulag*. Above all, I am indebted to my friend Patricia Blake, who, from her vast research on Solzhenitsyn's life and work, has given me generous and invaluable help again and again.

Of course, the responsibility for all errors of fact or outrageous opinions is mine.

Solzhenitsyn's Art

by Michel Aucouturier

While it still was possible to speak freely about Solzhenitsyn in the USSR, the liberal critics enjoyed mocking those who attacked his work for its "one-sidedness" (*odnostoronnost'*), a euphemism signifying that he had not sufficiently balanced off the dark with the rosy, "the negative aspects of Soviet reality," that is, the world of concentration camps and its bureaucratic setting, with the "positive aspects," such as clearing the virgin lands or raising the level of life of the masses.

Solzhenitsyn's partisans have had good sport deriding this statistical conception of realism, which would require that a writer could not select his subject without also portraying everything else; otherwise he would risk falsifying proportions by losing sight of the historical, global situation into which the tableau he wished to depict must fit in order to find its entire meaning. These critics were right to the extent that they defended the artist against the ideologues, the naked truth of the facts against the tortuosities of a system. But in full logic, they were in error: their arguments would have been valid only for the defense of a minor writer. For a great writer, even a realist, is not a reporter whose sole task is to inform us with exactitude about an unknown territory. Doubtless the accidents of his own life have provided him with rare and deeply felt subjects, but the truth which he expresses is not limited to the range of a particular experience, however exceptional and dramatic. Solzhenitsyn's grandeur consists not in having portrayed with exactitude the Mavrino Special Prison, the forced labor camps of Kolyma or Magadan, or the cancer ward of a Tashkent hospital. To do so would indeed require both courage and talent. But neither courage nor talent makes a great novelist. No, the source of Solzhenitsyn's grandeur, and the thing for which they cannot forgive him, is not that he described directly, from his own personal

"Solzhenitsyn's Art" by Michel Aucouturier. From Georges Nivat and Michel Aucouturier, eds., *L'Herne* 16, Série Slave, *Soljénitsyne* (Paris: Les Editions de l'Herne, 1971), pp. 346–51. Reprinted by permission of the publisher and the author. Translated by the editor and Sima Godfrey.

experience, a dark and hitherto ignored (or at least unexplored) aspect of Soviet reality; it is that he dared to make this particular experience the point of departure for a great literary work, to make this particular reality the center of a powerful and coherent fictional universe, that is, a network of symbols and new meanings, projected, of course, on today's Soviet society, but also more widely, on the whole of reality and the problems of existence. In other words Solzhenitsyn's grandeur, and his unpardonable crime [in official eyes] is to have made of the concentration camp experience the hallowed setting for reflection—to which no one can remain indifferent—reflection on Russia, on today's world, and on ourselves.

What was unforgivable in Solzhenitsyn's work was not its documentary content but its symbolic breadth. For however much Solzhenitsyn has defended himself as not having wished to make Ivan Denisovich or Matryona symbols of the Russian people, or to make cancer an allegory of the sickness which gnaws at post-Stalin Soviet society, nevertheless it is clear that the character whom he has placed at the center of his concentration camp chronicle has not been chosen at random, and, by the same token, that his individual character traits acquire a symbolic value; that it is not for its anecdotal interest that he tells us the story of the peasant, Matryona; that it is not a fortuitous connection which the reader feels between Oleg Kostoglotov's slow recovery from cancer (or should one not call it remission?) and the signs heralding de-Stalinization as they are revealed in the cancer ward.

Solzhenitsyn was certainly right to reply to his detractors that the cancer in his novel is far too "solid," too real (and he should know!) for a symbol.[1] He was right to rebel against an interpretation which impoverished his work, which drained it of its concrete and factual essence: a realist by temperament and aesthetic conviction he concerns himself, in fact, only with the concrete, individual Shukov or Matryona, or with the hard and hideous reality of cancer in all its forms. But let us recall here what Albert Thibaudet has written on "the symbolism of the realists": "Realism attains the level of art only if its details, its particularities are meaningful to the point of releasing undefined powers of suggestion or of appearing as vital images of an entire system."[2] Every great novel, every great work of art is symbolic, and all the more so perhaps when they do not proclaim any doctrine

---

[1] [The reference is to statements made by Solzhenitsyn at a session of the Secretariat of the Board of the Union of Soviet Writers, held on September 22, 1967, at which the possible publication of *Cancer Ward* in the USSR was debated.—ED.]

[2] Albert Thibaudet, "Symbolisme et roman," *Le liseur de romans* (Paris: 1925), p. 59.

of philosophic or literary "symbolism": not by the private and privileged meaning which the author attaches to certain images, situations, or characters (although, as we shall see, it would not be difficult to find symbols of this kind in Solzhenitsyn's work) but simply by the perspicacity with which he has chosen from the amorphic totality of experience the "important" elements, those which lead to great truths or at least to great historical, philosophic or moral questions. "A realistic work," to cite Thibaudet again, "attains its perfected level of art when, from its intense truthfulness, we pass naturally and inevitably to a great symbolic intuition." [3] Insofar as Solzhenitsyn's novels are linked to the great "epic" realism of Flaubert and de Maupassant (or of Tolstoy and Dostoevsky)—which Thibaudet contrasts to the "anecdotal" realism of Daudet and the Goncourts —his work quite naturally brings to mind a symbolic interpretation, an interpretation which is all the more convincing, all the more illuminating, as it has not been deliberately contrived.

Solzhenitsyn's accusers have been placed in an embarrassing dilemma, for that which makes the force of his symbols lies in an actuality for which he cannot be held responsible.

This ability to surmount the disorderly chaos of personal experi- ence, to extract its meaning and widen its scope to the dimensions of an entire society and an entire epoch, is all the more remarkable in Solzhenitsyn's work in that it hardly ever draws on the resources of fiction. Not just the material on which Solzhenitsyn's work is founded, but even the structure itself is documentary. His novels have almost no plot: the events are not hierarchically arranged or organized in a meaningful order, but only juxtaposed in their chronological succes- sion. This is clearly evident in *One Day in the Life of Ivan Denisovich* and in *Cancer Ward*, less so in *The First Circle* which is, it should be noted, the only one of his works which Solzhenitsyn has called a "novel." The chain of events separating the diplomat Volodin's fatal phone call from his arrest constitutes, in fact, a significant "plot," since it reveals the tragic alternatives of the Stalinist world: to be the victim or the executioner. But does this plot truly constitute the skeleton of the novel? Does it justify the breadth of the fresco with which we are presented? Does it not rather seem a somewhat artificial frame which allows the isolation and depiction, after "one day" in a labor camp of "four days" in the special prison of Mavrino?

This documentary structure of the narration is even more apparent in the short tales ("Zachary-the-Pouch," "Matryona's Home," "The Right Hand," "The Easter Procession") in which the author-witness

---

[3] *Ibid.,* p. 60.

hardly even takes the trouble to conceal his identity under the traits of a fictional narrator.

The almost total suppression of plot, the realm in which the creative imagination of the novelist generally presides, gives Solzhenitsyn's work that stamp of truthfulness which enabled his first readers to believe that they were reading a purely documentary work rather than an artistic one. And to be sure, this impression is not a mere illusion. All happens as if, having deliberately deprived himself of the resources of plot, Solzhenitsyn must focus elsewhere his talents as a novelist, that is, his ability to transform the real and to make matter the receptacle for meaning.

This focal point he finds at first in the constancy of a certain narrative progression, highly personal and highly characteristic. One cannot but be struck by the extreme chronological compression of an action, however teeming and many-sided it may be, which is the common trait of his three major prose works. Where it is most apparent—in *The First Circle*, in which the action described in six hundred pages takes up four days—the compression seems the most forced and the least natural: indeed, we feel that it is an artifice of construction, however adroit, which allows Solzhenitsyn to show us a sort of detailed slice-of-life of the Stalinist world in its police and prison structuring. At any moment a "parenthesis" may open up in the limited time span of the narration, for an account of the past life of one or another of the characters. There is, to be sure, something analogous in *One Day in the Life of Ivan Denisovich*, which also presents us with a large number of individual destinies, brought together by a kind of synchronic slice-of-life in a concentration camp. Here, however, the time span of the account acquires a proper value, a sort of dramatic fullness: the day is not an arbitrary frame but a real portion of the incessant combat in which Shukov must engage, both to survive and to safeguard his integrity. As a result, the manner of the narration is notably toned down. Its sole object is to lead us, as naturally as possible, from one character to another, from one destiny to another. The narration is no longer simply the guideline by which the author, both conductor and demiurge, leads us through his Hell. It moves forward step by step, slowly, stubbornly linear; it details the moments for their own sake, each one of which may be a victory or a defeat for Ivan Denisovich; it gives to each object, each gesture, each word, its full weight of reality, its duration in all its fullness, only letting go, it would seem, when all the meanings and all the resources have been exhausted. One thinks here quite naturally of the daily, hourly progression, the gait, of the life of the "zek" as Solzhenitsyn has depicted him, for whom the smallest bit of wood or metal, the slightest observation or bit of news has its value, because they provide material and moral furnishings in the destitution to which he has been consigned, and also establish with the objects surrounding him that active and creative contact which alone permits him to survive, morally as well as materially, in the cold and hostile world of prison and exile. The concentration camp experience, then, here imposes its own style in the broad sense of the term; this style, or narrative progression, expresses by its meticulous slowness a sort of sensual attachment to the most earthly, naked and elementary reality—(one thinks especially of the passage in which the art and pleasure of eating is described).

This feeling which, like a ray of light, illuminates the frozen horror of the Siberian prison camp, brings to Solzhenitsyn's moral and philosophical reflections, in the general debacle of values which the experience of the camp imposes, a sure and stable point of departure: the certitude of the intrinsic value of life itself, revealed in life's starkest deprivation.

One finds this return to an elementary, primordial relationship with the things of life also clearly sketched in the scene in *The First Circle* in which the intellectuals, Nerzhin and Sologdin, go to saw wood with the porter Spiridon. But what seems, in *The First Circle*, something of a symbolic gesture, is the very action of the tale in *Ivan Denisovich*, thus revealing the profound meaning of the work through its structure.

In its narrative structure *Cancer Ward* makes a kind of synthesis of the two preceding works. One finds there, on the one hand, the juxtaposition of biographies which characterized *The First Circle*, and on the other hand the validization of the moment as in *Ivan Denisovich*. But here the amplitude of the moment, suggested by the minute slowness of the narration and of descriptions (emphasized once again by the brevity of paragraphs, which at times transform sentences into breathlike rhythms, in the manner of Claudel's verses)—this amplitude is no longer dramatic but poetic. One need only reread the fine scene of the blood transfusion, without doubt one of Solzhenitsyn's most extraordinary successes, and also a scene in which one best grasps the originality and poetic quality of his narrative progression: a scene whose realism is microscopic, slow, interminable—and beautiful precisely for its interminability, with its cadence deliberately retarded to allow the hero to savor the moment of relaxation, of peace, of repose, of harmony with the world and with himself, which comes to him through the presence, the voice, the sure and measured movements of the beautiful and gentle Doctor Gangart. Here the moments are no longer just the stages of a struggle (although they are still that, as witness the opening of this same scene when Oleg, mistrustful, resists the transfusion which another doctor wishes to give him)—here the moments are also the pulsations of a return to life. The very same poetic sense of the moment was also present in *The First Circle*: suffice it to recall the happiness which the first snowfall in the prison courtyard brings to the prisoner Rubin at the moment of his most acute moral . and physical distress. But these moments of grace, of plenitude, these signs by which life discovers in a moment its meaning and its justification, are in this work only islands. In *Cancer Ward* they are everywhere: in the ray of sunlight which plays on Avieta's sweater, in the puddle of spring rain which is reflected on the ceiling of the blood transfusion room; they strike us in a turn of phrase and remain with us throughout an entire description; they resound in the last chapter of the book: in the splendor of the *ouriok*, the longed-for apricot tree in bloom, which is finally seen behind the walls of old Tashkent; and then in the swarming diversity of the zoological garden, where prodigal nature spontaneously blossoms forth in symbols. In the same way, in this—one might say—apparently useless piece of bravura, emanating, however, from the inmost substance of the book, Solzhenitsyn's descriptive style also blossoms forth in poetry, thus finding its broadest reach in this last of his works which is also his most mature and most serene.

This feeling of the plenitude of the moment, of the immanence of the meaning of life, this poetic—at times even religious—feeling of the beauty of the world grasped in the wondrousness of discovery, Solzhenitsyn has sought to express directly in his études and prose-poems. It is far from certain that the use of a mixed genre, the poem in prose, has genuinely enriched his work. One can ask if Solzhenitsyn's lyricism is not too closely bound to the narrative progression which characterizes his work as a novelist, to be able to flourish elsewhere than in the epic frame of an expansive narrative work.

Solzhenitsyn's art, that is, the originality and perspicacity of his view of the world, is also demonstrated at a level still more spontaneous than that of language and style. Some day it will surely be possible to measure more precisely Solzhenitsyn's contribution to the Russian literary language. As of now, however, the very shock which his language has provoked is an indication of its importance. In the only article from his pen which has appeared in *Literaturnaya Gazeta*, Solzhenitsyn has himself explained his preferences and the meaning of his own studies in this field. He calls on writers to react against the weakening of the written language by a transplanted international vocabulary, through a return to the national and folk sources of the Russian language. Of course, he may be accused of nationalism, of linguistic chauvinism, of recalling the conservative and retrograde endeavors of Admiral Shishkov who, even at the beginning of the last century, was trying to defend the Russian language against the invasion of Gallicisms. But Solzhenitsyn is too intelligent not to see the limits of his system: he has caricatured it in Sologdin, that hero of *The First Circle* who seeks Russian equivalents for such foreign words as "history" or "evolution." In fact, he objects less to the origin of foreign words than to their content: most often they represent abstraction, the ready-made cliché, in other words either the indolence of the creative intellect or falsehood. A return to Russian means a return to the living, organic, concrete word, which cannot become an instrument of deception or tyranny. He himself does not hesitate to delve into the buried treasure of dialects; he draws extensively on colloquial processes of linguistic derivation to form, if he needs them, words not found in the dictionaries; he opens wide the door to the highly colored slang of the camps.

More than the Russian word, however, he seeks for the Russian turn of phrase, the inimitable syntax of the spoken language, its suppleness, its ellipses, its anacoluthons.[4] This direct, spontaneous language resists all logical analysis; we must learn to recognize and appreciate it despite our bookish habits; there are many Russian readers whom it will shock by its seeming incorrectness. Here again Solzhenitsyn's traditionalism is in fact a highly audacious modernism which shatters the fixed formations of the literary language to make room for the vigorous élan of the spoken language.

Seemingly very crude, very spontaneous, hardly literary at all, coming straight from the streets and the camps, this language is in reality very knowingly controlled: the distribution of its elements varies from one work to another, in accordance with the general design of each. The language of *The First Circle* is, for example, much more neutral than that of *Ivan Denisovich*, whose expressive, verdant freedom is in accord with the hero's personality and his peasant origins. We touch here upon one of the most remarkable essential features of Solzhenitsyn's style. His extreme sensibility to the expressive nuances of the spoken language allows him constantly to glide imperceptibly from one point of view to another, permitting him to identify himself with one character and separate himself from another, in the middle of one chapter, one paragraph, sometimes even of a single sentence. Thus Solzhenitsyn solves in a new and original fashion

---

[4] ["*Anacoluthon*. A sentence in which there is wrongly substituted for the completion of a construction something that presupposes a different beginning." H. W. Fowler, *A Dictionary of Modern English Usage* (Oxford: 1965), p. 26—ED.]

a problem which has preoccupied other great novelists, notably Tolstoy, the problem of the equilibrium between the objectivity of the epic genre and the writer's sense of *engagement*, of moral obligation. Solzhenitsyn manages to let his characters act and speak; he manages also to place himself above them as a judge. But his most characteristic manner is the monologue reported in a semidirect style, which permits him to see things and events through the eyes of his characters without, however, allowing them full say, and without losing the privilege of distance and irony. In this regard *Cancer Ward* seems to mark a step forward from *The First Circle*. It is as if, having tested in *Ivan Denisovich* (with only one character) the possibilities of the semiindirect style, Solzhenitsyn is applying them to all the characters of *Cancer Ward* so as to surmount, by means of the synthesis of the author's language and the reported speech, the distance which in his first novel still separated the omniscient demiurge from his characters.

Indeed, in *The First Circle* one still feels too much the imperious hand of the guide who leads us through the infernal corridors: the characters seem diminished, reduced to the dimensions of those figures in classical painting who serve only to animate a splendid landscape. In *Cancer Ward*, on the contrary, each character in his turn himself alone fills almost the entire picture. In identifying himself with them, in presenting to us the world of the hospital through their eyes, the author makes them closer and more comprehensible to us. They gain in our view, in human density and in human warmth. Each—even the infamous Rusanov—constitutes an independent world which has its internal coherence, its organic justification.

Nevertheless, even while identifying with his characters, Solzhenitsyn never renounces judgment on them: by a parenthetical phrase, by the ironic intonation of a sentence, one feels the author is watchful that the novel which takes shape before our eyes should be not just a performance in which all the actors are equal, but rather a test which some pass and others do not.

We have noted above that in *Cancer Ward* Solzhenitsyn's narrative progression expanded into a poetic vision of the world in which this method found its fulfillment and its complete justification. Similarly, we see here how the technique of the semiindirect style issues forth in the creation of flesh and blood characters more complex and true to life than those of *The First Circle* and, above all, closer to us. One may illustrate this double evolution through the character of Oleg Kostoglotov. Hardened by seven years of forced labor, contemplating life with a stubborn mistrust, but ready for softening and rebirth at the first breath of life and love, Kostoglotov embodies the revelation of the immanent meaning of life in beauty which is Solzhenitsyn's fundamental poetic intuition. With his paradoxical mixture of mistrust and naivete, of roughness and gentleness, of wary astuteness and moral rigor, Kostoglotov is also the most living and successful of Solzhenitsyn's characters. As formerly one perceived Tolstoy through his Bezukhov, Levin and Nekhlyudov, here again one divines the author behind his character: a man who—by the spontaneous vigor of a talent which seems to spring from a vital instinct, by the obstinacy with which he sets forth in the face of and against all the world in the search for truth—is not so far from Tolstoy.

Epic and Dramatic Structure
in Solzhenitsyn's Work

by Wolfgang Kasack

The gravamen of Alexander Solzhenitsyn's literary creations lies in the long narrative prose works. Therefore an analysis must begin with *The First Circle, Cancer Ward,* and *August 1914. One Day in the Life of Ivan Denisovich* should also be included, despite its brevity, not only because it established Solzhenitsyn's fame but also because in its structure it prepared the way for the subsequent long epic prose works. Despite their artistic quality the short sketches constitute an exception in the author's work; they are, perhaps, a compromise with the difficulties of publication, and ultimately give the same effect as chapters of the large works. In the following attempt to comprehend the macrostructure of Solzhenitsyn's art, they remain unconsidered. The two plays which, however, have been published (up to 1971, the time of the composition of this study), *The Love Girl and the Innocent,* and *Candle in the Wind,*[1] and which have received little attention thus far,[2] will be included, in order to do justice to the breadth of Solzhenitsyn's talent.[3]

In the following essay the structure of the four prose works and the

"Epic and Dramatic Structure in Solzhenitsyn's Work" by Wolfgang Kasack. *(Die epische und dramatische Struktur im Werk Solschenizyns.)* Reprinted from Elizabeth Markstein and Felix Philipp Ingold, eds., *Über Solschenizyn* (Neuwied and Berlin: Luchterhand, 1973), pp. 184–202. Copyright © 1973 by Hermann Luchterhand Verlag, Darmstadt und Neuwied. Reprinted, with omissions, by permission of the publisher and the author. At the author's request the omissions have not been signified.

[1] [Translations of *The Love Girl and the Innocent* exist in English under that title and also under the titles *The Tenderfoot and the Tramp* and *The Prisoner and the Camp Prostitute.* A translation of *Candle in the Wind* has recently appeared (under that title).—ED.]

[2] [For an interesting discussion of the plays and references to the (scant) existing critical literature in English, see Gleb Zekulin, "The Plays of Solzhenitsyn," in J. Dunlop *et al.,* eds., *Aleksandr Solzhenitsyn,* pp. 303–16.—ED.]

[3] References are to the edition: A. Solzhenitsyn, *Sobranie sochinenii v 6-i tomakh* (Frankfurt a-Main: Posev, 1969–71). *Avgust chetyrnadtsatogo* is cited from the first edition (Paris: YMCA, 1971).

two plays will be examined in some of their aspects which seem to me essential. Solzhenitsyn calls *One Day in the Life of Ivan Denisovich* (which is very much shorter than the subsequent novels) a *"povest'*," thus choosing that specifically Russian narrational genre which is usually differentiated from the concept of the *"rasskaz"*[4] not so much by its greater length as by the renunciation of a focal point (in the Kleistian manner) and of a dramatic point of climax (in Staiger's meaning).[5] In comparison with the concept *"roman"* [novel] a *"povest'"* is, as a rule, many-faceted while having but one thread of action. Paustovsky has used this concept in his six-volume *Story of a Life*.

A single plot runs throughout the work, the experiences of the camp prisoner, Ivan Denisovich. He is portrayed in the most varied situations, but the structure consists of a series (or row) of more-or-less autonomous parts; the "many-threaded plots" so typical of Tolstoy and Dostoevsky, are not present.

Let us look briefly at the beginning and ending of *One Day in the Life of Ivan Denisovich*, a method of analysis which often reveals what is typical of a work:[6]

"At five o'clock in the morning, as always . . ." the tale begins. "There were 3653 such days in his sentence. Three days extra were added because of leap-years." So it ends.

A single day in the life of Ivan Denisovich is described. The "as always" in the first sentence makes clear that it is a typical day, as does the "such" in the conclusion. Solzhenitsyn does not want to present a special occurrence, an exceptional situation in which a character either succeeds or fails (as, for example, Pushkin does in his stories). Rather, the fictive world (to use Käte Hamburger's term)[7] which he creates is to encompass the ordinary, the typical. Nadezhda Mandel'stam writes in her memoirs, *Hope Against Hope*: "The only reason one could have to go on living [behind barbed wire] was to remember it all and later tell the story. . . ." [8]

Solzhenitsyn lives under this obligation, and, as his bounden duty,

---

[4] [*"Povest'"* is usually translated into English as "tale" or "novella"; *"rasskaz"* as "story" or "short story."—Ed.]

[5] See E. Staiger, *Grundbegriffe der Poetik* (Zurich[2]: 1951).

[6] For the methodological question of the study of the ending of a prose narrative, see W. Kasack, "Die Funktion der Erzählschlüsse in Pasternaks *Doktor Zhivago*," in *Zeitschrift für Slavische Philologie*, 35 (1970), pp. 170–186.

[7] K. Hamburger, *Die Logik der Dichtung* (Stuttgart[2]: 1968). (Käte Hamburger, *The Logic of Literature*, transl. by Marilynn J. Ross, 2nd, revised edition (Bloomington: Indiana University Press, 1973).

[8] N. Mandel'stam, *Hope Against Hope*, transl. by Max Hayward (New York: Atheneum, 1970), p. 383.

chooses to express the whole truth by describing ordinary, everyday life. The book's great effect in the Soviet Union confirms that what he described was felt to be representative. *One Day*, however, remains an excerpt and does not present the camp theme in its entirety. Ivan Denisovich is a simple man, no intellectual. Despite the variegation of the people around him, the view remains one-sided because the author has restricted himself to this one central figure. Censorship may also have been a consideration, as is shown by a comparison with the forbidden play, *The Love Girl and the Innocent*, for there a greater completeness is achieved through the inclusion of members of the intelligentsia.

Lukács has expounded the functional use of detail as the special characteristic of this work and has explained the wealth of such details by the fact that in the camps "every detail meant an alternative between preservation and downfall." [9] If we think of the little piece of saw-blade that Ivan Denisovich smuggled into the camp, or of the last granule of millet in the bowl of the continually starving prisoner, we may find a verification of Lukács' interpretation in these details which, as never in freedom, are a matter of life or death.

The principal work based on Solzhenitsyn's camp experiences is *The First Circle*. The foreground action, which in his first work was limited to "one day" in 1951, here encompasses four days, the 24th through the 27th of December 1949. All Solzhenitsyn's prose is characterized by the very long time of narration in proportion to the short time actually taken up by the events in the narration.[10] In comparison to the 128 pages of *One Day in the Life of Ivan Denisovich*, Solzhenitsyn relates *The First Circle* even more slowly: here the 798 pages correspond to three ($\frac{1}{2} + 2 + \frac{1}{2}$) days. For *Cancer Ward* the ratio is 582 pages to three ($1 + 2$) weeks, for *August 1914*, 579 pages to eleven days.[11] Solzhenitsyn loves the exact definition of dates; he interlaces his fiction with the historical events of the chosen days.

The time structure of *The First Circle* forms only the external frame of the novel. The author draws into the presentation years and decades of preceding time. Two forms are typical: (1) the concise personal record, chiefly of characters who appear only briefly in the action (*e.g.* of Engineer Potapov, who had confessed under interroga-

---

[9] G. Lukács, *Solzhenitsyn* (Neuwied and Berlin: 1970), p. 17.

[10] See G. Müller, "Erzählzeit und erzählte Zeit," in *Festschrift für Paul Kluckhohn und Hermann Schneider* (1948), pp. 195–212.

[11] These page enumerations are based on the Russian texts of the editions cited above in note 3. In order to render the differing type-sizes comparable, the printed page of *Rakovyi korpus* [Cancer Ward] was taken as a basis, and the works *Odin den' Ivana Denisovicha* and *Avgust chetyrnadtsatogo* were calculated upon it.

tion to having personally sold the Dneprogres Dam to the Germans [chap. 27] or of Isaak Moiseevich Kagan, who had finally been convicted of failure to inform [chap. 49]); and (2) the longer biographical flashbacks, as, for example, of Clara, the third daughter of Major General Makarygin, a state prosecutor in the security service. Solzhenitsyn uses a single chapter to recount Clara's school days during the evacuation, her literary studies, and the shattering encounter of the unsuspecting young girl of the privileged class with the educated prisoner who, watched over by a soldier, was scrubbing the stairs of the apartment building occupied by top K.G.B. officials (chap. 40).

The flashback is one of the techniques employed by Solzhenitsyn to achieve in his work the totality which the epic poem, as a segment of world history, demands.

Two characteristics which particularly draw attention to the structure of *The First Circle* support the view that it is an epic work, in the sense of Tolstoy's *War and Peace*, Cervantes' *Don Quixote*, or Homer's *Odyssey*.

One is the seemingly unending number of participating characters. Solzhenitsyn has relinquished a central figure. In different chapters he places different characters in the central role, chapters which are seldom connected as to action; in addition, he introduces new characters again and again. Such multiplicity and loose grouping of people is fundamental for the epic. The Russian people are to be comprehended in their entirety. The number and variety of the figures, which reveal Solzhenitsyn's striving for epic totality, correspond in scale and function to the interpersonal relationships in this work: they are abundant, yet episodic; overall, not one is dominant.

The second characteristic of the epic is that emphasized by Schiller in his letter to Goethe in 1797, that is, the autonomy of the individual parts. Every chapter is complete in itself, forms an artistic whole and is primarily connected to the rest by simple addition. The episode is the decisively constructive element. Individual chapters are remembered by the reader, independent of their place in the action, *e.g.*, the chapter in which Nerzhin is offered "amnesty" in return for scientific achievement correspondingly useful to the state, and in which he expresses one of Solzhenitsyn's basic ideas: "Let them admit first that it's not right to put people in prison for their way of thinking, and then *we* shall see whether we will forgive them" (chap. 9). The idea of the prisoner's inner freedom is expressed no less powerfully in the conversation between Abakumov and Bobynin, in which the prisoner proves to be more free than the high official who is dependent on

Stalin (chap. 17). In the same way, it is the dialogue which gives
poetic strength to such a self-sufficient scene as that in which
Solzhenitsyn lets Nerzhin's wife meet the Camp Commandant,
Klimentiev, in the Metro (chap. 26). The description of the subsequent meeting between Nerzhin and his wife (chap. 37); Innokenty's
arrest and incarceration in the Lyubyanka (chaps. 82–84); Rubin's
pseudotrial of Prince Igor based on the *Lay of Igor's Raid* (chap. 50);
the legend of Mrs. Roosevelt's visit to the prison (chap. 54): all are
entities complete in themselves.

The episodes which are autonomous parts of the action usually also
present autonomous problems. In the chapter about Clara's life until
1949, Solzhenitsyn elucidates the adulteration of 19th- and 20th-
century literature by Soviet literary scholarship of the early 1940s:
("And then they made a survey—all in a heap—of some sort of writers
no one had ever heard of: Stepnyak-Kravchinsky, Dostoevsky,
Sukhovo-Koblynin. Though of course one didn't have to bother
remembering the titles of their works" [chap. 40]). The very difficult
position of the Church, the misuse of the concept of the "people," the
mendacity of war correspondents (whom, by the way, even Korne-
ichuk brands in his play, *The Front*) are further examples of whole
chapters devoted to specific problems. Several other questions are
raised sporadically, such as the positive spiritual effects of imprisonment (*e.g.*, in chaps. 24, 42, and 48) or the moral problem of working
for the regime, *i.e.*, for the perfection of human enslavement (chaps. 29
and 79).

If in a work the episode as an isolated action or problem forms the
structural element, then it requires counterforces to render the parts
an artistic whole and to preserve the work from the danger of
formlessness. Solzhenitsyn has renounced the old manner of achieving
unity by means of the central figure and also the device of the journey
which Homer, Dante, and Cervantes chose. In the foreground action,
very brief in its time-span, he unifies the parts through several threads
of action which are to some extent suspenseful and thus contrary to the
basic epic principle: notably, the action line which leads to Nerzhin's
virtually impossible meeting with his wife, and Innokenty's telephone
conversation in the first chapter which links the beginning of the novel
to the end—his arrest on the basis of his "voiceprint."

The high artistic quality of *The First Circle* and its leading position in
Solzhenitsyn's work may ultimately rest on the fact that the episode
and the flashback are the techniques best suited to the content of the
material portrayed. For a prisoner exists only in the moment, the
episode. He has no influence on his future. Thus he has only memory,
and the possibility of flashback. Necessity then induces the prisoner to

ascribe greater profundity to each unique human encounter than is usual in life in freedom. Hence in each part the question of truth and of the meaning of life is posed anew.

In contrast to *The First Circle*, Solzhenitsyn's next novel, *Cancer Ward*, poses throughout the question of the future. It is the question of death—or, of the awareness of the inevitability of death—which here determines the thinking of all the characters.

If we employ Jean-Paul's conceptions of the epic and dramatic novel,[12] then *Cancer Ward* is the most dramatic of Solzhenitsyn's fundamentally epic novels. The number of characters is again extraordinarily large: educated and uneducated; beneficiaries, henchmen, and victims of the regime; patients, doctors, and the doctor as patient.

Perhaps the altered time structure in itself indicates the different nature of this work. The foreground action of Part I encompasses the 3rd to the 10th of February 1955; Part II is separated from Part I by about three weeks and again spans a relatively long—for Solzhenitsyn—narrated time-span. Only the beginning of this second period is dated (March 3, 1955). The end may be reckoned to be March 19, 1955. In this novel Solzhenitsyn requires time for the development of the plot. The foreground action—Kostoglotov's gradual recovery and release, Rusanov's admission and release—requires a greater time-span.

The number of flashbacks is fewer; the foreground action is weightier. New, and employed chiefly for Kostoglotov, is Solzhenitsyn's technique of multiple, achronological flashbacks into the character's past life. Thus there is a gradual opening out of the character of Kostoglotov, who at first was seen only in the fictional present and from the one-sided perspective of the Stalinist Rusanov. While in the ideal model of epic, episodes are interchangeable or even omissible (and this holds true for many parts of *The First Circle*), in the ideal model of dramatic narration every sentence has its own unequivocal and necessary place. The number of such functional parts is greater in *Cancer Ward* than in any other of Solzhenitsyn's works.

Interpersonal relationships play a correspondingly greater role: for example, Kostoglotov between the two women: the doctor, Vera, and the nurse, Zoya. Kostoglotov cannot indeed be called the central figure of this novel, not all the threads of the action lead to him, but he is more conspicuous than any figure in *The First Circle*. The most recent

---

[12] [Jean Paul Friedrich Richter (1763–1825), German writer of fantastic fiction, generally referred to as Jean Paul. His theories on art may be found in *Vorschule der Ästhetik* (1804).—ED.]

novel, *August 1914* (published in Paris in 1971) departs for the first time from themes related to the author's personal experience as a prisoner in Soviet concentration camps. In this work too, the epic poet's desire for the total presentation of life in a selected historical segment of time, which we saw in the earlier works, suggests Solzhenitsyn's strong historical interest. In *August 1914* he has chosen the First World War as the theme, and in the first volume, which he calls the first "Knot," he has concentrated solely upon the great Russian defeat in East Prussia. Behind the printed pages of this book there also stands the author, struggling for "sincerity in literature" (in the sense of Pomerantsev's postulate of 1953),[13] the author who here presents, as truthfully as possible, "the most important theme of our recent history" as he calls it in the "Afterword." In view of his previous works, with their many accusations against the subjugation of man in the Communist system, works throughout which his poetic strength seems to have grown out of personal pain, it is astonishing that Solzhenitsyn should now say [in this same Afterword] that he has always considered the presentation of this historical theme as "the chief purpose" of his life. This being so, it is particularly tragic that sources and library archives in the Soviet Union were not made available to him.

The work may be characterized as epically structured in the same sense as *The First Circle*. The similar time structure, eleven days from the 23rd of August to the 3rd of September (the 10th to the 21st of August, according to the old calendar) confirms the view that this structure is a specific characteristic of the author's epic style. The very large number of characters and the independence of the parts are, on the other hand, fundamental stylistic criteria for any epic novel. Both are fully provided. Nevertheless, the book differs greatly in its macrostructure from Solzhenitsyn's previous prose.

First, Solzhenitsyn almost completely relinquishes the technique of the temporal flashback, that is to say, the inclusion of the previous histories of leading or episodic figures. This change of technique may be founded in the nature of his conception of the historical novel. Of the important figures, the single fictional (nonhistorical) character, Vorotynsev, makes what one might call a typical exception. If, despite this renunciation of descriptions of the past, the description of the "historical present" has the effect of being the result or outcome of the foregone epoch, this effect is a consequence of the numerous

---

[13] V. Pomerantsev, "Ob iskrennosti v literature," *Novyi Mir*, 12, 1953, pp. 218–245. This article, which was sharply criticized from the official Party standpoint, is introduced into two conversations in *Cancer Ward* (chaps. 4 and 21).

reflections included in the configuration of the foreground events.

If (with reference to Wolfgang Kayser)[14] we differentiate the speech forms of report, description, speech and reflection in fiction, then direct speech and report predominate in the prose on the camp theme. In *August 1914* reflection, chiefly in the form of narrated monologue which Solzhenitsyn had used in *One Day in the Life of Ivan Denisovich*, becomes the dominant and scrupulously differentiating stylistic instrument.

Thus Solzhenitsyn permits the individual characters to ponder the military events, by which means he changes the perspective again and again, and in an even more important way than in *Cancer Ward*: from one general to a second to a third, each of whom, limited in information and by personal character has different views, to the simple soldier (who links the work to Tolstoy's *War and Peace*) to the sergeant and to the colonel; from the revolutionary and potential deserter to the reactionary *Chernosotenets* [Black Hundredist]; from the conservative landowner to the "progressive" school directress. The technique of changing perspectives is intensified by the constant permeation of the independent reports of the fictional narrations (in the precise concept of *Erzählfunktion* established by Käte Hamburger) with the reproduction of the subjective thoughts of the character accorded (for a time) a central position in a particular chapter.

The same diversity as is achieved by the very different figures chosen for the novel is produced by the multiplicity of the military events selected for inclusion. Every sphere in the material as in the moral world is drawn into the work. His desire is to attain truth through diversity.

Solzhenitsyn as author fundamentally expresses no opinion on the events. All of the reflections reproduce the stream of consciousness of the fictive figures; they are not given by means of fictional narrations. Not one of the long prose works has the structure of a first-person narrative; thus the question does not arise to what extent the first person narrator is fictitious in relation to the author. Of Solzhenitsyn's short prose works, only "The Right Hand" and "Matryona's Home" have a first person structure. If one judges from the brief autobiography which Solzhenitsyn published in connection with the award of the Nobel Prize,[15] the degree of the fictitious may be trifling, that of the autobiographical great.

As to the question of author's commentary, it is of decisive importance that even in those works which do have a first person

---

[14] W. Kayser, *Das sprachliche Kunstwerk* (Berne[2]: 1951).
[15] [See Dunlop *et al.*, *op. cit.*—ED.]

narrator, Solzhenitsyn does not comment on the events surrounding the first person figure. In all his work Solzhenitsyn maintains as objective a stance as possible with respect to the narration. He lets the fiction speak for itself, and the reader judges for *him*self. This attitude especially links him with Chekhov, who also consciously avoided taking a specific stance, although in other respects their narrative styles differ considerably.

The single exception to this principle occurs in the 40th of the 64 chapters of *August 1914.* Here Solzhenitsyn inserts his own reflections on the historical facts which are the material of his fiction; for example: "Could a novelist possibly be believed if he wrote that General Kluyev, who led the central corps deepest of all into Prussia, had NEVER before BEEN IN BATTLE!" [16] Moreover, it is only here that Solzhenitsyn leaves the temporal milieu and goes into the future, when he says that the mass graves of the fallen Russians would be cared for by the Germans until the Second World War (chap. 40). This long section of the chapter (which ends with a brief scene objectively narrated) is the only case of intervention by the author. Its function is similar to that of the Afterword.

In contrast to his first long prose works, Solzhenitsyn has interspersed further chapters, which possess a completely different structure, into the mosaic of the narrated chapters (in which, from chapter 10 on, the place of the action and the central figures almost continually change). Twice he inserts newspaper sections (chaps. 7, 60). Four times he summarizes the events of one or two days from the historian's point of view (chaps. 23, 32, 41, 49). Just as frequently he introduces lyrically impressionistic pictures which most powerfully reflect the tragic events of the war (chaps. 30, 51, 52, 56). He titles these sections "Film Screens." Their texts are not a scenario but they transpose into language two characteristics of the film as an art form: the visual image and also the possibility of swift change. Thus, in the microstructure of these parts, as well as in that of the chapters with the newspaper extracts, there is revealed the same epic principle of simple addition as is found in the macrostructure of the whole. Finally, Solzhenitsyn has included six documents (commands of the Tsar and similar memoranda from the highest authorities) whose assertive strength comes from their crass "No comment" contrast to the true, factual portrayal of the course of the war itself (chaps. 25, 43, 55, 56, 63). All these differently structured sections, inserted into the objectively narrated chapters, are set in different types, an optical device which Solzhenit-

---

[16] [The emphasis by capitalization is Solzhenitsyn's.—ED.]

syn has employed in the past, *e.g.* for specific camp expressions.[17]

The interpolation of historically contemplative, lyrically impressionistic, documentary and similar sections conforms to the epic principle of the autonomy of parts. The special characteristic of *August 1914* is that the autonomous transcends place, time, people, action and perspective, and enters into the realm of an independent language structure.

Solzhenitsyn's three plays were written at the same time as the epic works. He has rejected the earliest, *The Feast of the Victors*; *The Love Girl and the Innocent* belongs to the same period as *Ivan Denisovich* and (as of 1971) he had not yet given permission for the translation of *Candle in the Wind*.

In a comparison of the *povest'* One Day in the Life of Ivan Denisovich with the drama, *The Love Girl and the Innocent*, besides the previously noted difference in the level of intelligence of the major characters, what is most striking is the considerably greater density of action in the play. Solzhenitsyn has composed a play with several threads of action: Nemov's fall from labor-supply director to prisoner without privileges; his relationship to Lyuba and her decision to become the "camp wife" of the characterless prison doctor for the sake of her love for Nemov; Brigadier Gay's struggle against the criminals *(blatnye)* with the support of the murderess, Granya; and also the production problems in the foundry. The diversity of the action, like the abundance of the characters (62 plus "extras") permits inclusion of the play in the category of "open drama" (in the terminology of V. Klotz).[18]

It is also in accordance with the principle of the open drama that the fundamental structural unit of this play is the scene and not the act. Solzhenitsyn has divided it into 4 acts and 11 scenes, without, however, subsuming the scenes under the acts, but rather numbering them, quite appropriately, 1 through 11. Thus each scene forms a unity of place and action. There are time segments between the acts which Solzhenitsyn, who sets the play in 1945, indicates as "several days." The fictive time amounts to about two weeks. In contrast to Solzhenitsyn's long prose, it is a matter of a greater stress ratio between the narrated time and the time of narration. When one considers the relatively long narrated time in *Cancer Ward*, then it follows that there is a dependence of the density of the action on the time prolongation: the longer the narrated time in relation to the time of narration, the greater the density of action.

---

[17] For further detail on the camp expressions, see E. Shilyaev, "Lagernyi yazyk po proizvedeniyam A. Solzhenitsyna," in *Novyi Zhurnal* 95, New York, 1969, pp. 232–247.

[18] V. Klotz, *Geschlossene und offene Form in Drama* (Munich⁴: 1969).

We find both indoor and outdoor scenes, and in all, unity of place [or locale] is preserved. Scenes 2, 7, and 10 are set in the foundry; 1 and 11 at the entrance gate. The symmetrical placement of the same places of action (1:11, 2:10) serves the unity of the artistic work and forms a counterpoint to the open structure of the drama. The motifs of arrival, at the beginning, and departure, at the end, which in themselves are rather of an epic nature, round out the whole, but also open out the conclusion and let the drama reveal the same structural characteristics as the prose. *The First Circle* ends with the removal of prisoners to an unknown camp. Kostoglotov's departure concludes his time in the hospital and therefore is the most firmly conclusive ending in Solzhenitsyn's works. It also, however, opens our imagination to Kostoglotov's future life in exile—until his readmittance to the hospital, which we anticipate.

The dramatic structure of *Candle in the Wind* (The Light Which Is in Thee) can be called similar, although not exactly the same. It accords with the open type of drama. The play is organized into 6 scenes (called "pictures") without division into acts, and has 14 performing characters and several threads of action. With respect to content, it is the setting of the place of action in an abstract land which differentiates it from Solzhenitsyn's works of the same period. To be sure, the factor of unjust deprivation of freedom for many years enters into the play in an abstract way, and parallels to the Stalinist system are clearly evident, but neither the social picture nor the social critique is related solely to the Soviet Union. As the play progresses, the problem it raises becomes even more clear: has the scientist the right to interfere in mankind's spiritual sphere by means of biological (or other) methods? A human being's nerves are "stabilized"; the personality is destroyed. The grave question which Chekhov had posed in "The Black Monk" is answered anew with an affirmation of man's inviolability.

The solitary appearance of the poor, elderly Christina, who, viewing her dead brother, quotes from the Gospel according to St. Luke (11, 35): "Take heed, therefore, that the light which is in thee be not darkness," also belongs to the category of Solzhenitsyn's self-sufficient unities of action. For several reasons it is justifiable to see this quotation as embodying the drama's essential statement. Solzhenitsyn has used its nucleus, "the light which is in thee" as a subtitle. Each of the individual threads of action in the play is ultimately subsumed under this Biblical quotation. It forms the climax of the Christina scene. It is a surprising feature of the structure here that within the fictional action the Biblical statement is not prepared for by any formulation, nor is it taken up again later. It is precisely the fact that it is unrelated to the rest which creates the intensity of the artistic effect, its continuing existence in the imagination of the reader and/or the spectator.[19]

The action of the play is compressed, as in *The Love Girl and the Innocent*. The time-span is long, encompassing over half a year. The time breaks between the scenes are functional. The character structure is the most complicated of all Solzhenitsyn's works. Interpersonal problems, friendship and its dangers, marriage and adultery, love and self-sacrifice: all are essential to the action. Thus this play has more elements of the closed drama than the other; nevertheless it too belongs to the type of open drama. Moreover, at the end, the question remains open as to whether science is successful in finding models for a reasonable ordering of society.

If Solzhenitsyn's realism in his prose can to some extent be understood as a reaction against socialist realism (that is, against the unrealistic idealization of reality in accordance with the patterns imposed by the CPSU), similarly the form of his plays reveals a reaction to Soviet drama of earlier periods. In the first decade of Soviet literature, the variety so characteristic of that time is also evident in its plays. Along with such typically closed dramas as *Lyubov' Yarovaya* by Trenev or *Squaring the Circle* by Kataev, stand such typically open works as Mayakovsky's *Mystery-Bouffe* and Olesha's *A Conspiracy of Feelings*, probably the last significant drama of this epoch. The typical dramas of socialist realism, however, have so tightly closed a form that one can "count off" in them every formal characteristic of classical drama. Their conjunction with ideology means that the entire plot is given beforehand, along with the exposition, and so the plays become unbearably boring. The first plays after Stalin's death, such as Shtein's *A Personal Affair*, despite new themes, retain these stereotyped dramatic structures.

If Solzhenitsyn writes open dramas which have no exposition and no predictable plot outcome, this is a revolutionary development, not in comparison with the development of West European drama, but rather in the context of Soviet drama. It finds its parallels in the work of the most important contemporary Russian dramatist, Victor Rozov, who—in such plays as *Before Supper* and *On the Road*—employs an even more open structure than Solzhenitsyn.[20] For Rozov, who writes only

---

[19] Gleb Zekulin analyzes the characters appearing in the center of the action, independent of the focal point of the Christina scene; "Solzhenitsyn's play: *The Candle in the Wind (The Light Which Is in Thee)*," *Canadian Slavonic Papers*, 13 (1971), pp. 179–192.

[20] V. Rozov, *Pered uzhinom*. In *Teatr* 24, 1963, pp. 165–192; *V doroge*, in V. Rozov, *Moi*

plays, this development can be interpreted solely in relation to the
history of Soviet drama up to 1954, while for Solzhenitsyn it is closely
linked to his prose: it is the epic principle, the determining element of
the prose, which also underlies the structure of his dramas.

---

shestidesyatye (Moscow: 1969), pp. 5–82. See also, W. Kasack, "Viktor Sergeevich
Rozov," in *Zeitschrift für Slavische Philologie*, 38, No. 1, 1974.

On Solzhenitsyn's Symbolism

by Georges Nivat

Kondrashev (. . .) pulled out a small canvas (. . .) and brought it over, holding out to Nerzhin its gray underside.

"You—you know about Perceval?" he asked in a muffled voice.

"Something to do with Lohengrin."

"His father. The Keeper of the chalice of the Holy Grail."

"It's an opera by Wagner, isn't it?"

"The moment I portray here isn't in Wagner, nor in von Eschenbach, but it's exactly the one I imagine. A moment any man might experience, when he suddenly sees the Image of Perfection. . . .

Kondrashev closed his eyes and chewed his lips. He was preparing himself.

Nerzhin was surprised that the painting he was about to see was so small.

The artist opened his eyes.

"This is only a sketch. A sketch for the major painting of my life. It is the exact moment when, for the first time, Perceval sees—the castle! The Castle of the Holy Grail!!!"

> Alexander Solzhenitsyn, *The First Circle* (chap. 42)

"And have you found what we were seeking?" asked Perceval.

"Not at all," replied Bohort, "but I think that we shall never separate again before completing this quest."

> Anonymous author of the 13th century, *The Quest for the Grail*

"On Solzhenitsyn's Symbolism" by Georges Nivat. From Georges Nivat and Michel Aucouturier, eds., *L'Herne* 16, Série Slave, *Soljénitsyne* (Paris: Les Editions de l'Herne, 1971), pp. 352–64. Reprinted, with omissions, by permission of the publisher and the author. Translated by Sima Godfrey; translations from the Russian by the editor.

Solzhenitsyn's work has a hypnotic effect. We are fascinated by the immensity of a cruel universe, a universe we would like to think foreign to us, but which overwhelms us because it is, in truth, close to us. (. . .) Stalinist Russia was part of our experience, whether we were Stalinists or not. It pressed on our souls, it was for us what Persia was to Greece in the fifth century: an awesome fate, at once hostile and imminent, on the very threshold of our consciousness. (. . .) The shadow continued to bear down. Only the work of Solzhenitsyn succeeded in defying it; because Solzhenitsyn at one stroke plunged into the interior immensity of forbidden Russia, obscured by twenty-five years of darkness. (. . .) But more than just our thirst for the documentary was satisfied. Before we were even conscious of it, we felt that in these two books not only was a piece of history being revealed to us, but that all history was in fact being rejudged in the dark light of our twentieth century. His work was not just an immense fresco, it was also a Judgement. (. . .) On rereading Solzhenitsyn, we are struck by the references to past history, to the legacy of culture, to the memory of disasters of old: Epicurus, Thomas More, Hobbes, the Russian chronicles of the fifteenth century, the Decembrists, Anna Karenina and Stavrogin—a multitude of references to the past which serve here as signs. Signs of an overturn of human history: reassessed in the dark light of the concentration camp society, the entire body of history cracks, and like a gigantic iceberg, totters. (. . .) Let us listen to the conversation between Nerzhin and Sologdin on that cold December morning in 1949:

> (. . .) "But if they send you to a camp," asked Sologdin, "what will become of your work on *times past?*" (This meant, history.)
> "Well, what? Even here I'm hardly pampered. Keeping a single line of my notes puts me in danger of the dungeon as much here as it will there. I've no access to the public library here, and till I die, I'll have none to archives. If you mean paper, well even in the taiga I'll find birch or pine bark. And my greatest advantage no spies can ever take from me: the grief which I've experienced myself and see in others, can't that be a powerful prompter to my speculations about history?" [*F.C.*, chap. 24]

Even if it must be on Novgorod birch bark, history will still be rewritten, Solzhenitsyn tells us, and not only the history of our time, but that of all times. Just as Grotowski in his "theater of poverty" reassesses the "classics" of the past in the light of concentration camp destitution,[1] so Solzhenitsyn proclaims that no fact of past history can

[1] [Jerzy Grotowski (1933–) is the director of Theater Laboratory, Poland's best known experimental theater. He has been acclaimed for his theoretical writings, his

avoid being rejudged in the light of the present. And the past is
rejected as a harmless myopic witness. This is not to suggest, of course,
that wickedness has not existed in prior times; it is that never before
did such a concentration of wickedness take place. And from this
scientifically accumulated wickedness, something irremediable
emerged which upset the former even flow of things, which cancelled
out all that could be called "the march" of history, the values of
history or cultural heritage. Where is the age of *"Testis unus, testis
nullus,"* when the accused himself becomes his own accuser? Where is
the age of [the Decembrist wife] Marya Raevskaya, receiving the right
to travel by carriage to farthest Siberia to settle near her deported
husband? Where is the age of an Anna Karenina who had the leisure
to opt for a passion that would ultimately destroy her? Where is the
monster Kitovras whom Solomon tricked into chained enslavement,
and before whom all houses had to be razed:

> And in his path there chanced to be the house of a widow. The widow
> burst out crying and begged Kitovras not to destroy her poor little
> house—and she touched his heart. Kitovras started twisting and
> turning—so that he broke his rib. But the house remained standing.
> And then spake Kitovras: "A soft word can break your bone, while a
> harsh one rouses anger."
>
> And Oleg reflected: this Kitovras and those scribes of the Fifteenth
> Century. They were men, and compared to them we are wolves. [*C.W.*,
> chap. 29]

Thus, as though adventitiously, the entire past history of humanity
is measured against the new standard of the twentieth century. Nor is
this just Dante's allegorical Inferno: everything is perfectly real,
verified by the intersection of destinies and witnesses. Moreover, it is
only the first of the circles: what will the ninth be like? No doubt, too
unbearable for us, who have not been there at all. (. . .) But the
allusion to Dante is not limited to the quotation from the Fourth
Canto of *The Inferno.* (. . .) Like Dante's great three-part work,
Solzhenitsyn's epic cycles have a governing principle; their architec-
ture is not a matter of chance, but of Symbol.

(. . .) In *Cancer Ward* an immense network of apparently
subordinate signs links the abandoned creatures to one another. These
are the details to which one gives little consideration at first and which

daring adaptations of European plays (Marlowe's *Doctor Faustus*, Calderon's *The
Constant Prince*) and of the classics of the Polish repertory (Wyspiański's *Akropolis*, which
Grotowski set in a concentration camp) and for his production *Apocalypsis cum figuris*,
whose text consists of quotations from the Bible, Liturgical Chants, Dostoevsky, T. S.
Eliot, and Simone Weil.—ED.]

would take long to examine. For instance, the opera *The Sleeping Beauty* which Oleg, dying, exhausted by his tumor, wanted so much to see before passing through the fateful gate of the hospital; weeks later, Vera Gangart in the gray darkness of her room puts a record on the phonograph:

> It was a suite from *The Sleeping Beauty*. The Adagio, then "the entrance of the fairies."
>
> Vera listened, but not for herself. She was trying to imagine how it might have been for the rain-soaked man, swollen with disease, condemned to death and never having known human happiness—how he, from the balcony of the Opera Theater, might have listened to the Adagio. [*C.W.*, chap. 25]

There is also this curious coincidence: Yakonov had imagined a nickname for that strange girl called Agniya, who seemed to kindle everything she approached with a flame of contained despair: "Forest Brook." It is this same fire that enflames the picture which Nerzhin admires in Kondrashev's "studio" on the landing of an abandoned staircase of the *sharashka*: "Now full of attention, Nerzhin began studying Kondrashev's latest painting—done in the four to five proportions of the Egyptian quadrangle, an Autumn Brook or, as the painter himself called it Largo in D-Minor" (*F.C.*, chap. 42).

There is also the symbol of the *ouriok* in *Cancer Ward*: marvel of the Orient, this immense [flowering apricot] tree blossoms forth in an enormous pink ball, six meters across. The *ouriok* first appears, to Oleg, in the letter from the Kadmins; next in Vera Gangart's daydream when, inexplicably happy, she goes to town seeking the miraculous tree. Finally, in chapter 35, the vision of the pink marvel is bestowed upon Oleg, during the reprieve he is granted on leaving the hospital. (. . .) Music, in a more than casual way, also plays a role in this network of secondary signs, often intervening to express a strong, overwhelming emotion. For example, when Nadya Nerzhin, after her meeting with Gleb, finds herself in the horrible solitude of Room 418, it is the Liszt Étude in F-Minor that reaches her faintly from the neighboring room: "She herself had played it as a girl—but had she understood it? The fingers had played but the soul had not responded to the notation—disperato—*desperately*. (. . .) Desperation. Impotent desperation, trying to rise from its knees but again falling down! That insistent, high D-flat, a cry torn from a woman—a cry, a cry—finding no answer!" (*F.C.*, chap. 47). Music also appears in *Cancer Ward* as the "difficult and disquieting" first movement of Chaykovsky's Fourth Symphony, that melody "in which the hero, perhaps having just returned to life, or perhaps, just recovering from blindness—peering or groping to slide his hand over objects or over a dear face—as if he touches them but still fears to trust his happiness, fears to believe that the objects are really there, that his eyes have begun to see" (*C.W.*, chap. 11).

These musical symbols announce deep-seated resonances: through them, people are not so alone, something in them responds to a call, to a harmony. Along with these secret signs, there are also the triggers of memory that give Solzhenitsyn's heroes a sudden depth, a strong and unexpected resonance. (. . .) In the whitish hours of an early hospital morning, Ephrem Podduyev stares at the pale ceiling of his room: "there came to him with a jolt, with naked clarity—and for no particular reason—a trivial and utterly forgotten event from the past" (*C.W.*, chap. 15). From the white ceiling which he sees lying in bed, three faces emerge. Three anxious faces on which snow is falling and sticking. They are in the camp. Ephrem is the overseer and he leans over the trench which the three men must dig in the insufferable cold. "Listen, comrade-captain, do us a favor and give us the last few centimeters. We're out cold, we've reached the end of the line." The snow enshrouds the already dead faces. Ephrem does not grant them the favor. Then from the grayish ditch, from the chalky ceiling of this early hospital morning comes a frail and almost childlike voice: "All right, but wait your turn; one day, overseer, you too will die." The white shadows fade away on the white screen of the ceiling; only an accusing voice remains, within the very marrow of the man. In chapter 66 of *The First Circle*, Rubin, after the exhausting ideological debate with Sologdin, plagued with insomnia and a migraine, paces the corridor faintly lit with blue light bulbs. He pounds in vain on the guards' desk to go to the infirmary. Each trek up and down the corridor triggers another old painful memory from the spiral of his migraine. First the muffled sound of boots kicking the body of an inmate in the central prison of Kharkov twenty years ago, and bursting forth from the cells the staggering, improvised choir of voices singing "The International." Then the "innocent" interrogation in the Party Secretary's office, and that quiet person who at the end of the interview politely instructs: "Now, just sign here. . . ." And Rubin signs away his cousin's life. Another trigger-click, Rubin is now in charge of the collectivization of a village. Revolver at his side, he tries to erase the "error" and terrorizes the village. And here is the wagon of the dead passing by. It now passes every morning at dawn, through the dead bloodless village. The wagon-driver cracks his whip on the first window-shutter: "Hey! Got any dead bodies? Chuck 'em over!" Then a second shutter: "Hey! Got any dead bodies? Chuck 'em over!" And then he passes again, this time shouting: "Hey! Got any

live bodies?" The migraine pounding in his head, Rubin trembles and
wonders if he is not expiating these apocalyptic voices shouting from
the depths of his past. (. . .) These voices are echoes from within the
man at the hour of silence. Their subsurface connection reconstitutes
the true totality of past history, that which the false literature of
camouflage (so much hated by Solzhenitsyn) would never dare
imagine: the history of the human conscience. Frightened, deafened
by the "silent bell" that Nerzhin hears, Solzhenitsyn's characters
group together, grasp at each other, and the best of them manage to
build an "Ark" which saves them from the chaos of despair:

> Those who floated on the ark were themselves weightless and their
> thoughts were weightless. They were neither hungry nor satiated. They
> did not possess happiness and thus had no fear of losing it. (. . .)
> Love, from time immemorial comprising the delight and the torment of
> humanity, was powerless to affect them with its thrill or its agony. Their
> terms of imprisonment were so long that no one of them could even
> imagine the time when he would go forth to freedom. Exceptional in
> intellect, education, and experience of life, they were men who had
> always devoted themselves too much to their families to have time for
> friends. Here they belonged to their friends.
>
> (. . .) From here, from this ark confidently making its way
> through the darkness, one could easily look out on the tortuous
> blundering course of accursed History—one could survey it whole, as if
> from an enormous height, and in detail, to the very pebbles at the
> bottom of the stream. [*F.C.*, chap. 48]

Solzhenitsyn himself invites us to recognize his two great novels as
privileged moments in the salvation of man, as—like the Biblical
Ark—moments of intense human communion. (. . .) It is clear that
Cancer Ward derives its unity from that room full of patients where so
many destinies converge. (. . .) The protagonists of the debate are
Rusanov, Oleg, Podduyev, and Shulubin. There are moving moments
of communion between these men: for example when Oleg dictates
the recipe for the miraculous infusion of "birch mushrooms" to the
feverish little troop of patients, united all in their common terror of
death and their fragile, almost foolish common hopes. It is the great
debate that inspires the frustrated Podduyev to read the fable of the
master and the cobbler in Tolstoy's "What Do Men Live By?" The
question captivates the poor sentenced victims and each tries to
imagine the answer. (. . .) The argument is re-echoed in chapter
11, when Oleg reveals to the patients that there exist "spontaneous
cures for cancer:" "Something stirred through the chamber. It was as
if a great book had been flung open and spontaneous cure had floated

out, like a palpable, rainbow-colored butterfly, and everyone held up
his forehead, his cheek, to receive its healing touch as it flew by." In
the innermost depth of Podduyev there lurks the fear that the tumor
on his neck is the punishment for his crimes: "All remained silent,
holding up their faces to the butterfly; only gloomy Podduyev moved,
creaking his bedsprings and hopelessly morose, and said in his hoarse
voice: 'For that, though, I suppose you need—a clear conscience'"
(*C.W.*, chap. 11). It is this gauche, amateur debate that creates for us
and actually brings to life this little community of men. It re-emerges
in Part II, in chapter 29, when a dispute occurs over socialism and
equality of means, an anachronistic debate that seems to be a
carry-over from "War Communism" somehow displaced into Stalinism. Here the "duel" between Oleg and Rusanov acquires its full
dimensions, when Oleg accuses the most orthodox champion of class
hatred of being, in fact, a racist.

In truth, this sick room is not the real "Ark." Solidarity in the face
of death is not enough. (. . .) No, the real ark is the community of
devotion and pity established by the other patients, the two admirable
women doctors and the woeful Elizaveta Anatol'evna. From the gentle
smile of the condemned Sigbatov to the anguished smile of Dontsova,
the doctor who is herself afflicted by cancer, there forms an active and
moving alliance: " 'You see, Sharaf,' said Dontsova's eyes, 'I've done
what I could. But now I'm wounded and I too am falling.' 'I know,
mother,' the Tartar's eyes replied, 'and the mother who bore me could
not have done more for me. And now, I am helpless to save you'"
(*C.W.*, chap. 32). But at the heart of this book lies Oleg's whole
internal debate, in search of the true life, in search of the genuine Ark
of Salvation. And it is this struggle that gives the work its essential
dynamic. Having reached middle age, Oleg reckons that he has never
known happiness. And his heart and soul, both insatiate, search for a
direction to take.

Instinctively Oleg thinks that the real men are those of the "secret
order," those who have known the world of the concentration camp,
where "ninety-nine cry and one alone laughs." (. . .) Nevertheless,
the encounter with Shulubin teaches him that this criterion alone is
insufficient. In the course of twenty-five years of deprivation, acquies-
cence and deterioration, Shulubin had become that "strange owl"
with the mad look of Pushkin's miller in *Rusalka*, and all his
accumulated years of speechlessness suddenly explode in a torrent of
words, in a fury of self-destruction. Hearing the breathless confession
of a man who has experienced the ultimate degree of self-negation,
Oleg finally understands "the other Russia," the one that broke backs
and in so many meetings elected "in one voice" to send the black

sheep to Hell. Quiet *autodafés* in the calm of libraries, the denial of science, the damnation of children, the withering of man: can it be that humanity is actually turning backwards to the obscure cavern of idols "under the base sky of fear, covered with gray clouds"?

No; for the singular night bird suddenly rises up and in another voice, gives him hope: to cease hating, to change biological man, to take up once again the example of the liberal thinkers of the nineteenth century, the theocracy of Solovyev, the anarchism of Kropotkin, the populism of Mikhailovsky. Then, everyone based their system of values on the human exchange of mutual aid, on the generosity of human beings, on voluntary sacrifice for a common cause. A reflection then flashes across Shulubin's dilated pupils, a reflection of that flame of sacrifice of the munificent generations of Russia's populists. Vladimir Solovyev taught that history is a path to perfection, from the purely biological realm right up to the realm of God.[2]

"Happiness is impossible" Shulubin cuts in. In yet another domain, Oleg must once again revise his thinking. He comes to the hospital convinced that only the carnal love of a woman can count in a man's life. But a woman teaches him that desire is not everything in love and that abstinence is sometimes more noble. A silent battle follows between Zoya the nurse and Dr. Vera Gangart; a battle which Vera wins because she touches at what's purest and most hidden in Oleg: memories of childhood. This land of childhood is in fact the secret ark whereon those who are saved embark; all who possess, in Solzhenitsyn's work, a seed of that noble generosity which is, for him, the criterion for everything. (. . .)

Despite the immense complexity of *The First Circle*, the symbol of the Ark appears clearly throughout and organizes the whole structure of the *poema*. Despite the juxtapositions, the concomitances, the digressions, the book appears clearly centered, like a medieval romance, on two symbolic banquets: the *sharashka* feast organised in honor of Nerzhin's thirty-first birthday and the "antifeast" of Makarygin, the Prosecutor, in his substantial, sumptuous apartment. (. . .) Through a number of allusions, Solzhenitsyn suggests to us that the

---

[2] A close study should be made of this thirty-first chapter of *Cancer Ward* and of the ideological sources of Solzhenitsyn's "moral socialism." It derives both from the highly personalized voluntaristic ethic of Lavrov and Mikhailovsky, the two populist "thinkers," and from Solovyev's "Theoandry" which saw all progress of human history as the establishment of the "City of God" illuminated by the universal. In *The National Question* one finds a chapter entitled "Idols and Ideals" where the idea is developed of a humanist culture founded on the organising principle of helping one's neighbor.

men of the *sharashka* are forming a new chivalric order and new Arthurian table, without precedence, which contrast to the "free" world (. . .): they are the unfathomable "Rosicrucians" for their superiors and guards, they roam about in an "ark," insensible to the vicissitudes outside. These are the *real* free men.

The feast, called "the Lycée Banquet" in memory of the annual fraternal reunions of Pushkin and his former school-fellows at the Imperial Lycée of Tsarskoe Selo, is the central episode of the book (chap. 53). While the jailers, gnawed with envy or fear, have returned to their bourgeois homes, Gleb Nerzhin's friends gather round the table at their feast of fortune. They are seven in all. There is Potapov, the timid and intransigent hero, there is Adamson, the sceptic veteran of many prisons (the *Chateau d'If* makes him smile), there is Pryanchi-kov, the most ingenuous and childlike of the engineer-prisoners, and there is Kondrashev, the mystical artist, whose job is to supply his superiors with flattering, realistic portraits. Finally, completing the picture around Gleb, are the two brother-enemies, Sologdin and Rubin, who symbolise Russia's two eternal combatants: the mystical, chivalric, and Slavophile; the materialistic, Westernizing, and liberal. Sologdin represents the former; with his beautiful, inspired face and cold blue eyes, he resembles Alexander Nevsky, he is a "sergeant" of Old Russia, a man of Kitezh, the [folk-legendary] pure city, swal-lowed up. Rubin is the latter, the impetuous talkative southerner, convinced that violence must be done to Russia to extirpate the mirages of Kitezh. At this improvised banquet, at this privileged moment of manly friendship, a kind of absolute freedom reigns in the intellectual exchange: ideal Russia lives again. Having begun with the burlesque parody of the trial of Prince Igor, thus lightened and purified by laughter, the day finishes as in the Middle Ages, with an impassioned tournament. But the tournament here is ideological. It is the ancient combat between faith and materialistic reason, between Slavophilism and Westernism, which abruptly enkindles and bursts into flame.

The second feast, called "The Dinner Party" (chap. 56), brings together symbolically the "free" world of the privileged and the satiated. In the luxurious dining room, around a table collapsing under the weight of many dishes and worthy of Muscovite merchants of yore, Makarygin the Prosecutor has gathered his family and several friends, or aspiring suitors of his daughter. With truly Tolstoyan irony, worthy of *Resurrection*, Solzhenitsyn shows us a new patrician society, preoccupied with idle chatter, last night at the opera, and flirtations. But the real discussion takes place between the Prosecutor's two sons-in-law: the writer-male-courtesan Galakhov and the lively diplomat Volodin. Galakhov represents that false literature, draped in its turgid style and in its nonreality, which Solzhenitsyn condemns so harshly. Volodin represents the new *dolce vita* of a certain elite. The entire episode might well remain at the level of social satire, were it not for the fact that, secretly, Volodin, this elegant playboy, this agile disciple of Epicurus, had not already been marked for seizure by the vile hand of Hell.

The pronouncement comes only much later, at the beginning of chapter 78: "He had accomplished his feat by a swift flight of feeling, emotion—and now feeling had plunged him into devastation and exhaustion." The Russian word *"podvig,"* a moral or spiritual feat, explains to us Volodin's behaviour. For in *The First Circle*, between the two stages on which the two symbolic banquets take place, it is he, the lively young man for whom everything indicated easy happiness, who sets in motion the profound dynamic of the book: hurled from the upper circle into the lower by a thrust of pity to which he had yielded for an instant. Innokenty is not prepared for his "feat."

He already regrets it. How could he, in one short telephone conversation, shatter his career and ruin his life? Why did that minute of simple pity make him violate the brazen law of the "class struggle"? In fact, unknown to him, Innokenty Volodin has become the "athlete" of whom St. Paul speaks: he runs, but not to adventure, he struggles, but not in the void. This "feat," however brief, which brings him across the Styx into Hell, sends him at once down the dizzying descent into the trap of history and upwards towards the Ark, where he will find Nerzhin, Spiridon, and Gerasimovich. This "feat" did not happen completely spontaneously; it is the fruit of an old seed implanted by his mother who was both the ardent revolutionary and the cultured woman of the refined "Silver Age" of Russia, who fifteen years before, in her notebooks, had bequeathed to her son these words: "What is the most precious thing in the world? In fact, this: to know in your conscience that you will not take part in iniquities." Obeying his impulse, Innokenty tries to save a man because, if one is granted life only once "one is granted a conscience only once."

Volodin's descent into Hell sets the Mavrino prison in motion. The prisoner-experts are placed in charge of identifying the voice guilty of compassion. Are Rubin's "phonoscopy" and Sologdin's "absolute cryptograph" accomplices of the forces of darkness? In the secret hearts of the *sharashka* Volodin's spiritual feat causes much doubt and torment. In fact the experts are neither guilty nor absolved by their science. The only thing that counts is their innermost determination at the hour of choice. And that hour is not the same for everyone. Innokenty Volodin, in violating the law of hatred, had joined the true ark of the Just, the invisible ark to which each in his own way proceeds—Gerasimovich, Nerzhin, and Spiridon, the blind porter who during a zigzag lifetime of calamities and reverses, always conducted himself with utmost certitude in his soul, never knowing doubt or torment, in accordance with the simple "criterion" of the people: a naive version of the Evangelic law: "The wolf-hound is right, but the cannibal is wrong." In other words, do not be a "wolf-man." When he rejects the offer to work on a tiny piece of photographic equipment for espionage, Gerasimovich first thinks of his wife's worn face and then, without any appeal to pathos, takes his stand with Volodin: "I am not a hunter of men."

Like Oleg in *Cancer Ward*, Nerzhin occupies the central place because he symbolises the quest for truth, a quest which leads him to the humble Spiridon, as it does to the mystic Kondrashev. At the same time he is above the struggling impassioned pair, Rubin and Sologdin. Symbolically, at the very end of the book, it is he who reconciles them and shows them the way: that of renunciation. A renunciation different from that of Oleg Kostoglotov, but also achieved with the aid of a woman, his wife, the tender and radiant Nadya. Nadya's unconditional fidelity uplifts him as much as Vera's pure resigned love saves Oleg. In both cases woman, excluded from the manly world of camp camaraderie, can, when faithful to her profound destiny as woman, inspire from afar, and spark man's courage. (. . .) "Among women, Larisa Nikolaevna, there is a special category. They are the beloved of the Vikings, the sacred Isoldes, with souls of diamond" (*F.C.*, chap. 30). Solzhenitsyn draws an inspired portrait of this Isolde with a diamond soul in the strange and beautiful chapter 23 of *The First Circle*: "The Church of St. Nicetas the Martyr." This long past episode which Colonel Yakonov recalls when "the abyss beckons him once again" represents a kind of digression quite superfluous even in the biography of Yakonov himself. Its role is symbolic: Agniya symbolises all the fiery women who, on the edge of Solzhenitsyn's universe, urge man to accomplish his mission. Agniya—Greek for purity, chastity—"was a girl not born of this earth." (. . .) One day she takes Yakonov into a church on the upper bank of the Moscow River. From the outer courtyard, with the suddenness of a miracle, they discover the whole city at their feet. The setting sun sets the entire panorama ablaze. Inside, shadows of the worshippers intone a hymn in praise of the Virgin Mary: "No soulless church dogmatist had written this litany, but a great unknown poet confined by the monastery; and he had been moved not by a transient lust for a woman's body but by that lofty rapture a woman can inspire in us" (*F.C.*, chap. 23). Agniya, the shy girl frightened by carnal love,

symbolises the inspirational Woman, who sends forth the knight to
great distant feats and dangerous quests. She is the secret model for all
Solzhenitsyn's Isoldes—Vera Gangart, or Nadya Nerzhin. Like Isolde
of the legend, she likes to escape to the depths of forests: "She would
simply wander around and then sit, pondering the secrets of the
forest" (*F.C.*, chap. 23).

The "secret of the forest," this burning secret of nature, represents
the essential element in Solzhenitsyn's symbolism. It is closely linked
with the theme of the mysterious Ark of the Just, and with the theme
of the Holy Grail that comprises chapter 42 of *The First Circle*. The
[silent] command heard by Oleg Kostoglotov on his arrival at
Ush-Terek, "Take up thy bed and walk," is addressed to a man
hunched over, disillusioned, paralysed. Man only need stand up
straight, and fill himself with the freshness of the world and the "secret
of the forests" will be his. Intense and poetic, several episodes in the
two novels describe this religious discovery of the beauty of the world.
It is Oleg's long walk through the city in the morning "on the first day
of creation," it is also Rubin's brief, exhilarating walk through the
prison yard, snowflakes on his happy lips, and the sudden "communion of his whole soul with the freshness of the world." We rediscover
here the poetry of some of the "Etudes" and "Prose Poems," and the
most beautiful passages of *One Day in the Life of Ivan Denisovich*, and
"Matryona's Home." The baptismal beauty of the world is not the
object of simple passive contemplation. On the contrary, the beauty of
the world burns as the soul of the Just burns, like the rebellious birch
fire in Kondrashev's "Autumn Brook." "Understand this! (. . .)
We've got used to thinking of our Russian nature as impoverished,
deprived, just modestly pleasing. But if our nature is only that—then
tell me, where have all our self-sacrificers, self-immolators come from?
The rebel-*streltsy*? Peter the Great? The Decembrists? The revolutionaries of *The People's Will*?" (*F.C.*, chap. 42). In the beauty of the
Russian forest, Solzhenitsyn senses all the beauty of ardent souls.
What he sees in the frigid water of this brook are all the barks of fire
drifting down Russian rivers, carrying in their floating coffins the
eternal, dauntless rebels of Russia. For him, this symbolic river still
flows and continues forever to carry the fiery Ark. History can
therefore recover its meaning. The sacrifices of intrepid souls are
therefore not absurd. (. . .) There *is* a rebirth of value and culture
for man. But for this renaissance to take place, man must be
completely stripped bare, deprived even more starkly than Job, to the
extent of a kind of annihilation of history and all pre–concentration
camp cultures hitherto transmitted to man. We evoked at the
beginning of this essay the reversal of History, the new Judgement

which the "silent bell" heralds. Nothing that Solzhenitsyn evokes or quotes is by chance. Epicurus is there at first as just a simple allusion—the game of a society searching within itself, rather mockingly, for cultural values. Then, when Volodin understands the message of Epicurus more profoundly, we realise that Epicurus is there because he symbolises all of ancient wisdom without God. He represents that which humanity, without God, found to be its most solid rampart. And for Volodin, this rampart turns out to have no meaning. Solzhenitsyn's universe is a reinvention of Christian culture, of Valor and of Grace. And for this reason, only the Middle Ages, that is the new Christian Age, could provide him with the symbols capable of making us understand. (. . .) For the great message of Solzhenitsyn is that the chain of history has been broken, that a methodical concentration of perversity has broken the line of generations, and rendered void the heritage of culture. But, let man strip himself bare, let him thereby enact a new gesture of valor and courage, let him follow the example of Nerzhin or Volodin, and slowly, History will be reborn. And it will be reborn precisely at that point of juncture between the pagan heritage and Christian renaissance as it occurred in the twelfth century, when from out of a cruel disorder there emerged the highest mystical values, and of all values, the most precious: that of Integrity of Self.

The documentary richness of Solzhenitsyn's work would be nothing without this vision of the rupture of History and renaissance of values. All Solzhenitsyn's most memorable characters have, however momentarily, that presentiment that out of the depths of Abandonment everything is reborn. Unforgettable is the cry of Shulubin dying, the tormented Ugolino[3] of Solzhenitsyn's world, whispering in his final breath: "I shall not die completely, not completely." And a moment later: "A flash, ah, a flash. . . ." This is the most dramatic form given by Solzhenitsyn to his message: somewhere in the depths of the circles where we do not see, history is being reborn and man, by his achievement, builds a new foundation "deep in the forest."

[3] [Ugolino della Gherardesca (c. 1220–89) immortalized by Dante in the "Ugolino episode" of the *Inferno*.—ED.]

"Matryona's Home": The Making of a Russian Icon

by Robert Louis Jackson

"O, Rus! My wife! Our long road lies painfully clear ahead!"

> Blok, "On the Field of Kulikovo"

"It chewed 'em all up. Can't even pick up the pieces."
"That's a detail. The nine o'clock express nearly jumped the track, that would've been something."

> Solzhenitsyn, "Matryona's Home"

The years pass, and what is not recalled grows ever dimmer in our memory.

> Solzhenitsyn, *Gulag Archipelago*

Alexander Solzhenitsyn's tale, "Matryona's Home"[1] (1963), consisting of three little chapters, begins with a prologue that is brief, factual, yet tense with significant drama.

One hundred and eighty-four kilometers from Moscow, and a good half year after it happened, all trains slowed down their course almost to a crawl. The passengers pressed to the windows, went out into the vestibule: were they repairing the tracks, or what? Was there a change in schedule?

No. Past the crossing, the train again picked up speed and the passengers settled back.

Only the engineers knew and remembered what it was all about.

And I.

" 'Matryona's Home': The Making of a Russian Icon" by Robert Louis Jackson. Used by permission of the author. This essay appears for the first time in this volume.

[1] The Russian title is *"Matrenin dvor."* The word *"dvor,"* in this context, has the more inclusive meaning of "homestead," or "farmstead," that is, it suggests the house, yard, and the whole domain.

These lines have a dramatic impact upon the reader: his curiosity instantly aroused, he peers ahead in order to learn what has happened, what will happen—what in fact will turn out to be the dramatic and ideological core of the story. The mystery is deepened by the narrator's cryptic and somewhat unconventional way of alluding to the cause of the slow-down: *"esche s dobrykh polgoda POSLE TOGO vse poezda zamedljali svoj khod,"* literally, "a good half year AFTER THAT all trains slowed down their course . . ." (My capitalization—RLJ). What is "that"? As the reader learns in chapter 2 of the tale, "that" is the accident which occurs when "two locomotives coupled together, without lights and moving backwards—why without lights nobody knows"—crash into a tractor, two sledges loaded with lumber and sundry people at a railroad crossing, creating a havoc of organic and inorganic matter. Matryona, too, the central figure in the tale, is crushed. A terrible accident. On the story's deeper symbolic plane of meaning, however, the accident is no accident; it is more than a chance error in the moving of railroad stock, more than a "mistake." The accident is the fated expression—in the story the central metaphor—of vast social and national catastrophe. The accident emerges out of Russian life and history, most immediately out of the years of revolutionary upheaval and change—for Solzhenitsyn profoundly tragic years involving the disfiguration and dislocation of Russian life. The narrator himself, though a marginal actor in this tale, in his own destiny is a bearer of this theme of disfiguration and dislocation: one of the "distant ones" who has spent a good ten years in prison, he "came back at random from the dusty, hot desertlands—simply to Russia." [2] This "random" movement of the narrator is philosophically of the same order as the strange movement of the "two locomotives coupled together without lights, and moving backwards": both movements, seemingly unmotivated and senseless, are in fact symbolic expressions of one violent historical explosion. But the random movement of the locomotives embodies the terrifying amoral force of history; the haphazard movement of the narrator—the reaction of one of those unfortunates to whom such history happens.

The accident is history. Matryona is the focal point of the historical action.

"I wanted to work my way into, and lose myself in, the very core of Russia—if ever there was such a place," observes the narrator in the opening lines of chapter 1. These words signal the pilot effort of

---

[2] The time of the narrator's return to Russia is given as 1953: the date of the dictator Stalin's death. After Stalin's death, masses of amnestied convicts were released from Soviet concentration camps.

Solzhenitsyn's "Matryona's Home": an effort to make a fundamental statement about Russian man and reality. Solzhenitsyn's story is socialist realism turned on its head: it seeks to depict man not in the perspective of the future, but of the past, its myth and reality; it is a look at the old Adam and at the same time an attempt to restore in men's minds the lost outlines of the iconographic image, the concept of a viable ideal, one that is accessible and humane. Matryona's "home" is at the mythic core of Solzhenitsyn's Russia; Matryona herself—the heroine of this fabled, but ailing land, is ill; doomed to perish she is nonetheless its restorative force, the bearer of the theme of its moral reformation. But the "core" of Russia is above all problematic, ominously complex in the contemporary and historical perspective of Solzhenitsyn; its ideal incarnation, its mythopoetic *figura* Matryona is not only challenged, symbolically, by a "second" and "substitute" Matryona (the wife of Faddei) but by the old peasant Faddei himself—an incarnation of darker forces in the core of Russian life; it is challenged, finally, by the metallic era of socialist primary accumulation. The theme of disfiguration in "Matryona's Home" runs from past to present—from the ancient Russian peasant with an axe to the modern "excavators snarling about in the bogs."

The narrator's predilection for the pastoral ideal is prefigured in a scene curiously reminiscent of Turgenev in *A Sportsman's Notebook* (1852): the narrator sitting on a stump in the gentle rolling hills and woods of *Vysokoe Pole* (High Meadow), surrounded by "an unbroken ring of forest;" he wishes that he could live and die in such a place, do nothing but commune with nature "with the whole world silent." But Solzhenitsyn's Russia provides no such total immunity for man from man. "Torfoprodukt [Peat Product]?" ponders the narrator a little later as he scans his official orders directing him to a community of that name where he could find work. "Ah, Turgenev never knew that one could put together such a thing in Russian." [3] The modern place name "Torfoprodukt" and all it connotes signals the end of the Russian idyll. It abruptly announces the theme of disfiguration in the heart of Russian culture: its language. "Torfoprodukt." A terrible accident. Language here anticipates the author's picture of social catastrophe. This "thematic" use of language is characteristic of

---

[3] "Torfoprodukt"—a compound of two words brought into the Russian language, *"Torf"* (German-Austrian dialect for "peat") and "produkt" (product). Turgenev, perhaps, is the greatest prose stylist in Russian literature. The reference to Turgenev, however—the only Russian writer mentioned in "Matryona's Home"—has deeper significance. "Matryona's Home" in certain features—its open form, its use of a narrator-observer, and its oblique critique of the social order—recalls Turgenev's sketches in *A Sportsman's Notebook [Zapiski okhotnika]*.

"Matryona's Home," as it is in other works of Solzhenitsyn, where the typically rich, colloquial speech of Russian life enters into a veritable war with the mutilating jargon of bureaucracy and propaganda.

A growing rumble of imagery announces a curse of disfiguration on this land: the very "stump" upon which the narrator first sits in Vysokoe Pole; the jarring name "Torfoprodukt"; the strange signs at its railroad station, "scratched with a nail," and "carved with a knife"; the once dense and impenetrable prerevolutionary forests "cut down by the peat exploiters and the neighboring collective farm"; acres of timber razed and sold at a profit in Odessa. And in the midst of these peaty lowlands a scene of urban-industrial blight: "a settlement sprawled out in disorder" (barracks of the 1930s and the little houses with glass verandas of the 1950s), yet oddly skewed by a narrow gauge railroad which "here and there" ranged through it. Factory chimneys. Thick smoke. Piercing whistles. And in this typical industrial settlement the narrator could assume "without fear of error" that in the evening the "loud speaker" over the doors of the club would "screech forth in lacerating tones" *(budet nadryvat'sya radiola)*, that on the streets the drunkards would brawl, "not without thrusting at each other with knives." This imagery of social disfiguration foreshadows the impending tragedy.

Torfoprodukt: this was where the narrator's dream of a "quiet little corner in Russia" brought him. Torfoprodukt with its mutilated landscape is a last stop. "It was easy to arrive at Torfoprodukt, but not to leave." But Torfoprodukt is not all of Russia, at least not yet. The landscape of disfiguration is immediately offset by an atmosphere or setting such as that encountered in Washington Irving's "Legend of Sleepy Hollow" or "Rip Van Winkle." At daybreak, after his night at the railroad station, the narrator wanders to the market place and encounters a peasant woman selling milk. He takes a bottle and starts drinking it right away. . . . A new world unfolds. "I was struck by her speech. She did not speak, but sang in a sing-song way and her words were the very ones I was longing to hear when I left Asia." And from this peasant the narrator learned that not everything was peat production, that beyond the railroad "was a hill, and behind the hill—a village, and this village was Talnovo, which had been here from time immemorial, even when the 'gypsy woman' lived there and the enchanted forest stood all round." And beyond Talnovo, "deeper into the hinterland, and farther from the railroad toward the lakes," follow a whole region of villages with "soothing" names that "promised me age-old Russia." Thus do the magically mellifluous words and drink of a Russian peasant woman in a "tiny market place" open the broad way, as in a fairy tale, to Matryona's little homestead with its "two or three willows, a lopsided house" and a pond with ducks and geese—a place that is close to the narrator's heart. And out of age-old Russia, out of the enchanted forest, out of Talnovo, out of her house emerges Matryona—a figure whom the narrator himself compares with one of the "grandmothers in fairy tales"; she emerges to survive and die in a world "turned upside down."

Matryona's strange little lopsided world with its quaint, almost grotesque interior might seem disfigured in the way of Torfoprodukt; yet it is in every respect its antithesis. Outwardly battered by use and nature it has the warmth and humanity of its mistress, the simple rhythms and shapes of a workaday life. The dirty white goat with the twisted horn, the lame cat, the mice that run rampant behind the five loose layers of wallpaper, the tubs full of odd rubber plants, the food with its occasional litter of peat and cockroach legs—everything is touched by the benign and tangible presence of Matryona. Everything is manifestly what it is; of the noisome cockroaches and mice the narrator observes significantly that "there is nothing evil in them, no lie in them." It is here that the narrator "hermit" finds his cot, his refuge; it is here that he begins to discover his ideal.

The "lustreless mirror," like a Gogolian artifact, reflects the "bleary" eye of Matryona; it was plain, notes the narrator, that illness had exhausted her (her illness is almost a motif in the tale). Yet her much emphasized "roundish face" with its quixotic expression points to an almost legendary spiritual health and goodness.

There is more than a touch of Gogol in Matryona's immediate surroundings, in her life and in her person;[4] yet this is no "vegetable life," no tedious world of physical satiety and slumber, no world in which the vitality of things parodies the slumber of man. Food is conspicuous by its absence or meagreness. And the narrator reconciles himself with his diet because "life had taught me not to find the meaning of everyday life in food" (an outlook, of course, quite distinct from that of the hero of *One Day in the Life of Ivan Denisovich*). In this, of course, the narrator mirrors the life view of Matryona. In an existence that is marginal to the engulfing life of the new social and economic forms of the collective farm and state enterprise (she had worked for the collective farm for twenty-five years, but was dismissed when she fell ill), Matryona scours about for food and fuel, potatoes, peat and stumps; yet her essence is not in the Gogolian accumulation of things, in drawing everything towards herself, but in what might be called a

---

[4] We may note, as another example, the fleeting, but touching mention of how Matryona, on receiving her pension money at last, orders from the "hunchbacked tailor" a "wonderful coat."

proliferation of selfless activity. With wondrous energy she aids others, individuals and enterprises, who invariably call on her in their moments of need. This goodness that is neither humble nor dumb, this simple nature that also feels pain and injustice, seems powered by an organic earthly force. In Matryona (her name is etymologically connected with the Russian word *"mat'*,*"* or "mother"), in this peasant possessed of incredible physical strength, one recognizes those indefatigable laborers of Russian life: Russian women. Plain and simple in her half-pagan, half-Christian religiosity and ethic, Matryona is also a type that finds persistent embodiment in Russian literature, one of that class of simple and unpretentious people who do not preach but live their values. Such are the Mironovs in Pushkin's *The Captain's Daughter,* or Samson Vyrin in "The Station Master"; such, too, are Maksim Maksimych in Lermontov's *Hero of our Time*, Devushkin in Dostoevsky's *Poor Folk*, Captain Tushin in Tolstoy's *War and Peace*, or even Chekhov's Samoylenko in *The Duel*—people whom everybody takes for granted, but upon whom everybody depends; people whose reliability rests on their complete freedom from any kind of self-interest or opportunism.

The theme of disfiguration which is heard so emphatically at the opening of chapter 1 rises to a crescendo in chapter 2 with the dismemberment, first, of Matryona's house, and then of Matryona herself in the accident. These two events—which form the structural and ideological center of the story—are part of the tangled skein of past and present. From Matryona herself the narrator learns her tragic personal history: the disappearance of her betrothed, Faddei, in the First World War; her subsequent marriage to Faddei's brother, Yefim, and then the sudden reappearance of Faddei, axe in hand: "If it weren't my very own brother I'd cut you both down with this axe." And then the sequel: her luckless family life with Yefim (six children born and buried, the unfaithfulness and, finally, disappearance of Yefim in the Second World War). Under pressure from Faddei and his daughter and son-in-law (the young couple need a building in order to buy and keep a plot of land), Matryona agrees to yield in her lifetime what she had willed to her niece: the top room of her house. The house must be torn apart. "It was an agony for her to start about smashing that roof under which she had spent forty years," the narrator observes. "Even I as a tenant felt sick at the thought that they would tear out the boards and yank out the beams of the house. But for Matryona this was the end of her whole life. Yet those who were insisting on it knew that her house could be broken up even while she was alive."

The mutilation of Matryona's house and the events leading up to the accident are described in detail. The mood is apocalyptic. Faddei with his sons and son-in-law turned up one February morning and began hacking away with their "five axes," setting up a screeching and creaking as they ripped off the boards. They worked feverishly, left chinks in the walls, and "everything indicated they were wreckers—not builders." Old Faddei came to life in this work of destruction, his eyes "gleamed." Two weeks later the dismembered room is piled onto two sledges. "All were working like madmen." But before leaving the mutilated house they celebrate with drink and leave behind them a scene of "desolate carnage."

The railroad accident itself, the final episode in this drama of destruction, is a terrible mauling of men and material. "It chewed 'em all up. Can't even pick up the pieces," remarks one observer. The locomotives "came flying up and crushed to a pulp the three people who were between the tractor and sledges." Tractor, sledge, tracks, and locomotives are churned into a chaos. The remains of Matryona, covered with a dirty sack on a sled, are "jumbled together. The feet, half of the trunk and the left hand were missing." "The Lord has left her her right hand," observes one peasant woman. "She will say her prayers there." This motif of the reformation of the spiritual image of Matryona—at the opening of chapter 3—follows directly upon the last lines of chapter 2 which speak of the fatality of the tragedy: "For forty years [Faddei's] threat had idled in a corner like an idle broadsword— and then struck at last . . ."

Solzhenitsyn's use of the railroad and of the railroad accident in the ideological design of "Matryona's Home" follows in the rich tradition of Tolstoy and Dostoevsky. For these two great novelists the railroad symbolizes the commercial and capitalist disfiguration of Russian life. The railroad is part of the apocalyptic imagery in Dostoevsky's *The Idiot*. The apocalyptic note is struck in the very first lines of the novel—in the ominous image of the train rushing through the fog, bearing Myshkin and Rogozhin into the chaos of Russian life. The theme of the railroad is used with consummate artistry in *Anna Karenina*. The railroad accident at the opening of the novel—a guard is crushed by one of the trains—is not an "accident" on the deepest level of the novel's meaning: both the death of the guard and the subsequent suicide of Anna on the tracks emerge as ultimate expressions of profound dislocations in a life in which "everything is topsy turvy" (Levin's words), in which new and destructive social and economic forces, spearheaded by the railroad, are overtaking traditional Russian life, tearing up what for Tolstoy is its rich communal and patriarchal fabric. Anna's suicide, in the last analysis, is inseparable from the general social tragedy in Russian life.[5] The same may be said of Solzhenitsyn's conception of the death of Matryona. Her fear of railroads points not simply to her superstitious nature, but to an elemental sense of alienation from all that this railroad and its creation, Torfoprodukt, represent.[6]

The railroad crossing in "Matryona's Home," then, is the tragic junction between all forces in Russian life: those fated to destroy, those fated to perish and those fated to bear witness to the disaster and, perhaps, record it. The accident is but the focal point of a tragic action which embraces all society. The remorseless realism of Solzhenitsyn in developing the theme of disfiguration in "Matryona's Home" prefigures his *Gulag Archipelago*. What dominates the consciousness in a reading of "Matryona's Home," however, is not only the mutilated house and body of Matryona—obvious symbols of a much larger edifice—but the elemental and irrational character of the mutilating forces, senselessness and moral anarchy reaching deeply into men and history. The tragic destiny of Matryona is not alone the product of a "new" upheaval in Russian life. Woven into that destiny is the record of men driven by crude impulses of need and greed, men who have accepted the rituals of Christianity but who have remained alien to its ethic of love and self-sacrifice. The tragedy of botched life in "Matryona's Home" is the more overwhelming because of the disparity between the real and the ideal that it exposes not only in society at large, but in man himself. In this connection the figure of Faddei occupies a central place in Solzhenitsyn's tableau. The dark counterpart of Matryona on the mythic as well as the real plane of the story, Faddei is the legendary Russian peasant with an axe. How does he use that axe: as a "builder or destroyer"? Faddei, too, emerges out of the "core" of Russia; he threatens Matryona with his axe, seeks out another woman with the name of Matryona to marry, as though, in malice, to scratch out the very existence of the "first" Matryona; finally, eyes gleaming, he lays an axe to Matryona's house and, in effect, to Matryona herself. This strange figure carries the motif of *demonism* in the story—not without reason is the epithet "dark," *chernyj*, applied seven times in the opening two lines of the description of Faddei; yet he is not without a deceptive potential. The narrator

[5] See my discussion, "Chance and Design in *Anna Karenina*," in *The Disciplines of Criticism*, edited by Peter Demetz *et al.* (New Haven: Yale University Press, 1968), pp. 315-29.

[6] The narrator, clearly, is very close to Matryona in his basic outlook on contemporary industrial society. His purely social perspectives would seem to turn backwards into Russian history, rather than forwards. In this respect, his interest in photographing "somebody at an old-fashioned handloom" is indicative.

outlines the sad state of affairs in Faddei's life after the accident: his
daughter's sanity has been shaken, his son-in-law faces a criminal
charge in connection with the accident, and his son, as well as his first
betrothed, Matryona, are dead. Faddei stands by the coffins only
briefly, then leaves. "His lofty brow was clouded by painful thoughts,
but what he was thinking about was—how to save the timbers of the
top room from the flames and from Matryona's scheming sisters."
Faddei's "lofty brow," struggling with thought, seems to promise
something more worthy of the destiny of man than acquisitiveness. But
the promise is a lie.

"Going over the people of Talnovo in my mind," the narrator
continues, "I realized that Faddei was not the only one like that."

Faddei's choice of evil arouses in the narrator the following
speculation: "The [Russian] language strangely calls property our
good, [*dobro*] whether it be the people's property or personal. And yet
losing any of it is considered disgraceful and stupid by the people."
(The Russian word *"dobro"* signifies both "goods," property, and
ethical "good.") The line of thought here is tragic: the only "good"
that man understands is property, material goods, whatever is *good for
him*, whatever serves his self-interest; his feeling of "shame" in giving
up property, therefore, parodies that feeling of shame man is supposed
to feel when he deviates from ethical good, from his supposed inner
sense of what is right or just. In like manner Faddei's "painful
thoughts," in their inner essence and genealogy, sharply parody and
contradict the lofty spiritual attribute arbitrarily assigned to the "lofty
brow" by the indulgent observer. The demonism of Faddei, then,
consists in the fact that he, like so many others around him, stands at
the fringe of moral evolution, a troubled and uncertain realm
where—as Dostoevsky repeatedly demonstrates—acquisitiveness, violence and sensuality constitute an entangling syndrome.[7]

Even the religious conventions and rituals would seem only to mask
man's moral and spiritual immaturity. "I observed in the weeping a
coldly thought-out time-worn pattern," the narrator observes of the
lamentations over the body of Matryona. The striving for goods set the
tone of these "political" lamentations. "At her burial all sang, 'Worthy

---

[7] The ambiguity of the word *"dobro,"* we may note here, is brought out by
Dostoevsky in Raskolnikov's dream about the beating of the mare. "My property!"
(*moyo dobro!*) screams the peasant Mikolka repeatedly as he beats his horse. Mikolka's
crude "ethic" is plain: what I covet and own releases me from all obligations because
it is *my* good (property). See my discussion of this problem in "Philosophical Pro and
Contra in Part One of *Crime and Punishment*," in *Twentieth Century Interpretations of "Crime
and Punishment*," ed. Robert Louis Jackson (Englewood Cliffs, N.J.: Prentice-Hall, Inc.,
1974), pp. 34–35.

is She.' Then again thrice over: eternal memory! eternal memory! eternal memory! But the voices were hoarse, discordant, their faces drunk and nobody put any feelings into the eternal memory." And after the special guests left, the remaining relatives "took out their cigarettes, smoked, exchanged jokes and laughter." In such a world Matryona, who "never tried to acquire things for herself," who "never struggled to buy things and then treasure them more than life," who "never tried to dress smartly," was inevitably considered a "ridiculous creature"; in such a world Matryona, who would work for others without pay, who even accompanied her dismembered house to the railroad crossing (as though to her crucifixion), was inevitably pitied and scorned; in such a world, as the narrator concludes, Matryona was the only true "righteous" one. "All of us lived alongside her and did not understand that she was that very righteous one without whom, according to the proverb, no village can stand. Nor city. Nor our whole earth."

Matryona, clearly, was the only true Christian; in the language of her time—the only true communist.

The Russian word for image or form is *obraz,* and it carries the implication of the highest beauty; it also stands for "icon"; its antithesis in the Russian language is *bezobrazie*—disfiguration, the monstrous, literally, that which is "without form or image." These two moral-aesthetic opposites structure Solzhenitsyn's story and invest much of its imagery with their deeper symbolic meaning. Matryona is mother Russia. Her death, in the symbolism of Solzhenitsyn, signifies Russia's martyrdom.

> Matryona is no more. Somebody precious had been killed *[ubit rodnoj chelovek].* And I had reproached her the day before for wearing my jerkin. The ornately drawn red and yellow peasant woman in the bookstore advertising poster smiled joyfully.[8]

Matryona, real and tangible, nonetheless has a mythic aura; but she is infinitely more real in all her moral and spiritual health, than

[8] The word *"rodnoj"* has several related meanings: one's own (a close, blood relationship); close in spirit or way of life; native; dear; precious. The phrase, then *"ubit rodnoj chelovek"* (literally, "a dear or closely related person has been killed") suggests an intimate family relationship between the narrator and Matryona, and between a mother and son. It may be noted here that the intimate and chaste relationship between the narrator and Matryona is suggested symbolically in the last lines of section 2 of the story, after Matryona's death. The narrator imagines Faddei on the threshold declaring: "If it weren't my very own brother I'd cut you both down with this axe." He is alone in the hut, but at that moment Matryona is "invisibly fluttering about in the hut and bidding all farewell."

the "joyfully smiling" woman who looks down at the narrator from the poster on the wall of the hut, that Soviet madonna who knows no home in the real world as she knows no suffering. Matryona, horribly disfigured in the accident, yet emerges a symbol of transcendent spiritual beauty. Solzhenitsyn's final description of Matryona in death suggests precisely the triumph of *image (obraz)* over disfiguration *(bezobrazie)*. "Matryona lay in her coffin. Her lifeless, mangled body was neatly and simply covered with a clean sheet. Her head was enveloped in a white kerchief, but her face, undamaged and peaceful, seemed more alive than dead." Matryona's death completes the making of a Russian icon.

A premonition of catastrophe pervades the prologue to this story. "Only the engineers knew and remembered what it was all about. And I." The author Solzhenitsyn here merges with the narrator, memory with conscience, history with art. Of course: precisely on this level of art, in the creation of moral-aesthetic form, the aching disparity of the real and ideal is bridged, the disfiguration of history is overcome, suffering is redeemed, and the possibility of moral progress in society restored. Such is the action of all significant art.

The Debate over *August 1914*

by Nikita Struve

More than a year has passed since the appearance in the West—and subsequently in *samizdat*—of Aleksandr Solzhenitsyn's latest novel, the first fascicle ("knot") of a projected series of works devoted to Russia's fate over a span of more than forty years. In the short period since the appearance of this novel, many different and contradictory opinions have been expressed. Openly and sometimes in veiled fashion, a controversy has arisen around the novel both in Russia and in the West. From this controversy certain definite conclusions can already be drawn.[1]

The appearance of a literary genius is, for various reasons, always accompanied by a certain amount of uneasiness and distrust. There is in mankind, and perhaps in each individual man, a reluctance to acknowledge that which is superior; we fear that a phenomenon of a higher order will degrade us, and, therefore, something unquestionably low and sinful within us struggles against the recognition of such phenomena. But we also possess an opposite and conscientious desire to examine ourselves and make certain that we are not victims of self-delusion, illusion or infatuation, that we are not, in a fit of uncontrolled enthusiasm, elevating something which is really unworthy. Uneasiness and distrust, as well as enthusiasm and paeans of praise, have accompanied the appearance of each of Solzhenitsyn's works. When Solzhenitsyn's first two short works, *One Day in the Life of Ivan Denisovich* and "Matrena's Home" appeared, they immediately

"The Debate over *August 1914*" by Nikita Struve. From *Vestnik Russkogo Studencheskogo Dvizheniya* 104/105: 197–210. Copyright © 1972 by *Vestnik*. Reprinted from John B. Dunlop, Richard Haugh, and Alexis Klimoff, eds., *Aleksandr Solzhenitsyn: Critical Essays and Documentary Materials*, translated (in slightly abridged form) by Olga V. Dunlop (Belmont, Mass.: Nordland, 1973). Translation copyright © 1971 by Nordland Publishing Co. Reprinted by permission of the publisher.

[1] These remarks were written before an excellent *samizdat* collection of critical studies on *August 1914* reached the West. (N.S.) They have been recently published by YMCA Press in Paris as *Avgust chetyrnadtsatogo chitaiut na Rodine* [*How* August 1914 *Is Read in the Homeland*].—J.D. *et al.*

struck everyone by their close kinship, in terms of truthfulness and depth, to the great tradition of Russian classical literature (i.e. Dostoevsky, Chekhov, Turgenev). At the time readers remarked, "Yes, these are marvellous works, but they are only short narratives. Will the author be able to cope with the larger genre of the novel?" This legitimate question was answered in the affirmative when *The First Circle* and *Cancer Ward* made their appearance. But, although all now agreed that Solzhenitsyn had succeeded with both the long and short narrative form, new doubts arose. In his novels Solzhenitsyn describes what he has seen with his own eyes and has personally experienced. It was questioned whether he was capable of writing a novel not based on his own life; whether, like a true novelist, he could recreate through his imagination the heroes, mores, and life-style of another epoch and of other worlds. And, as if in answer to this no less legitimate question, there appeared *August 1914*, a novel written half a century after the historical events it describes, just as, incidentally, half a century separates the publication of Pushkin's *The Captain's Daughter* from the Pugachev rebellion and *War and Peace* from the Napoleonic wars.

Being, as it were, the final and supreme test of Solzhenitsyn's claim to recognition as a great writer, it is not surprising that *August 1914* has only served to sharpen those sentiments of approval and enthusiasm, on the one hand, and distrust and censure, on the other, which accompanied the appearance of all his works. (. . .)

The most basic objections which were expressed in the press, in private letters and in discussions concerned the following aspects of the novel: its literary form, which, in the eyes of some, was insufficiently rich in images; its formal structure with its preponderance of war over peace; an alleged inaccurate portrayal of the spirit of the times; an excessively mannered language. And, finally, many disliked the theme itself—the author's attitude toward Russia.

Some readers, especially in the Soviet Union (we know this from private letters and from the response of recent émigrés to Israel), were put off by the realistic manner of *August*, which they considered too akin to the notorious and detested method of socialist realism. Aside from the incorrectness of this judgment, it would seem that we are here dealing with an "overreaction," where a justifiable aversion to socialist realism has passed directly into a denial of realism as such. But it is of course quite obvious that socialist realism fails not because of its realism (there has never been a trace of realism in it) but precisely because of the absence or rather perversion and desecration of reality by political fiat. In this sense socialist realism is also a caricature of idealism. The "ideal" always has been and always will be the subject of art, including realistic art. In depicting a world compatible with

Communist ideology, socialist realism has to describe that which does not exist in nature. Furthermore, even if such a world were actually to come into existence in the future, it would represent nothing but a gross reduction and distortion of man. Even without the presence of political demands, socialist realism, by denying the metaphysical foundation of existence, inevitably becomes philosophically flat, a false oversimplification of life. In other words, socialist realism fails because it is socialistic and materialistic. But realism as an artistic method is just as unchanging and eternal as the fantastic or other experimental forms of expression. It should also be obvious that the historical or historio-philosophical novel can only be realistic.

But there are different kinds of realism, different in the degree to which they encompass reality. While socialist realism perverts and impoverishes reality, its literary predecessor, naturalism, was satisfied merely to reflect nature, to copy its contours without stepping beyond its boundaries. Only a higher realism encompasses human existence in its fulness, from mundane details to the transcendent laws of life.

A perusal of the first few lines of *August 1914* is sufficient to convince us as to which of the three above-named types of realism this novel belongs. From the very start Solzhenitsyn uses this higher form of realism to describe his heroes and the action of the novel. The transcendent mountain range [*Khrebet*] which Sania Lazhenitsyn sees so clearly as he departs for the war is a many-sided symbol: on the historical plane it is a symbol of Russia's highest hour before a fateful break;[2] on the metaphysical plane it symbolizes something higher and purer than man and his creativity. In this remarkably successful introduction, with its depth and variety of meaning, Solzhenitsyn defines from the outset both his perception of the world—unquestionably Christian—and his creative approach, which is not simply to reflect history, but an attempt to penetrate to its deepest meaning. It remains for us, however, to demonstrate to what extent Solzhenitsyn has been successful in carrying out his intentions, in embodying his perception of the world, and in sustaining his artistic approach.

One should first of all keep in mind that *August 1914* is only the first of several fascicles projected by the author. As Solzhenitsyn states in the foreword of his novel, he does not claim that the novel is complete, nor even that the characters are sufficiently developed. "Except for the military operation of Samsonov's army," the author explains, "this is only the preliminary layout." Since the majority of the characters are only barely outlined, we are not justified in making the same critical demands on them as we would on those of a completed novel. We are

---

[2] In Russian *khrebet* means both mountain range and backbone.—Tr.

dealing here with a most difficult genre, the novel-in-many-parts, one which has no counterpart in Russian literature. Even in world literature few have successfully used this form (with the possible exception of Galsworthy). Moreover, such works usually trace the fortunes of one family through several generations rather than dealing with a variety of unconnected characters. On the basis of the first fascicle we cannot yet pass judgment on Solzhenitsyn's ultimate success or failure, but we must emphasize that he has taken upon himself a titanic task unprecedented in world literature.

Every great writer has his own unique approach to time and space, his own personal experience of these two dimensions of existence. In Gogol's works, for instance, time does not exist; his characters do not develop but are depicted in an immobile state, and Chichikov is not fated to be reborn. Space, therefore, is also illusory in his works; Chichikov travels extensively in *Dead Souls*, but he is only circling a monochromatic and undifferentiated area. In Tolstoy time unfolds smoothly. Despite the fateful events which are described, there are no discontinuities; time and space are unlimited; a landlord walks or drives the length and breadth of his estate for hours. In Dostoevsky time and space progressively build up in intensity, become concentrated, are brought to a climax and contract to a few fateful moments in a limited area (most often a room or staircase). Then comes an abatement or release in the form of a temporal-spatial lapse (Raskol'nikov's unconsciousness, the Idiot's journey which is not described to us, etc.). Just as Tolstoy's perception of time derived from the patriarchal way of life, so Dostoevsky's was a product of his experience of the last minutes before death on Semenovskii Square and of the momentary illumination preceding an epileptic seizure. Chekhov also has a unique experience of time: leisurely and slow, it changes pace only in extreme circumstances.

Solzhenitsyn has his own experience of time, one which, as far as I know, is unique in literature and which probably grew out of his extended concentration camp experience. Like Dostoevsky, although, as we shall see, in a somewhat different manner, Solzhenitsyn concentrates time to the utmost and maximally limits space. The camp life of Ivan Denisovich is described within the duration of one day, *Cancer Ward* lasts several weeks, and *The First Circle*—only four days. *August 1914* is compressed into eleven days. These telescoped time dimensions correspond to an increased density in space: a prison-camp, a railroad station, a home, a hospital, a sharashka or a small corner of Eastern Prussia . . . This constancy of vision and uniformity in the pattern of the temporal-spatial dimensions already attests and defines the imagistic nature of Solzhenitsyn's thought. This alone would make of him an important and original writer.

Following the laws of tragedy, Dostoevsky depicts his protagonists at a moment when their fate has already been internally determined and is building up for the denouement. With Solzhenitsyn it is different; his characters depend not so much on their own spiritual development as on external events and stimuli. They are part of a social and historical whole and come into conflict with each other and even with themselves as a result of external circumstances. The diverse representatives of Soviet society in the Tashkent hospital are brought together by illness. Technical training or plain chance has assembled the prisoners in the Moscow sharashka. The same is true of *August 1914*; war intrudes into the peaceful and mundane existence of the novel's future protagonists, catching them by surprise, making no distinction among them, and bringing some of them together on the first battlefield of the war. Obviously the author cannot fully develop his protagonists in the ten or eleven days which are described; they only begin to live. Therefore we shall be able to judge the final success or failure of each protagonist only after the completion of other volumes, if not at the end of the entire work. The one exception is General Samsonov, the chief and only fully developed hero in the first fascicle of the novel. *August* begins as a great and tragic epic about the history of the Russian people and state; in all probability, each subsequent volume of this epic will contain its own particular and completed tragedy. We may assume that the protagonists of the work will gradually become clearer and better defined against the background of these specific and self-contained tragedies.

In *August* the death of Samsonov and the destruction of his army is such a self-contained tragedy. It is on the basis of this tragedy that we must judge the whole work. And here, we believe, all must concur— both those who praise *August* and those who are critical of it. Piotr Rawicz, the literary critic of the French evening paper *Le Monde*, who published an enthusiastic review of Solzhenitsyn's novel, speaks of a "Shakespearian resonance" in the depiction of Samsonov. Even the harsh and unfair critic of *August*, Roman Gul', admits that "these scenes in the novel raise Solzhenitsyn to the summits of Russian classical literature." [3] Indeed, perhaps in no other of his novels was Solzhenitsyn able to penetrate so deeply into the secret depths of man's soul (except perhaps in the description of Volodin's arrest in *The*

---

[3] The reference is to Roman Gul's article "Chitaia 'Avgust Chetyrnadtsatogo'," ["Reading *August 1914*"] which appeared in the émigré *Novyi Zhurnal* 104 (1971): 55–82.—Tr.

First Circle) and to unite so convincingly in one person the private with the corporate, the real and historical with the transcendent. Certainly no one can speak of "non-imagistic thought" here. General Samsonov is portrayed simultaneously on the psychological, historical, historiosophical and religio-ethical planes.

A conscientious, reasonable, modest, and honest general, he becomes by the will of Providence at once the perpetrator and victim of the catastrophe which will result in the fall of Russia. He is not directly responsible for the disaster since he did not conceive the absurd plan involving a premature offensive; nevertheless, as commander-in-chief, he carries responsibility for it. With extraordinary psychological insight Solzhenitsyn shows how Samsonov, sensing defeat, divests himself of everything he has accumulated during a long military career. He descends deeply into himself, to his childhood memories, and then rises upward in prayer, preparing himself for sacrifice. On this deep level Samsonov approaches a kinship with Christ, experiences his own Gethsemane. Like Dostoevsky, Solzhenitsyn was not afraid to superimpose the image of Christ onto a protagonist of his novel—and onto the fate of a Russian general at that. While kneeling in prayer, Samsonov wipes off a heavy sweat—compare this to the bloody sweat of Christ in the Gospel account. Like Christ in the Gospel, Samsonov experiences an hour of absolute isolation. When he rises from prayer, "no one had come for him either with a pressing question or with a cheering or bad report." And descending even deeper, Samsonov is granted a vision of his own impending death . . .

In comparing Samsonov with Christ, Solzhenitsyn has masterfully avoided any labored moments, any sentimentality or artificiality inherently possible in such a bold comparison. Colonel Vorotyntsev calls Samsonov a "seven-pood lamb." With this unusual word-combination Solzhenitsyn promptly defines the limits of his comparison and, at the same time, expands Samsonov's image to the dimensions of all Russia. This Shakespearian protagonist, having divested himself of all glory and earthly dignity, turns out to be a profoundly Russian hero, a symbol and sign of the approaching fate of Russia—at once guilty and innocent, sacrificed and self-sacrificing.

The days preceding Samsonov's death, his "pre-Petrine" and "pre-Muscovite" farewell to the army, become a singular rite of forgiveness and the high point of the novel. Nevertheless, the conclusion drawn by some critics (in particular Roman Gul') who think that this moment overwhelms the rest of the novel is wrong. On the contrary, Samsonov's monumental and in-depth portrait does not stifle but rather elevates the entire body of the novel to an appropriate height. In the light of Samsonov's death, we can understand the real significance of the army's prolonged and senseless advance and of its staunch resistance even to death. Between the tenth and twenty-first of August, through the fault of its obdurate leadership and partly through no one's fault, but according to the mysterious laws of inscrutable destiny, all Russia was going to the slaughter amid the sands and lakes of Eastern Prussia. The movements of the many different regiments are described in precise detail, and Solzhenitsyn forces us to march with them over the sandy roads of Prussia because he wants us to witness and to participate in Russia's national Golgotha.

In the light of what has been said, the objections of those who complain that the chapters describing the military maneuvers are not well integrated with the rest of the work, that they stand alone and are written for the military specialist rather than the average reader, pale to insignificance. Furthermore, in addition to their image-creating, unifying function, the military chapters also have other qualities. Solzhenitsyn is an unsurpassed portrayer of battle. He succeeds as few others in simultaneously showing both the mass nature of modern war and its deeply personal character. Despite the detailed description of the planned or disorderly movements of the troops, they never create confusion or swallow up the individual and personal aspects. Following Stendhal, Tolstoy described a small section of the battle through the eyes of one of his protagonists or ascended with the army command to some observation point from which he observed the battlefield. Solzhenitsyn, on the other hand, is always in the very thick of movements, skirmishes or battles. I am not aware of any other work in Russian or world literature in which the personal and the corporate are so harmoniously combined, or which gives such a complete picture of a military operation, from the high command down to the innumerable and nameless soldiers.

It is appropriate here to touch upon the question of Solzhenitsyn's insertion of special chapters into the fabric of the novel—the montages of newspaper items of the time, the "survey" chapters which exclude the fictional characters and, finally, the "screen" chapters. These chapters, which stand out both graphically and stylistically, seemed to many to be an unnecessary tribute to the literary modernism which was the rage in the Western novel of the twenties. Solzhenitsyn, they said, included these chapters in order to disarm those critics who accused him of excessive traditionality. It seems improper, however, to pose the question this way. Solzhenitsyn had need of these chapters not in order to answer his critics but to encompass as fully as possible that reality which he had undertaken to describe. The newspaper clippings allow him, in an unusually concise way, to throw light on those aspects of Russia which remain outside the scope of the narrative, i.e. beer-hall patriotism, a banal belief in progress, the general smugness which reigned on the eve of the fateful catastrophe, the lack of mutual understanding between the home front and the army, etc. Furthermore, the newspaper clippings introduce an element of healthy and objective humor, which every tragic epic needs like a safety vent.

The survey and screen chapters expand the panorama of the war. The survey chapters, which are, incidentally, not obligatory for the indolent reader, allow the author to single out in an impartial fashion high-lights of the advance and the defeat which would otherwise be lost in the course of the narrative. They serve as a kind of bird's-eye view of events—distant in both time and space. The screen chapters, on the other hand, offer a close-up view; they direct the eye to details and heighten the emotion of the moment. The alternation of different kinds of chapters adds a rhythmic movement to the novel: the survey chapters slow down the rhythm, the screen chapters accelerate it. We are not then dealing with an antiquated modernism or the employment of devices allegedly rendered illegitimate after their use by Dos Passos. It is true that Solzhenitsyn did not invent these devices, although it would be difficult to find in world literature an exact analogy to the screen chapters, with their distinct focus on sound, long-distance shots, details, and direct speech. Moreover, is the criterion for accepting a literary device merely its originality and not its appropriateness? Surely not only that which is novel is worthwhile and justified but also that which finds an appropriate and organic function. Why should one hold that Dos Passos discovered a literary device suitable only for himself? Like all major writers, Solzhenitsyn has absorbed the novelistic techniques of many different eras . . .

The military chapters stand out in still another, no less important way—by their remarkable and almost scientific precision. Perhaps nowhere did *August* elicit such approval as among the veterans of World War I in the Russian emigration. In the opinion of these eyewitness-specialists this military operation of some fifty years ago is described with unimpeachable exactitude. Here we encounter one of the peculiarities of Solzhenitsyn's genius: his scientific cast of mind. We should observe, however, that in this respect Solzhenitsyn has only brought to perfection a quality possessed by all true novelists. Since Pushkin had no historical materials which he could easily draw upon, he became a historian to write *The Captain's Daughter*; he recreated the Pugachev period solely on the basis of carefully collected and meticulously examined materials. Tolstoy also studied the era of Alexander I for several years, although in the long run his poetic and polemical talent overcame the historian in him. Solzhenitsyn has a similar approach. He did not need to write the history of the Prussian campaign (there were already many such studies), but he did study the existing materials with great thoroughness. Therefore the reproach of some critics who accuse him of inaccuracy is comical. We must distinguish here between reproaches for specific factual errors and a more general charge of an inaccurate grasp of the spirit of the time. Pushkin's *The Captain's Daughter* was also reproached for containing a number of anachronisms, but does this in any way diminish its literary worth? After more than a century not a single reader can any longer notice these anachronisms. It is also a fact that the veterans of the campaign of 1812 were indignant at the inaccuracies in Tolstoy's descriptions of military operations in *War and Peace*, but this has not the slightest significance for us. Therefore the question, raised by one critic, as to whether Varsonof'ev could have lured two young students into a beer-hall and drunk beer with them is of little importance. This may now seem like an anachronism to some, but in twenty years not a single reader will notice this detail. Moreover, if one must accuse Solzhenitsyn, I would rather reproach him for having an insufficient number of anachronisms, for reproducing the period too exactly . . . Perhaps every work of art needs a little poetic fantasy . . .

The question as to whether the author has faithfully reproduced the spirit of the time described is more substantial, since it touches upon matters of aesthetics. We know that *War and Peace* was widely criticized for showing the epoch it depicts in a false light. Konstantin Leont'ev wrote that Natasha Rostov is more characteristic of the spirit of the eighteen-sixties than of 1812. That may well be true. But the mistake lies in the way the question is posed. All historiosophical novels throw light simultaneously on two historical periods—the period they describe and that in which they are written. Pushkin undertook *The Captain's Daughter* in an attempt to illumine and rethink the socio-political relations between the gentry and the people in the light of the Pugachev rebellion. The rather unlikely friendship and mutual respect between Grinev and Pugachev reflect the hope for harmony between the classes prevalent in the eighteen-thirties. Similarly, the starting point for Tolstoy's *War and Peace* was the return of the Decembrists from exile and the writer's desire to return to the epoch which gave them birth.

Solzhenitsyn has the same approach. Like his great predecessors he sees the past through the present. It is not by chance that the same time span of half a century separates the three novels we have mentioned from the events they describe. The historical novel is born naturally of a gap in time in order to reestablish a lost connection. There was little of Catherine's epoch left in the reign of Nicholas I and little of the Alexandrian era in post-Emancipation Russia. Much more awesome is the gap between pre-revolutionary and contemporary Russia. Solzhenitsyn himself emphasized this break when he said in the novel that one no longer meets the same smiling, trusting faces as before. The events described in *August* are not only interesting in and of themselves but even more as a key to the understanding of the present. A dialogue with the present is an important element of the novel.

When Roman Gul' writes that no one in 1914 would have said, as Sania Lazhenitsyn does in the novel, "I feel sorry for Russia," he is wide of the mark. "No one would even have entertained such an idea," Gul' maintains. In the first place, I would like to ask the critic how he can be so omniscient. Perhaps the war did awake uneasy presentiments in some Russians (one person experiencing such presentiments was, for example, Rasputin), if only because of its analogy with the defeat in the recent Japanese war. But that is not really the point. "I feel sorry for Russia," is more than just another point in the controversy between pro-war and defeatist factions. It has a more general, trans-temporal significance. It is one of those threads that bind eras together. What is appropriate in a work of art is not that which seems most plausible to the average reader but that which can raise the moment above the flow of time, without contradicting the essence of the epoch which it describes. The statement "I feel sorry for Russia," especially in reference to 1914, may express not only Sania Lazhenitsyn's feelings but also the author's and even our own, since we know the events which followed. Konstantin Leont'ev once remarked that Pierre Bezukhov is not a man of 1812 but of a later era, since one can discern echoes of Gogol' and Dostoevsky in his thoughts. Certainly Pierre is not believable from the point of view of pedestrian realism; but from the artistic point of view he embodies that mutual penetration of different historical epochs which is a sine qua non of any true historical novel. Konstantin Leont'ev also stated that Tolstoy made the psychology of the generation of 1812 more complex than it actually was, since he was viewing it through the prism of his own time. It is possible that the opposite has occurred with Solzhenitsyn: he may have somewhat simplified the psychology of pre-revolutionary Russia by viewing it through the prism of the nineteen seventies. It could not be otherwise and to complain of this is in vain. (. . .)

Equally unjustified are those who reproach Solzhenitsyn for using a modernized form of the Russian language. It is obvious that Solzhenitsyn could not and should not have written in the language of 1914; the result would have been an archaeological, and hence artificial, reproduction of the past and not a novel. Pushkin used a contemporary rather than eighteenth-century language in *The Captain's Daughter*, and only occasional lexical archaisms remind us that the narrative is dealing with the past. From the artistic point of view it is important for the author to capture, both in his language and his concrete details, the spirit of the period he describes in what is basic and most important, not in minute details. A historical novel is not a photographic reproduction but an artistic recreation in which many levels of language play a role. The reader of the work must be aware of a distance in time, but, at the same time, this distance must to some extent be capable of being disregarded; otherwise one is left with a dead copy and not a living narrative. Despite their differences the time which the novel describes and period in which it is written become one. A historical novel must also not be too contemporaneous. Perhaps this will help us to understand why Solzhenitsyn's quest for a language peculiarly his own is more noticeable in *August* than in his other works.

However, it is precisely this distinctive language of the novel which has been criticized so strongly for being pretentious and mannered. This view ignores the problem of language which confronts the contemporary Russian writer. The Russian language has become gray, impoverished, and faded in the Soviet period. The degeneration of the language is only a reflection of the general degeneration of the country. In all of his works Solzhenitsyn has taken up the difficult task of returning vitality, verve, and color to the Russian language. This was especially needed in *August;* it was unthinkable for the author to describe pre-revolutionary Russia in his contemporary language. And so Solzhenitsyn evolved a language of his own. *August* is striking in its dynamic use of syntax. There has probably never been such select, terse, tense speech used in Russian prose, with the possible exception of Marina Tsvetaeva. At the same time Solzhenitsyn, like Leskov, has expanded the lexical pool of the language. It is difficult to determine at present whether all the words that Solzhenitsyn has picked up from actual speech or culled from dictionaries are successful. (. . .) It is difficult to dispute about language with a great writer possessing a sharper instinct for words than his critics. Besides, whether Solzhenitsyn's every lexical innovation is justified is not vitally important. What is important is that the Russian language in *August* appears renewed, shines with new color, acquires new strength and power.

Solzhenitsyn's language expresses one of the particularities of his literary genius: his overwhelming will-power. Russian literature has never known a writer of such forceful will. Pushkin and Lermontov were first of all poets, and their will-power was therefore of necessity weakened. Tolstoy also did not express a forceful will in his fiction; again and again his poetic gift overcame his will. Thus *War and Peace* gradually changed from the pacifistic novel that the author had originally intended into a poetic apology for war. Dostoevsky did manifest will-power, but it was limited by his illness. Goncharov, Turgenev and Chekhov were all in their own way devoid of will. But Solzhenitsyn's fate, life and work are characterized above all by will. To survive four years at the front, live through the Soviet concentration camps, overcome serious illness, struggle to become a writer, gain a world reputation against inhuman odds, and finally unswervingly to follow his path—all this is a miracle of rare will-power. Ivan Denisovich, Matrena, Nerzhin, Kostoglotov, Vorotyntsev are characters of supreme will-power whom Solzhenitsyn presents as examples to his readers. And to some extent this volitional element somewhat overcomes the poetic element in Solzhenitsyn, or, rather, it adds a peculiar and, on occasion, somewhat brusque nuance to his work.

We have already stated that Samsonov's death is the high point of the novel. But there is another high point in the book which parallels it and is no less important—the breakthrough of the small group led by Vorotyntsev through the Grunfliess forest. Just as the decay and the foredoom of Old Russia are graphically depicted in Samsonov's death, so the breakthrough serves to offer us hope for a better future. All is lost, all is destroyed, but there is still action, even if on the most insignificant scale. Vorotyntsev, who at one point traversed the entire front in an effort to save the situation, can now save only himself and the handful of men left to him. Thus Solzhenitsyn shows that in all circumstances, in the words of his prayer, "not all the paths of goodness are closed." Vorotyntsev's breakthrough embodies the author's philosophy of the will, one relevant for all periods of time but especially appropriate for the present. Even when confronted with total destruction one must continue to act wherever possible. The conditions necessary for a successful result of such activity are also indicated—a close bond to the soil and to heaven. The exhausted Vorotyntsev, upon awakening from sleep, feels "the grass, so pristine, uniform, silky, from which purity flowed into him." And the same Vorotyntsev takes part in a memorial service under the open sky before the body of the heroically fallen Colonel Kabanov. Downward, to the earth, to childhood, to the past, and upward, to what is higher, toward the future and the eternal, and between them, supported by and nourished by both—there remains an effort of will and action in the present. Such is the philosophy of the will in *August* and to it both the structure of the novel and its imagery and language are subordinated.

We have not yet touched upon the last of the disputed questions listed at the beginning of this essay: the author's attitude toward Russia. The essence of this has already been admirably expressed by A. Schmemann.[4] Solzhenitsyn disappoints those who have lost all hope for Russia, seeing her as a land of perpetual slaves and masters, as well as those who blindly and thoughtlessly extol her in the face of all evidence. Solzhenitsyn's "lucid love" (in A. Schmemann's phrase) knows that Russia has been both great and petty, holy and sinful, and also that she must be formed in the image of the free and wilful men who will recreate her. Solzhenitsyn does not give a final, conclusive judgment concerning the past and supplies no recipe for the future. But he does not turn away from the reality of Russia and calls on all to achieve the task set before her.

August 1914 will enter into the corpus of Russian literature as one of its most tonic works. The dispute which has broken out over the novel represents a first testimony to this fact.

[4] [The reference is to Alexander Schmemann's article, "A Lucid Love" in Dunlop *et al.*, eds., *Aleksandr Solzhenitsyn.*—ED.]

Solzhenitsyn
and the Theme of War

by Patricia Blake

The drama of war, with its incomparable range of grandeur and grief, has provided one of the most engaging epic themes in world literature. For Homer, Virgil, Shakespeare, and Tolstoy it offered the occasion for the accomplishment of their genius. Kierkegaard observed that the union of a great artist and a great theme "constitutes the fortunate in the historical process, the divine conjunction of its forces, the high tide of historic time." Solzhenitsyn, though mesmerized by the battle of Tannenberg of August 1914 while still in his teens, necessarily turned to the holocaust at hand, only much later seeking its cause in the portentous war that had preceded it. By then, the union of Solzhenitsyn and the theme of the concentration camps had already produced the masterwork of post-Stalinist Russian fiction, *One Day in the Life of Ivan Denisovich.* This short novel achieved what Camus had deemed impossible: it compelled the human imagination to participate in the imprisonment and murder of millions that has been the distinguishing feature of our age. Such a task could perhaps only have been accomplished by literature, performing what may be—after the historical cataclysm of Nazism and Stalinism—its highest cathartic function.

How fortunate was Solzhenitsyn's later choice of World War I as a fictional theme will probably only be fully appreciated when the multivolume cycle *August 1914* introduces is complete. Until *August 1914* he confined himself in his fiction to recording events and situations of which he had intimate knowledge. *August 1914* suggests that worldwide recognition of his earlier literary achievements has nerved him to risk the exercise of his imaginative powers beyond his immediate experience. Although by no means abandoning his role as a witness, he has now also assumed the duty of interpreter of a history

Soviet Russia has in large part been denied. The moral stimulus for his work remains the same; he is moved by a desire to restore history—and its lessons—to his people. In his Nobel Prize lecture, he called upon literature to act as "the living memory of a nation," sustaining and safeguarding her past history, in a form that is impervious to distortion and falsification. "In this way does literature together with language preserve the national soul." [1] This is the formidable task that Solzhenitsyn has now set for himself. And, in World War I, he recognizes the first essential "knot" [2] that must be unravelled before the sources of Russia's subsequent calamities can come clear.

Few serious historians would dispute the view that the war was the immediate cause of revolution in Russia. This, the first mass war in history, came as brutal shock to all of Europe. In Russia, however, where the social fabric was flimsy, and hence more vulnerable to stress, the chances of succumbing to the ordeal were far greater.[3] Russia's disastrous invasion of East Prussia in August 1914, while it made possible France's recovery on the Marne, cost the invaders a quarter of a million men. As Russian casualties mounted to a total of nine million, the initial surge of patriotism, and the often frivolous enthusiasm for the war turned into overwhelming fatigue and anger. Though mortally ill, the Romanov empire might have endured for a time had it not been for the death blow struck by the war. Essentially, the war destroyed the faith of the elite that had supported the throne and—in contrast to the Russo-Japanese war that had precipitated the revolution of 1905—it shattered any illusion that the Russian system of autocratic government was subject to reform. The result was an erosion of legitimate authority, political and social upheaval, and generalized chaos which persisted after the February revolution.

---

[1] Alexander Solzhenitsyn, "Nobel Prize Lecture," trans. Alexis Klimoff, in Dunlop, Haugh, and Klimoff, eds., *Aleksandr Solzhenitsyn*, p. 488.

[2] *August 1914* is designated *"Uzel I"* rather than Volume I of the historical cycle. This original use of *uzel* suggests a knot that may later be untied.

[3] An example of the debility of the imperial regime is cited in *The Gulag Archipelago*: the growing ineffectiveness of the prison system. "Tsarism lost its chance for survival—not in the street skirmishes of February—but several decades earlier when young men from rich families began to regard a prison term as an honor, and army officers, even guards officers, deemed it dishonorable to shake a policeman's hand" (p. 461; part 1, chap. 12). Such widespread disrespect for the prison system, Solzhenitsyn believes, reinforced the revolutionaries' positions. In *August 1914*, Solzhenitsyn offers a far more comprehensive picture of the regime's weakness in the face of crisis. The above cited quotation, and all other passages from *The Gulag Archipelago* quoted in this essay have been translated by the author from A. Solzhenitsyn, *ARKHIPELAG GULag* I-II (Paris: YMCA Press, 1974).

Driven by Lenin's energy and vision, the Bolsheviks now entered the vacuum of power. The chain reaction of civil war, foreign intervention, the consolidation of the Bolshevik regime, and the organization of a modern totalitarian state under Lenin and Stalin will no doubt be the subject of later volumes in Solzhenitsyn's historical cycle.

Evident as such a recital of causalities may appear in the West, they are scarcely perceived as such by orthodox Soviet historians. The seizure of power by the Bolsheviks is seen as inevitable, while all that was irrational, haphazard and fortuitous—so brilliantly rendered by Solzhenitsyn—is generally disregarded. (In reality, only the breakdown of the empire can be said to have been inevitable; the particular form the revolution took was accidental.) Solzhenitsyn treats the Marxist view of history with what the Russian émigré historian George Katkov calls "magnificent contempt." The philosopher Varsonof'ev in *August 1914* asserts that "history is irrational. . . . It grows like a living tree, while reason is an axe. You can't make history grow with reason" (pp. 376–77, chap. 42).[4] Varsonof'ev also makes this Tolstoyan observation: "history has its own organic structure that is perhaps beyond our understanding" *(ibid.)*.

At the same time, Solzhenitsyn takes issue with the Tolstoyan theory, formulated in the epilogues to *War and Peace*, that historical events are not made by the will, the cunning, or the genius of rulers. Tolstoy would have us believe that the ruler is governed by the event itself, in a process that is at once inevitable and incomprehensible, involving the interaction of all the persons participating in the event. In *August 1914*, Solzhenitsyn proposes to demonstrate that, in spite of "Tolstoy's conviction that it is not generals who command armies . . . not presidents or leaders who run states and political parties . . . all too often the twentieth century has proved to us that they do just that" (p. 350, chap. 40). Solzhenitsyn's shiftless General Blagoveshchensky sees himself as Marshal Kutuzov, as portrayed by Tolstoy. "Military matters go their own way," he muses, "there is an inevitable course of events." To justify his inertia, Blagoveshchensky further attributes to Tolstoy the notion that "there is nothing worse than speaking out on your own initiative—people who do that always get into trouble" (pp. 463–64, chap. 53). These are all, of course, simplistic extensions of Tolstoy's ideas. In spite of Tolstoy's belief in the inevitability of historical events, he held rulers and ruled alike *morally* responsible for their part in those events. Tolstoy was as keenly aware as Solzhenitsyn of the justifications men devise for collective and individual murder;

---

[4] All passages from *August 1914* quoted in this essay have been translated by the author from A. Solzhenitsyn, *Avgust chetyrnadtsatogo* (Paris: YMCA Press, 1971).

the examples he offered reach deep into our present century, as when he wrote ironically of the practice of killing a man "in recognition of his rights." [5] In their insistence on individual moral responsibility the two great Russian didacts resemble one another absolutely.

One of Solzhenitsyn's objectives in *August 1914* is to implicitly call attention to the similarities that obtain between the Russian defeats of 1914 and 1941. The most striking of these lies in the problem of conscience posed by the call to serve an autocratic—or totalitarian—regime if the homeland is to be defended. Here Solzhenitsyn turns to the experience of his father, an artillery officer at the battle of Tannenberg, to whom *August 1914* is conceived as a monument. For Isaaki (Sanya) Lazhenitsyn, a character modeled on Isai Solzhenitsyn, the problem is resolved by reference to simple patriotism and compassion for the nation. A sometime Tolstoyan, and a pacifist, Sanya explains his enlistment in the imperial army with a phrase that may serve as an epigraph to the whole of the novel: "I pity Russia" (p. 18, chap. 1). As Hitler moved to conquer Stalin's Russia in June 1941, Sanya *père* and Sanya *fils* are seen to merge as one man in defense of the nation.[6]

In 1941, however, the moral issue was beclouded by widescale unawareness of the evils of Nazism among a people deliberately kept in ignorance of those evils during the Stalin-Hitler pact. While the overwhelming majority of Soviet citizens rallied to the national cause, the first year of war found countless civilians welcoming the invader in the pitiful hope that he would bring relief from oppression. The Soviet military situation was disastrous. In the first month of war the Germans had seized control of Soviet territory more than twice the size of France. Six months after the invasion in June they held 3.8 million Soviet soldiers who had surrendered—mainly involuntarily—to the enemy. By the end of 1942 about 100,000 Red Army deserters had volunteered to fight on the German side for the "liberation" of their country. (Although only a minority actually saw action, over half a million Soviet citizens had served in a military or paramilitary capacity in the German forces by the end of the war.) Tens of thousands of civilians in occupied territories had enlisted to serve as

---

[5] L. N. Tolstoy, *War and Peace*, trans. Aylmer Maude, ed. George Gibian (New York: Norton, 1971), p. 1334.

[6] Several devices are used to suggest the interchangeable identities of father and son. Sanya is not a diminutive for Isaaki (or Isai), but for Alexander; yet Solzhenitsyn has chosen to give his own name to Isaaki Lazhenitsyn. The parallel is reinforced by Sanya Lazhenitsyn's assertion that "They [the Germans] have attacked us" (p. 17, chap. 1), in order to justify his enlistment. This was, of course, true only in 1941; Russia conducted an offensive war on German territory in 1914.

Ostarbeiter (Eastworkers) in Germany by the summer of 1942. But Nazi savagery in these territories soon turned welcome into resistance. And when news of the abominable treatment of deserters, POWs and *Ostarbeiter* in Germany got back to the Soviet Union, and, later, as the German military situation began to deteriorate, desertions and *Ostarbeiter* enlistments subsided.

While there was no such Russian collaboration with the enemy in World War I, the analogies between the Russian defeats of 1941 and 1914 have proved engaging for the Russian writer. A Red Army officer in Konstantin Simonov's war novel *The Living and the Dead* makes this observation: "We've all studied in our military academies the lessons to be drawn from our military disasters of August 1914. We've all poked fun at Samsonov and now we've crapped all over ourselves, just like him." [7] Other, more concrete, analogies spring to mind. In April 1914 the British Foreign Secretary, Sir Edmund Grey, told French President Poincaré that "Russia's resources are so great that in the long run Germany will be exhausted without our helping Russia." The major Soviet slogan of the 1930s, "The Red Army will win any future war with little loss of blood and will carry the fight into the enemy's own territory," supported by massive prewar Soviet mobilization, persuaded foreigners and Russians alike that Germany would never catch the Soviet Union unprepared. The analogy extends dramatically into the first year of Russia's entry into both wars, when the incompetence of the High Command, the obsolescence of weaponry, the breakdown in communication, intelligence and supply, and the low level of military training contributed to the magnitude and rapidity of the initial defeats.

So compelling are these historical parallels that when *August 1914* was published in the West in 1971, the Soviet press printed articles suggesting that Solzhenitsyn had cunningly contrived a libel on the Soviet leadership and the Red Army in the Great Patriotic War, in the guise of describing the ineptitude of the imperial command in World War I. In reality, Solzhenitsyn had no need of such contrivance, as *The Gulag Archipelago* has now made manifest. Here, Solzhenitsyn compares the annihilation of General Andrei Vlasov's forces in the spring of 1942 to the rout of General Samsonov's army in August 1914. "Vlasov's Second Shock Army perished," he writes, "repeating the fate of Samsonov's Second Army, which had been just as insanely abandoned when encircled by the enemy" (p. 258, n. 8; part 1, chap. 6). Solzhenitsyn goes further. He declares that "the blindness and lunacy" of Stalin and his diplomatic and military staff served as an

---

[7] K. Simonov, *Zhivye i mertvye* (Moscow: 1968), p. 32.

invitation to Hitler to invade Russia. Indeed, history bears him out as he asks: "Who, if not they, flung Russia into ignominious, unheard-of defeats, far worse than the defeats of Tsarist Russia in 1904 or 1915—defeats such as Russia had not known since the thirteenth century?" (p. 376; part 1, chap. 10). In *The Gulag Archipelago*, as in *August 1914*, Solzhenitsyn seems once again to address his father on the battleground of Tannenberg, and, drawing upon his experience of 1941, he mourns the redoubled tragedy that now enfolds them both.

Evolution of an Exile:
Gulag Archipelago

by Robert Conquest

A well-known American left-wing journalist, noted for the frequency, the variety, and the righteousness of his public interventions on every conceivable matter in the field of foreign affairs, recently remarked on his horror at reading *Gulag Archipelago*. For he learned from it facts hitherto unknown to him: for example, that in the Soviet Union large numbers of people had been executed or sent to labor camps during the period when Joseph Stalin held the post of general secretary of the party. Now, of course, to any but the most purblind or fanatical admirer of the Communist system, all this had been established and documented at the very latest with the publication in 1948 of D. I. Dallin and B. I. Nikolaevsky's *Forced Labor in the Soviet Union* (which Solzhenitsyn quotes). And even those compulsive ignoramuses had almost all come to learn of such facts when they were revealed by the then leader of the Communist party of the Soviet Union, Nikita Khrushchev, in February 1956. In the meantime, much further documentation of these horrors has taken place, including my own *The Great Terror* (1968), in which several thousand references, half of them from Soviet sources, established pretty firmly, I had thought, that all had not been well. And since then there have been such books as *Let History Judge*, by Roy Medvedev, with further details, almost all of them highly unpleasant.

But for all that, this journalist's reaction is, if in exaggerated form, something of very significant portent about the importance of Solzhenitsyn's book. Even if the book had registered no more than we know already, it is written by a man whose courage, whose integrity, and whose experience will give it overwhelming authority throughout the world. It is a truly exceptional work: For in it literature transcends history, without distorting it.

It is indeed an important aspect of Solzhenitsyn's book, though by no means the only one, that he confirms and further details many horrors that have been reported. (Medvedev, an ideological opponent of Solzhenitsyn, has, incidentally, gone on record as saying that all the factual material in *Gulag Archipelago* is true.)

Solzhenitsyn exposes, for example, the full frightfulness of the highly secret Sukhanovka prison, which (in my first edition)[1] I was only able to mention from the evidence of a single prisoner personally known to me—but which Solzhenitsyn had meanwhile spoken of in *The First Circle*; he confirms the summary execution of those serving prison sentences as the advancing Germans approached their camps, the obscure massacre of air force generals in 1941, the incredible crowding in prisons, the notorious "lists" under which the accused were sentenced under various categories, such as "Anti-Soviet Agitation." One of the categories I had noted was "Suspicion of Espionage," saying that this was a crime perhaps unique in the annals of world justice. Solzhenitsyn (once again) demonstrates my inadequate incredulity: For in addition to listing that, he names the even more extravagant charge of "Connections Leading to Suspicion of Espionage." He notes the groupings most liable to arrest, including the Esperantists, people connected with the Red Cross, Austrian Socialist refugees from the 1934 uprising in Vienna, etc. He confirms that in 1949 everyone who had previously been in camp and had managed to survive to the end of his sentence was re-arrested and re-sentenced without further charges.

The post-war categories of individuals sentenced on new charges—as against simply being dragged back to camp—are listed as: spies, believers, geneticists, and there were three special categories of intellectuals insufficiently hostile to the West, against whom the charges were:

VAT—Praising American technique

VAD—Praising American democracy

PZ—Abasement before the West (a more general charge)

Other war and post-war victims included those who had escaped from German prisoner-of-war camps, all classed as spies, those children of certain victims of the earlier purges who had been too young—even under Stalin's twelve-year-old law—to be charged at the time, the children of Spanish refugees from the civil war (as Anglo-American spies).

There is, in addition, useful material for the historian on important

---

[1] [The reference is to Robert Conquest, *The Great Terror* (New York and London: Macmillan, 1968).—ED.]

political cruxes in the USSR. For example, he gives us what appears
to be entirely new information about the notorious "Doctors' Plot."
This was planned, had Stalin not died, to have been the culmination
of the great anti-Semitic campaign of the time. All the Yiddish writers
and cultural figures had already been shot secretly in the "Crimean
Case" in August 1952, and it was only in January 1953 that a great
public propaganda campaign was mounted around the arrest of the
"murderers in white coats"—a group of leading Soviet physicians,
mainly Jewish, accused of the medical murders (or attempted
murders) of various Soviet personalities.

After Stalin's death, Beria repudiated it and released the doctors.
There has always been a mystery concerning two of the doctors, who,
though cleared, were not available to be released after Stalin's death.
About one of these, Dr. Etinger, a strange tale now emerges, obtained,
moreover, from an excellent source—a member of the prosecutor's
office who conducted the interrogation of various guilty police officials
after Stalin's death. Abakumov, the minister of state security (who
figures prominently in Solzhenitsyn's novel *The First Circle*), was
arrested near the end of 1951. We now learn that he and Ryumin,
assistant minister of state security, had a dispute. Dr. Etinger was
already under arrest, and Ryumin came to Abakumov and suggested
a "Doctors' Plot." Abakumov for some reason rejected this. Shortly
afterwards Etinger was found dead in his cell. It seems either that
Abakumov had killed him to avoid proceeding with the case or that
Ryumin had interrogated him to death. Stalin went along with
Ryumin, and Abakumov himself was jailed with a number of his
closest associates. Then came Stalin's death. Ryumin was arrested, but
Abakumov was not released by Beria. Beria was then arrested and
shot. The following summer Ryumin was shot, and Abakumov took
the view that he had been vindicated and would now doubtless be
released. However, he too was shot in December 1954, on a charge of
faking the earlier "Leningrad Case," in which politburo member
Voznesensky and others had been executed. Solzhenitsyn says that the
reason is not quite clear but that rumor has it that Khrushchev had a
non-political objection to Abakumov, since he had beaten Khrushchev's own daughter-in-law before she was sent to die in a labor
camp. Such motives need not be discounted, though there is no sign
that Khrushchev intervened in her favor at the time, any more than
Molotov or Kuusinen or President Kalinin did for their own arrested
wives while they themselves were continuing to serve in high positions,
or Kaganovich for his brother, a fellow member of the central
committee, who was lucky enough to get the chance to commit
suicide—when accused (though a Jew) of being Hitler's nominee for

president of a Fascist Russia. Nevertheless, there were also political motives for Abakumov's execution, in that the men he had had shot in Leningrad had been Malenkov's enemies and that Khrushchev was now working to remove Malenkov from the premiership.

So far, then, there are movingly presented accounts of the terror and certain material of great interest to historians of an obscure and gloomy period. But the present Soviet leaders themselves (as in speeches by Shelepin and others at the 1961 party congress) have told similar stories. And even though the present policy is to sweep them under the carpet, to condemn harping on the "errors" of the past, these things are not entirely denied. Other writers on them, like Roy Medvedev and Evgenia Ginzburg, though unpublished in Russia, have not been arrested. What is there about *Gulag Archipelago* that made it a kind of last straw and that drove the politburo to its reckless and arbitrary arrest and expulsion of the author?

First of all, Solzhenitsyn does not put the blame solely on Stalin and the "personality cult." He traces the long evolution of terror, showing that the labor-camp system, the frame-up trials, the mass shootings, the secret disappearances—all go back to early Soviet times. His brief description of the "trials" of the early Twenties, for example, would be regarded by any humane standards as the sign of a far worse regime, already, than most of the "reactionary" dictatorships of modern times. He departs from reasonable and orthodox criticism of Soviet terror by failing to restrict his complaints to the frame-up and execution of innocent Communists. He actually urges that it was wrong to do the same to non-Communist revolutionary socialists and even liberals. Since these were mainly wiped out in the earlier years, his "fifty-year-old" (as he puts it) juggernaut is the Soviet regime from its beginnings—he was writing in 1967. That is to say, a major aspect of Solzhenitsyn's book is that it breaks totally with the myth that has corrupted and deluded so many commentators on the Russian Revolution and the Soviet regime: the myth of a constructive and humane Lenin.

Solzhenitsyn compounds this "blasphemy" by a comparison between Soviet standards of terror and those of czardom. Czarist Russia was the most backward and despotic regime in Europe. Solzhenitsyn notes that those executed between 1826 and 1906 in Russia amounted to 894. In the revolutionary days of 1905–1908, 2200 executions took place. In Lenin's time, very incomplete figures for the central provinces alone estimate that 16,000 were shot in eighteen months. Even in December 1932, before the Stalin terror proper, he notes the shooting of 265 people at one time in the Kresty Prison in Leningrad.

And, in peacetime, at the height of the terror, a *minimum* of just under a million were executed in two years—that is, a rate about *fifty thousand times* as great as that of sixty years of czardom back to Nicholas I!

Moreover, the czars' victims had actually plotted against the state; their relatives were not also sentenced; the non-capital prisoners were not starved and sweated to death. (Indeed, Solzhenitsyn is inclined to attribute the collapse of Bukharin and other veterans in the hands of Stalin's police to the comparative softness of their previous treatment in czarist jails, which they had boasted of, and even thought of, as the utmost harshness possible.) These are comparisons that give offense to the beneficiaries of the Stalin system.

Solzhenitsyn has previously—as in his Nobel Prize speech—also pointed out that, if we are to judge regimes by a calculus of murder and terror, the Soviet state is, apart from Hitler's, in a unique category. To compare the sufferings under Greek and other right-wing governments with those of the Soviet Union is something in the nature of saying that a gross and unprovoked assault, such as punching someone on the nose, is the same as boiling him in oil.

Solzhenitsyn is particularly disgusted at the notion of the ruling group that if they describe the Stalin terror as a series of "mistakes" that they have apologized for once and for all and do not wish it to be referred to again, that settles the matter. During Khrushchev's ascendancy, the humorous Soviet paper *Krokodil* (July 20, 1956) once printed a picture of a mean-looking little boy saying to his teacher, "Why did you give me a failing mark? I have admitted my mistakes, haven't I?"

Solzhenitsyn compares de-Stalinization with de-Nazification. He points out that in Western Germany de-Nazification tribunals, up till 1966, in one way or another, penalized 86,000 Nazis. In Russia a handful of high police officials—and only those who took the wrong side in the struggle for power in the Fifties—were shot, while the vast bulk of accomplices, large and small, in the criminal regime of Stalin have survived unharmed. This has applied even to major criminals like Kaganovich and Molotov, who have actually been openly denounced by the public prosecutor in person as having been responsible for millions of murders. They were removed from power, having happened to lose a round in the struggle. But they were pensioned off quietly. Terror operatives on the winning side kept their jobs. So the Soviet taxpayers are still securing a serene old age for those who murdered their fathers and uncles—and to come to think of it, their mothers and aunts. It is to be remembered, moreover, that almost all the present leaders held posts under Stalin. Many of the current politburo and secretariat were members of Stalin's own central committee. The top figures—Brezhnev, Kosygin, Suslov—rose from the ranks to high position during the worst of the terror in the late Thirties.

Then again, Solzhenitsyn, it is true, denounces the terror with passion; but even more intolerable from the point of view of the *apparat* is the stinging contempt that he expresses for all concerned. They do not appear as men of a certain horrible grandeur, like Robespierre or Genghis Khan, but as vile little pygmies, bird-brained, sniggering torturers.

Perhaps the most important lesson, indeed, is how difficult it is for us in the Western political culture really to make the effort of imagination, as well as that of intellect, to conceive what the other lot are really like, what their background really is. I myself, as a student of Soviet politics for many years, and one not inclined to grant them unproven virtues, have found myself still tending, if I do not make that effort, to grant more common sense in the Western style, to make "natural" assumptions of conduct, however evil, in ways that do not necessarily apply. I remember once asking that profound student of Russia, the late Tibor Szamuely, himself a former inmate of the camps, a question about the military purges. I could see, I said, why Stalin had shot Marshal Tukhachevsky, but I did not see why he shot Marshal Yegorov. Tibor's answer was simple: "Why not?"

That effort of the imagination is made much easier for all of us by the power of Solzhenitsyn's writing in this book. Pasternak breaks off his *Sketch for an Autobiography* before the frightful years of the Yezhovshchina with the words "to continue it would be immeasurably difficult . . . one would have to talk in a manner which would grip the heart and make the hair stand on end. . . ." This Solzhenitsyn (in some sense Pasternak's successor) has done in *Gulag Archipelago.*

On Solzhenitsyn's
Gulag Archipelago

by Roy Medvedev

General Assessment

In this essay I have tried to express only brief preliminary thoughts about Solzhenitsyn's new book [primarily] because the author has published only the first of three or four volumes.

Solzhenitsyn's work is crammed with fearful facts. It also contains a number of assertions that are hard to believe, but these are far fewer. What has already been published is too considerable to grasp and to evaluate all at once. In this volume are depicted concretely the strange and tragic fates of hundreds of persons, which were, however, typical of past decades. The book is full of deep and true thoughts and observations, and some that are not so true but were born of the monstrous sufferings of tens of millions of people, sufferings never before endured by our people in the many centuries of their history. No one ever came out of the awful "Archipelago" of Stalinist camps and prisons the same as they went in, not only in their age and health but in their ideas about life and people. I think that few people would get up from reading this book the same as when they turned to its first page. In this respect, I can think of nothing in Russian or world literature to compare with Solzhenitsyn's book.

Facts on Which Solzhenitsyn's Account Is Based

A certain I. Solov'ev wrote in the January 14 *Pravda* that the facts given in Solzhenitsyn's book were not genuine and were either the product of a sick imagination or of a cynical falsification by the

"On Solzhenitsyn's *Archipelago Gulag*" by Roy Medvedev. From *Intercontinental Press*, 12, no. 11, March 25, 1974, 358–65. English translation copyright © 1974 by *Intercontinental Press*. Reprinted by permission of Dr. Zhores Medvedev and the publisher. Translation and footnotes by Gerry Foley.

author. This, of course, is not so. I cannot accept certain of
Solzhenitsyn's assessments or conclusions. But it must be said emphatically that all the basic facts in his book, and especially the details
about the life and torments of prisoners from their arrest until their
death (or in rarer cases, until their release) are completely authentic.

Of course, in [an artistic investigation] of such scope, which is based
not only on the impressions of the author but on the testimony and
first- and second-hand accounts of more than 200 former prisoners, it
is inevitable that there will be some inaccuracies. And that is all the
more true because Solzhenitsyn wrote his book under the most
clandestine conditions and was unable to discuss it, even with many of
his closest friends, before it was published. But such inaccuracies are
insignificant in the context of such a considerable work. I think, for
example, that the extent of the expulsions from Leningrad in 1934–35
(the Kirov wave) was less than Solzhenitsyn indicates. Tens of
thousands of people were expelled. But not a quarter of the two
million people living in the city. But I do not have exact figures. I am
only going by fragmentary testimony and my own impressions (I lived
in Leningrad for more than fifteen years). It is hard to believe the
story Solzhenitsyn got from an unknown informant that Ordzhonikidze[1] used to talk to old engineers with two pistols lying on the right
and left of his desk. In order to track down old Tsarist officials (and it
was not even looking for all of them but mainly those from judicial
bodies and the police), the GPU hardly needed to rely on random
notes by random people. All of these lists could have been found in
local archives and the reference books that were available. I think that
Solzhenitsyn exaggerates the number of peasants exiled in the years of
collectivization (he says there were fifteen million). But if to the
victims of those years we add the peasants who died of famine in
1932–33 (there were no less than three or four million in Ukraine
alone), then you can [arrive at] a figure higher than the one
Solzhenitsyn gives. After Stalin's death not ten but about 100 leading
officials in the MGB/MVD[2] were jailed or shot. (In certain cases there
were no open hearings.) But all the same, this is a tiny number in
comparison with the criminals in the *organy*[3] who went free or even got
various high posts. In 1936–37, Bukharin was no longer a member of
the Politburo, contrary to what Solzhenitsyn says, but only an
alternate member of the Central Committee.

[1] Sergei Ordzhonikidze, one of the organizers of the Five Year Plan, commissar of
heavy industries under Stalin. [N.B. All footnotes are by the translator.—Ed.]

[2] Ministerstvo Gosudarstvennoi Besopastnosti/Ministerstvo Vnutrennykh Del;
Ministry of State Security/Ministry of the Interior.

[3] The word *organy* (organs) is widely used to designate state security organs.

But these and some other inaccuracies are absolutely immaterial for such a tremendous work of background research as Solzhenitsyn has done. On the other hand, Solzhenitsyn's book has other "shortcomings," about which he himself writes in his introduction. He was not able to see everything, to remember everything, or to figure out everything. He writes, for example, about the rounding up of amnestied and repatriated Cossacks in the mid-1920s. But still more terrible in its consequences was the campaign of "de-Cossackification" and massive terror in the Don and Ural areas in the winter and spring of 1919. This campaign lasted "only" a little more than two months, but it prolonged the civil war, with all its excesses, no less than a year, giving the White armies dozens of new cavalry regiments. And 500 hostages were shot in Petrograd, which the *Ezhenedel'nik VCHK*[4] records in only two lines. To describe all this, many books are needed. I am confident that they will be written.

While *Pravda* tried to show that the facts given by Solzhenitsyn were not genuine, *Literaturnaya Gazeta* tried on January 16 to convince its readers that there was nothing new in the book. That is untrue. Although I have been studying Stalinism for more than ten years, I found many things in Solzhenitsyn's book that I did not know before. Except for former prisoners, Soviet citizens, even those who remember the twentieth and twenty-second party congresses of the Communist party, hardly know one-tenth of the facts Solzhenitsyn writes about. And young people do not know even a one-hundredth part.

Solzhenitsyn on the Vlasovites

Many newspapers write that Solzhenitsyn justifies, whitewashes, or even praises the Vlasovites.[5]

This is a deliberate and malicious distortion. Solzhenitsyn writes in the *Archipelago* that the Vlasovites became the pitiful hirelings of the

---

[4] The Weekly Report of the Vserossiiskaia CHrezvychainaia Komissiia po Bor'be s Kontrrevolutsiei i Sabotazhem (All-Russian Commissariat for Fighting Counterrevolution and Sabotage).

[5] General A. A. Vlasov, a Red Army commander captured by the Nazis, was persuaded by his captors to recruit fellow prisoners of war to form a Russian unit in the German army. His example was utilized a great deal in Nazi propaganda. As for the ex-Vlasovites' opinion of Solzhenitsyn's portrayal, one view appeared in the March 2 issue of *Novoe Russkoe Slovo*, an émigré daily published in New York. What was most distressing to the writer of this article, Riurik Dudin, was that Solzhenitsyn described the Vlasovites as a band of desperate and disoriented men rather than principled anti-Communists.

Hitlerites, that the "Vlasovites could be tried for treason" (page 249),*
that they took arms from the enemy and when they got to the front
they fought with the desperation of the condemned. Solzhenitsyn
himself, along with his battery, was almost annihilated in East Prussia
by Vlasovite fire. But Solzhenitsyn does not simplify the problem of
the "Vlasovites" and similar units of the fascist army.

In the many "waves" of Stalinist repressions, many of us have our
own special tragedies. I know, for example, that for A. Tvardovskii it
was the "de-Kulakification"—which claimed the life of his father, a
hard-working peasant from the poor stratum of that class, a recent
veteran of the Red Army, a defender of Soviet power, who was exiled
to the other side of the Urals with his entire family. The only one to
survive was his oldest son, who had happened to go into the city to
study. That was the one who was to become our great poet, A.
Tvardovskii. And he once had to deny his father. He wrote about all
that in his last poem, "It Is Right to Remember."

For my family, the tragedy was the repressions of 1937 and 1938, in
particular the purge of the commanders and commissars of the Red
Army. My father, a commissar of a division and a teacher in the
military-political academy of the RKKA,[6] was one of those who were
arrested and perished. Those people were totally devoted to Soviet
power, socialism, and the Bolshevik party. As participants in the civil
war, they were romantic heroes in my eyes, and I never believed that
they were "enemies of the people."

For Solzhenitsyn this deep, personal tragedy was not his own arrest
but the cruel and terrible fate of millions of Soviet prisoners of war,
Solzhenitsyn's contemporaries, the generation of October, who made
up a large part of our professional army in June of 1941. This army
was shattered and surrounded in the first days and weeks of the war
because of the criminal miscalculations of Stalin, who was unable to
prepare either the army or the country for war; because of Stalin's
absurd and stupid orders on the first day of the war and [then his
desertion of] his post in the first week of the war; and because of the
lack of experienced commanders and commissars, who had been
liquidated by Stalin. Nearly three million soldiers and officers landed
in prison camps, and one million others were later imprisoned in
"pressure cookers" near Vyazma, near Kharkov, on the Kerch
Peninsula, and near Volkhov. But the Stalin government betrayed its
soldiers even when they were in captivity, by refusing to recognize

---

* [Page references are to the Russian edition published by YMCA Press.—Ed.]

[6] From 1918 to 1946 the Red Army was officially called the Raboche-Krestianskaia
Krasnaia Armiia, the Workers and Peasants Red Army.

Russia's signature on the international convention on prisoners of war. As a result of this, no aid went to Soviet prisoners through the International Red Cross, and they were condemned to die of hunger in the German concentration camps. Those who survived were betrayed again by Stalin after the victory when they were all arrested and went to swell the population of the "Gulag Archipelago." This triple betrayal of Stalin's soldiers is what Solzhenitsyn considers the worst, gravest crime of the Stalinist regime—a crime unprecedented in the thousand-year history of Russian governments. "I felt," Solzhenitsyn writes, "that this history of several million Russian prisoners would hold me forever, the way a pin holds a cockroach." (Page 245.)

Only a tenth part of our prisoners joined the Vlasovite units, the police units, the work battalions, the ranks of the "voluntary" helpers of the Wehrmacht. The majority of those who joined sincerely hoped that once they had gotten food and arms, they could go over to the side of the Soviet army or the partisans. These were, as it soon turned out, false hopes. The chances for escape were too few.

Solzhenitsyn does not justify and praise those desperate and unfortunate people. But he asks the tribunal of their descendants to take into consideration certain extenuating circumstances. These young and often illiterate fellows, mostly from the countryside, were demoralized by the defeat of their army; and they were repeatedly told in the concentration camps: "Stalin has denounced you" and "Stalin doesn't give a damn about you." And they could see very well that this was true and that death by starvation awaited them in the German camps.

Of course, I can't agree with everything Solzhenitsyn says. I don't feel any pity, for example, for a certain Yuri E., a Soviet officer Solzhenitsyn tells about who did not starve in a prison camp and who went over to the side of the Hitlerites quite consciously, becoming an officer in the German army and even the head of a spy school. From Solzhenitsyn's book, we can see that this Yuri E. went over to the side of the Soviet army when he already foresaw the defeat of the Germans and not because he felt the call of the motherland. His idea was to hand over "the secrets of German intelligence" to our intelligence service, that is, in fact to switch from the German spy agency to the Soviet MGB. Moreover, this Yuri was convinced that a war would break out immediately between the USSR and its allies and that the Red Army would be quickly defeated.

As for the fierce battle that some large Vlasovite units waged at Prague against German units under the command of SS General Steiner, that is a historical fact that cannot be denied. What happened, happened.

Virtually all the "Vlasovites" were condemned to twenty-five years in the labor camps. They were not affected by any amnesty, and almost all of them died in prison or in exile in Siberia. I also think that for most of them this was too severe a punishment, because Stalin bore a far greater guilt in this tragedy than anyone else.

"Liberalism" of the Hitlerites and of Russian Tsarism

Solzhenitsyn is being accused of minimizing the atrocities of the Hitlerites and the cruelty of Tsarism. It was not Solzhenitsyn's task to examine the German "Gulag Archipelago," although he speaks in a number of places about the torture carried out by the Gestapo and the inhuman treatment of Soviet prisoners by the fascists. But he is not at all wrong when he writes that long before Hitler came to power, Stalin had started massive repression, deportation of millions, torture, and frame-up trials; and that all of this continued in our country many years after the defeat of German fascism.

The Russian tsars could hardly be compared to Stalin in this respect. Solzhenitsyn speaks a lot about tsarist prisons and exile in his book, since it was a frequent subject of conversation among prisoners, especially when an old Bolshevik turned up among them. (Prisoners from the other socialist parties had almost all died out already before the war.) In these conversations, the old system of repression, both in its severity and extent, seemed like a rest home to the prisoners of the 1940s.

During the revolution of 1905–07 and the years that followed, the tsarist executioners shot as many workers, peasants, and craftsmen in a year as were shot or died in the camps in one day. What can be compared with this?

The Best Chapters

I think it varies from reader to reader which chapters make the greatest impression. The ones that were most important for me were "The Blue Caps" and "Capital Punishment." Here the author achieves the greatest depth in psychological analysis of the behavior of both prison guards and their victims. In this respect, Solzhenitsyn goes deeper than Dostoevski. I don't mean at all to say that he is a greater artistic genius. I am not a literary scholar. But it is obvious that what Solzhenitsyn experienced—a hundred years later than Dostoevski's arrest and imprisonment—in his terms at hard labor in Stalinist prisons and camps, in transit camps on the road to penal exile, and in prison colonies gave the author of *Gulag Archipelago* ten times greater opportunities to study the various forms of evil in the human soul and human institutions than [were given] the writer of *Notes From the House of the Dead*. And, of course, Solzhenitsyn accomplished his task as only a great writer could.

Solzhenitsyn on Stalin

In several places, Solzhenitsyn's book has deep and exact observations about the personality of Stalin, which appear, however, almost as asides. The author considers Stalin's personal role in our country's disaster and even in creating the "Archipelago" so unimportant that most of his remarks on Stalin are not included in the essential text but in short comments and notes. Thus, in his notes to the next-to-last page, page 605, Solzhenitsyn writes: "In the years before I was imprisoned and while in prison, I also long considered that Stalin had given a fateful direction to the course of the Soviet state. But then Stalin quietly died. And how much in fact has our ship of state changed its course? He did add a personal note of dismal stupidity, petty despotism, and self-adulation. But otherwise he simply followed in the path that had already been marked out."

Solzhenitsyn speaks very briefly in the second chapter about the waves of repression in 1937–38 (why go into detail about "what has already been described at length and will be repeated again many times"?)—when the main cadres of the party leadership and intelligentsia, the commanding and political officers of the Red Army, most of the management personnel in big industry, and the Communist Youth leadership were annihilated in the prisons of the NKVD; when the top levels of Soviet administration, the top levels of the NKVD itself, the foreign service, and so forth, were changed by force. He writes (once again in a note): "Today, having seen the Chinese 'cultural revolution' (which also followed seventeen years after the decisive victory), we can surmise [with great certainty] that there is a historical law here. And even Stalin himself begins to seem only a blind and accidental agent." (Page 80.)

It is hard to agree with such a view of Stalin's role and his significance in the tragedy of the 1930s. Of course, it would be wrong to completely divorce the era of Stalinist terror from the preceding revolutionary era. There was no such sharp dividing line between these two periods, not in 1937, as many think, nor in 1934, as Khrushchev claimed, nor in 1929, as Solzhenitsyn himself [once] thought, nor in 1924, when Lenin died and the Trotskyist opposition was defeated, nor in 1922, when Stalin was elected general secretary of the RPK(B).[7] Nonetheless, in each of these years, and in a few others, there were very substantial changes in policy that require special study.

Of course, there is a line of continuity between the party that took power in October 1917 and the one leading the USSR in 1937, in 1947, in 1957, and in 1967, when Solzhenitsyn completed *Gulag Archipelago*. But this thread of continuity does not mean that the party did not change. Stalin did not follow "in the footsteps." Even in the early years of the revolution, he did not always follow the direction set by Lenin. And later on, with every stride, he carried the party away from this path. In this case, surface similarities only mask very great inner differences—in some respects, even opposites. And the transition to such opposites was not always regular, determined, and inevitable. A deeper, scientific analysis, to which the events Solzhenitsyn researched for his literary work will no doubt be subjected, will certainly show that even within the party and in the context of [the system of] the party-state [and social] relations that were established in Russia in Lenin's time, in some methods Stalin [accomplished by several devices a fundamental overturn,] preserving only the external appearance of the so-called Leninist norms, only the terminology of Marxism-Leninism. In many respects, Stalinism [is indeed] the negation and bloody extermination of all revolutionary forces. In a certain sense, it represents a real counterrevolution. Of course, I by no means think that the Leninist heritage and the Leninist period in the history of our revolution do not require the most serious critical analysis.

Solzhenitsyn does not set himself the task of studying the phenomenon of Stalinism, its nature, peculiarities, its development, history, its premises. Such a notion as Stalinism probably does not exist for Solzhenitsyn, who feels that Stalin "only followed in the path that had already been marked out." What might be called historical background is completely absent from Solzhenitsyn's work. The book opens with a chapter called "Arrest," through which the author emphasizes immediately that he is studying and describing only the world of prisoners, the world of outcasts, the mysterious and terrible country of Gulag: its geography, [its structure,] its social system, its written and

---

[7] Rossisskaia Kommunisticheskaia Partiia (Bolshevikov), Russian Communist party (Bolsheviks).

unwritten laws, its population, its customs, its rulers, and its subjects. And Solzhenitsyn has no great need of historical background, because his Gulag Archipelago came into being in 1918 and has been developing since then according to its own [inner] laws.

This one-sidedness, which, it is true, is relieved not infrequently by profound comments, is maintained throughout the volume. Of course, the author has every right to take this approach. Even without uttering a word about Stalinism, and seemingly denying the validity of such a concept altogether, by his literary study of one of the main components of the Stalinist system, Solzhenitsyn has greatly aided the examination of the whole criminal and inhuman system of Stalinism. Solzhenitsyn is wrong in claiming that in its essential features this system has preserved itself to our day. But it has not yet completely disappeared from our social, political, and cultural life. Solzhenitsyn's book deals a very powerful blow to Stalinism and neo-Stalinism. In this respect, none of us has accomplished more than Solzhenitsyn.

Solzhenitsyn on Lenin

While still a youth in the Komsomol,[8] Solzhenitsyn doubted the wisdom and integrity of Stalin. This doubt, expressed in one of his letters from the front, was the cause for his arrest and sentencing. But at that time he had no doubts whatever that "the October Revolution was splendid and just and was led to victory by people of high aspirations and utter unselfishness." (Page 229.) Now Solzhenitsyn is of another mind about the October Revolution and Lenin.

Of all the accusations that Solzhenitsyn raises either directly or indirectly today against Lenin, I will dwell on only two. Solzhenitsyn thinks that in 1917 Lenin insisted on carrying out a new "proletarian, socialist" revolution in Russia despite the fact that the Russian people were not ready for such a revolution and had no need of it. He also considers that Lenin wrongfully used terrorist methods in struggling against his political opponents.

It is easy to sort out a revolutionist's errors fifty years after the revolution. But the first socialist revolution was inevitably a step into the unknown. There was nothing to compare it with. Its leaders had nobody's experience to borrow from. In that case, it was impossible to calculate and weigh everything in advance. The basic decisions and methods of revolutionary struggle can be adopted and corrected only in the course of events. Lenin understood all this very well and often

---

[8] Kommunisticheskii Soiuz Molodezhi, Young Communist League.

repeated Napoleon's words: "First we have to join combat and then we will see." A revolution of this type [was impossible] without risks—without the risk of defeat and without the risk of errors. But failing to give the signal for revolution when the possibility appears is also a great risk for a revolutionary party.

It is not surprising, therefore, that Lenin and the Soviet government headed by him made many miscalculations and errors that prolonged the civil war in Russia and increased its cruelty. These miscalculations delayed the transition to NEP and increased the economic dislocation of the early years. Lenin's hopes for a rapid development of revolution in Europe, which would then have given Russia technical and educational assistance, were not realized. The Soviet government went too far in restricting democracy in our country.

This list of miscalculations and errors could be continued. But no computer can show that the armed uprising of October 24, 1917, was historically premature, or that all the subsequent crimes of the Stalinist regime flowed from this fateful error of Lenin. After Lenin's death also, the road ahead for the party had not been traveled by anyone before. Unfortunately, those who replaced Lenin at the head of the party did not have his intelligence, his knowledge, or his ability even in the most difficult circumstances to find the correct solution. Therefore, they failed to take advantage of even a small part of the possibilities the October Revolution opened up for a rapid advance to a genuine socialist and democratic society. Today we are still far from these goals. Stalin not only did not "only follow the path that had already been marked out" [(such "clearly marked paths" do not exist in history)] but, to judge from the steps Lenin indicated in his last remarks, Stalin very quickly went off that path.

In the conditions of revolution and of civil war no government can avoid using some forms of violence. But the most objective historian would have to say that a reasonable limit of violence was exceeded many times even in the early years of Soviet power. Starting in the summer of 1918, our country was swept by a wave of both White and Red terror. A major part of these acts of [mass] violence was absolutely unnecessary and even harmful from a rational standpoint and in terms of the class struggle. This terror only increased the cruelty of both sides, prolonged the war, and gave rise to new needless violence. Unfortunately, in the early years of the revolution even Lenin said the word "shoot" [very] much more often than the developing situation required. Solzhenitsyn does not distort when he quotes from Lenin. But his comments are always negative. But hardly anyone today would approve of the order that Lenin gave to the chairman of the Nizhgorod provincial soviet, G. Federov: "Strain every effort, apply mass terror immediately, *shoot and clear out* all the hordes of prostitutes who are consorting with soldiers, former officers and the like." [9] Clear out, yes, but why kill women?

Such abuses of power are deplorable; they must be condemned. Nevertheless, this terror in civil war times did not predetermine the frightful terror of the Stalin era.

Lenin made not a few mistakes; he himself acknowledged many of them on frequent occasions. An honest historian must certainly note all these errors and abuses of power. Nonetheless, the general result of Lenin's work, I am convinced, is positive. Solzhenitsyn thinks otherwise. That is his right. In a socialist country everyone must be able to express his or her views and opinions about the activity of any political leader.

Solzhenitsyn on Krylenko

In his book, Solzhenitsyn does not have any sympathy with any of the Russian revolutionary parties. The Social Revolutionaries were terrorists and windbags, who "never had a proper leadership." The Mensheviks, obviously, were only gasbags. But the ones who come in for the biggest condemnation from Solzhenitsyn are the Bolsheviks, who, however, were able to take power and hold it in Russia, but in doing so exercised excessive and completely unnecessary cruelty. Of the Bolshevik leaders, Solzhenitsyn singles out N. V. Krylenko, the chairman of the Supreme Revolutionary Council, who was the main prosecutor in many "show" trials in the early years of Soviet power. To these cases, Solzhenitsyn devotes almost two entire chapters ("The Law as a Child" and "The Law Matures"); and we often come across Krylenko's name in other chapters as well.

Of course, it can be said that the early years of Soviet power were the time of the Soviet republic's fiercest struggle for life. And if the revolution and Soviet power were necessary, then it was necessary to defend them from their many and merciless foes. And that could not be done without revolutionary tribunals and the VCHK. But in such arguments, one cannot overlook how unjust and how senselessly harsh these judicial and extrajudicial reprisals were in many cases, or how many unqualified, stupid, and utterly brutalized persons found their way into the VCHK and the tribunals. And in this Krylenko soon became one of the main stage managers. Krylenko differed little in

[9] PSS [Polnoe Sobranie Sochinenii] Vol. 50, p. 142. This is Medvedev's note. The phrase is partially illegible in the Russian text.

fact from the presiding judge of the Jacobin tribune Coffinhal, who, while he did send some royalists to the guillotine, also sent many ordinary citizens, including 70-year-old women and an 18-year-old girl, revolutionists dissatisfied with Robespierre, and the famous chemist Lavoisier. When Lavoisier asked for permission at least to finish an important series of experiments, Coffinhal replied, "We don't need scientists."

Of course, Krylenko was not exceptional among the Bolsheviks. But not all leaders of the party were like Krylenko. Unfortunately, it is not only the most honest and courageous persons of their time who become revolutionists. Also attracted to revolutions, especially in periods of rise, are the vain, the ambitious, the self-seeking, people with cold hearts and unclean hands, as well as many who are simply stupid and narrow-minded, fanatics capable of anything. But that is by no means a reason to condemn all revolutions and all revolutionists.

Another thing must be taken into account. For revolutionists, the main test is not prison or banishment to a labor camp, not dashing charges under the fire of the White Guards, not hunger and cold; but power, and power that in the initial period will be almost unlimited. It has long been known that power often distorts and corrupts the best people. It must be noted with regret that very many of the Bolsheviks did not pass this test of power. Long before they perished in the meat grinder of Stalinist repression, these persons themselves came to be leaders and participants in numerous, cruel repressions, which in the majority of cases were unjustified, unnecessary, and harmful. But from this it by no means follows that even before the revolution these Bolsheviks were as unjust and cruel, or as indifferent to human suffering; that they were not [then] guided by the finest motives and the highest aims and ideals.

Solzhenitsyn understands the [destructive] effect that power has on people. He has described his own case with complete frankness. After years of a hard and hungry life as a soldier, he writes, after years of drill and exhausting parading, after suffering many injustices at the hands of the most junior commanders, he completely forgot about all of this as soon as he became a lieutenant and then a captain. In his mind he began to set himself off from the soldiers under him. The memory of a front-line soldier's hard life became dimmer and dimmer. Increasingly he came to see himself as something apart from these men, a different kind of being, a member of a different caste. He unthinkingly took advantage of all his officer's privileges, spoke in a condescending tone to men old enough to be his father or even his grandfather, harassed his orderly, and sometimes even was so severe with the men that an old colonel thought he had to give him a lecture right in the middle of an inspection. "It turned out," Solzhenitsyn admits, "that the officer's epaulets that had been trembling, swaying on my shoulders for no more than two years had cast a golden, poisonous dust into the empty space between my ribs." (Page 551.) What is more, Solzhenitsyn almost became an officer in the NKVD. They had convinced him to go to the NKVD school; and, if they had pressed a little harder, he would have accepted. Solzhenitsyn is merciless with himself. "I considered myself selfless and self-sacrificing. And at the same time, I was thoroughly prepared for the role of a hangman. And if I had gone to the NKVD school in Yezhov's time, maybe under Beria I would have grown to find myself right at home." (Page 175.)

But if Solzhenitsyn changed so much in two years as a junior officer, what should we say about Krylenko, who in a still shorter time was catapulted from being barely an ensign to the top command of the entire Russian army, and then to the chairmanship of the supreme tribunal, to the post of deputy commissar of justice and the chief prosecutor of the RSFSR? Although Krylenko had completed two courses of study before the revolution, he was so dulled and intoxicated by such exceptional power as to become almost unrecognizable.

"Apparently crime," as Solzhenitsyn writes, "is also a matter of a threshold, like certain chemical reactions. Yes, for their whole lives people waver and are buffeted back and forth between good and evil; they slip, fall, struggle to their feet, repent, and once again lose their way. But as long as they do not overstep the threshold of crime, they can turn back. But when by the extent of wrongdoing or as a result of rank or absolute power they pass over this threshold, they step outside the bounds of humanity. And there may be no turning back." (Page 182.)

"Let any reader who thinks that this book is going to be a political indictment shut it right now," Solzhenitsyn writes in another place. "If it were only that easy! If it were just that there were some evil persons, people who have committed evil acts, and had to be identified and eliminated. But the line dividing good and evil runs through the heart of every human being. And who is going to eliminate part of his own heart? In the lifetime of one heart, this line shifts even within it, sometimes pressed by exultant evil, at other times opening room for the flowering of good. One person at different ages and in different situations can be a completely different individual. At times, he may be close to being a devil, at others to being a saint. But the name doesn't change and we attribute everything to him." (Pages 175–176.) In this profound observation of Solzhenitsyn's we see at least a partial explanation of the drama and the moral fall of [very] many Bolsheviks, who before they became victims of Stalin's terror were not unimportant gears in the oppressive machine that had been created.

What Does Solzhenitsyn Propose?

But if power distorts and corrupts people, if politics, as Solzhenitsyn thinks, "is not a science but an empirical field that cannot be described by mathematics and is even subject to ego and blind passions," if all professional politicians are only "boils on the neck of society preventing it from freely moving its head and arms," then what is it we should strive for [in order to] build a just human society?

Solzhenitsyn speaks about that in passing. He puts his ideas in parentheses without explaining or interpreting them in detail. From these brief comments, it is clear that he believes the most suitable social structure would be one "headed by those who can direct the activities of society most intelligently." (Pages 392–393.) That means primarily engineers and scientists (workers, in Solzhenitsyn's opinion, are only helpers of engineers in industry). But who will offer moral leadership in society? It follows from Solzhenitsyn's reasoning that moral guidance cannot be provided by any kind of political doctrine but only by religion. Only faith in God can serve as an underpinning for human morality, and it was always deeply believing people who were best able to endure all the privations of Stalin's labor camps and prisons.

But these thoughts [suggest] utopianism. They are not even very original. Solzhenitsyn has dealt mighty blows to all kinds of political deception. He rightly calls on the Soviet people and above all the youth not to promote falsehood, not to cooperate with lying. However, it is necessary not only to convince people of the untruth of a political doctrine but also to offer them the truth, to convince them of the truthfulness of some other views. But for the overwhelming majority of the Soviet people, the truth is no longer and can never be religion. And the youth of the twentieth century are hardly likely to find guidance in faith in God. Moreover, how can the engineers and specialists take control of the affairs of society, or even of the economy, without politics and without political struggle? But even if this were possible, how can such a society be prevented from degenerating into a dictatorship of the technocrats? And wouldn't turning the moral guidance of society over to religion lead to the worst kind of theocracy?

Speaking of the repressions of 1937, Solzhenitsyn writes: "Maybe 1937 was *necessary* in order to show the worthlessness of the whole *world view* that they strutted around drugging themselves with while they were plundering Russia, wrecking her bulwarks, trampling on her shrines." (Page 138.) He is talking, as can easily be seen, about Marxism. But Solzhenitsyn is wrong. Marxism did not produce the Stalinist deformation, and overcoming Stalinism will not mean the collapse of Marxism and scientific socialism. And Solzhenitsyn knows—he says it in another place—that religious ideology facilitated the Inquisition's two centuries of savagery, the burning and torturing of heretics.

I find these ideals of Solzhenitsyn quite unappealing. I am profoundly convinced that for the foreseeable future our society must be built on a combination of socialism and democracy; and that it is precisely the advance of Marxism and scientific communism that will make possible the creation of the most just human society.

Engineers and scientists must have a far greater weight in our society than they have today. But this by no means excludes a scientifically organized political leadership. It assumes, in particular, the abolition of all sorts of privileges for leaders, reasonable limitations on [political] power, self-management wherever possible, an increased role for organs of local government, the separation of executive, legislative, and judicial branches of government, limitations on the time any political mandate can be exercised, full freedom of speech and conscience—including, of course, freedom [of religious belief and teaching,] freedom to organize and freedom of assembly for individuals and groups of all political persuasions, free elections with full freedom for all parties and groups to put up candidates for every post, and so forth. Only such a society, which of course would also be free of the exploitation of one person by another and would be based on [social] ownership of all the principal means of material production, can guarantee the unhindered and balanced progress of all humanity and its individual members. As long as this genuine socialist democracy does not exist, our country will continue to develop in a slow and unbalanced way, and such giants as Solzhenitsyn will not often appear among us.

Before his arrest, Solzhenitsyn considered himself a Marxist. Having passed all of the cruel trials that are described with such merciless truth in *Gulag Archipelago*, Solzhenitsyn lost his faith in Marxism. That is a matter of his conscience and convictions. A sincere change of opinion [deserves understanding and respect.] Solzhenitsyn has betrayed or sold out no one. Today he is an opponent of Marxism, and he does not hide that.

Marxism will not, of course, collapse because it has lost one of its former adherents. I even think that Marxism can only benefit from a polemic with opponents such as Solzhenitsyn. It is much better to have an opponent like this than "defenders" like Sergei Mikhalkov or Aleksandr Chakovskii. A "scientific" ideology that has to hold people by force or the threat of force alone would be worth nothing. Fortunately genuine scientific socialism does not need compulsion.

How Solzhenitsyn
Returned His Ticket

by George Gibian

> They put too high a price on harmony. It's quite beyond my
> means to pay so much for admission. And that's why I'm in
> a hurry to return my admission ticket. If I am a man of
> honor, I am obliged to return it as soon as possible. That's
> exactly what I am doing. It's not that I don't accept God,
> Alyosha. I'm just most respectfully returning his ticket to
> him.
>
> Ivan Karamazov

Before *The Gulag Archipelago* was published, it was difficult to
imagine what Solzhenitsyn could have written in it that had not
already been said before. Scores of accounts of Soviet prison camps
had been published. Emigrés and residents of Soviet Russia, from
Evgeniya Ginsburg to Pyotr Yakir, described denunciations, arrests,
transports, camp conditions. A small library of books about this
subject exists in the West. Would Solzhenitsyn's book not be
anticlimactic? Isolated by the circumstances of the life imposed upon
him, he may not have been informed of how much was already known
in the West.

Yet *The Archipelago* turned out to be a very powerful book. External,
nonliterary factors may add to its force, but they do not suffice to
explain it. Even after we have allowed for Solzhenitsyn's fame, which
makes anything written by him of great interest, and for his heroic
conduct, which gives poignancy to every page of *The Archipelago*, we
are still left with the awareness that the book is different in kind from
every previous book about Soviet prison camps. It is stronger and
more far-reaching.

We shall have to pay attention to the structure of the work, even if Solzhenitsyn himself might disapprove of such analyses, judging by a passage in it. He describes how he listened to a fellow prisoner, Kostya Kiula, who

> recited his poems written in prison. His voice broke from excitement. The poems were "The First Package," "To My Wife," "To My Son." When you are in prison, straining your ears to catch verses which were also written in prison, you do not stop to think whether the author departed from the syllabo-tonic system and whether the lines end in assonances or full rhymes. These verses are the blood of *YOUR* heart, the tears of *YOUR* wife. People wept in the cell. (P. 595; part I, chap. 4) [1]

Granted, the power of *The Archipelago* derives first of all from the fact that like Kiula's poems, it conveys something we might call the blood of its author's heart. It overwhelms us with the sheer amount of human pain which it expresses. An exclusively technical analysis of a book saturated with suffering and bearing witness to a gigantic historical and national tragedy would be an exercise in callousness. But *The Archipelago* does affect us also by its quality. We have here not a transformation of quantity into quality, but an addition, or perhaps multiplication of quantity by quality. The latter has to do with literary genres and tones of voice, for Solzhenitsyn matches the vastness of human misfortune with the variety of the modes of discourse and styles which he incorporates and out of which he composes his book almost like a mosaic. His documentation of the jail-keepers' crimes and the jailed ones' calamities is paralleled by his amassing of various modes of addressing oneself to reality.

Solzhenitsyn deals with the problem of finding a true link, a real community, between people, something which would bridge the isolation of human beings, during a historical period in which the ruling ideology preached collectivism, but in actuality produced separation and inhumanity. The whole situation is contained in the dominant image of Solzhenitsyn's book: people being arrested and quietly led away during the night, while others in adjoining apartments knew nothing about it, or, when they knew, said and did nothing against it. Solzhenitsyn (unlike the vast majority of his fellow writers in Russia) sees no hope in a political reply or even in any other secular stance. His is a sweeping denunciation, from the position of religion, of this world as it exists.

[1] A. Solzhenitsyn, *Arkhipelag GULag*, 1918–1956, I–II. (Paris: YMCA Press, 1974). All page references are to this first Russian edition. Quotations have been translated by the author.

The subtitle is "An Attempt at Belletristic Investigation" *(Opyt khudozhestvennogo issledovaniya)*. This should alert the reader to the mingling of genres which will follow. It implies there will be at least three distinct elements (actually there are many more than three): expository prose of intellectual analysis, using the procedures of research; belletristic or artistic prose (using the techniques of fiction), and the tentativeness of an "attempt" or experiment—implying the provisionality and informality of a personal essay.

These three kinds of writing are present in the book, but so are many others. Perhaps the best way to begin will be to list some of the many distinguishable kinds of writing in *The Archipelago*. (Admittedly, they merge into one another almost imperceptibly, and some passages might fit under two or more rubrics.)

1. Autobiographical: narratives of how the author was arrested, brought to Moscow, questioned, sentenced, jailed. Numerous specific episodes.

2. Personal memoirs: the history of the author's intellectual development from a loyal Soviet citizen, through the stages of disillusionment, into a dissident hostile to Stalin and to the entire Soviet system; at first still preserving loyalty to Lenin, in the end utterly rejecting the Revolution from beginning to end. This category corresponds to the explicitly drawn conclusions of a *Bildungsroman*.

3. Countless stories of prisoners the author met: how they lived, were arrested, tortured, imprisoned.

4. Countless stories of individual prisoners whom Solzhenitsyn did not know personally, but about whom he was told by others.

5. Expository sections on various large topics:
   a. The history of political persecutions after 1917.
   b. The history of labor camps in the USSR.
   c. Synopses and analyses of the Criminal Code and its sections dealing with political crimes (Section 58).

6. Taxonomies and descriptions of methods of arrest, questioning, sentencing, imprisoning, transportation of prisoners.

7. Speculations on the causes of the various conditions described in other parts of the book.

8. Exhortations addressed directly to the readers, reproaching them (and the author himself) for weakness in yielding to terror and urging them to resist firmly in the future.

This list of the chief modes of discourse in *The Archipelago* far from exhausts its variety. A passage which starts as straight analysis (for example, of the Code) or a straight historical account (for example, of

General Vlasov's activities) may be interspersed with personal comments in quite a different manner. Sober "objective" summaries are followed by suppositions, hypotheses, interjections. There are interruptions in the guise of sarcastic questions, bitter comments, ironic suggestions, hortatory homilies. The narration also quickly turns into dialogue.

The polemicist is never far off the stage. Anything being spoken in one key may at any moment be commented upon by the ever-present eavesdropping accuser. The explicit indictment is not made in one continuous section; it is distributed throughout at scores of appropriate places.

Solzhenitsyn makes back-references to episodes he had recounted earlier. One meditative passage in which he alludes shorthand fashion to earlier incidents, similar to his earlier prose poems, lyrically evokes the entire country:

> "All this is Russia: the prisoners on the rails, refusing to complain; the girl behind the partition of the Stolypin railroad car compartment; the guard who went away to sleep; the pears which fell out of the pocket; the buried bombs; and the horse taken to the second floor." (P. 518; part 2, chap. 1)

The multiplicity of the book threatens to disunify it. However, the recurrence of two elements serves to hold it together: like a pendulum swinging between two points, Solzhenitsyn comes back time and again to specific illustrations (cases, names, trials, prehistories, posthistories) [2] and to his major conclusions (that everybody is guilty; that people should have resisted).

In its numerous interpolated case histories, its time span (1917 to date), and its sweeping conclusions, *The Archipelago* is the antithesis of *One Day in the Life of Ivan Denisovich*. The early novelette was strictly delimited. Solzhenitsyn centered it on self-denial and self-restraint. Understatement was his method. The action encompassed exactly one day; no general condemnations of the prison system or Soviet Russia were made by anyone, "author" or character; the authorial presence was subdued; the day chosen was a relatively good day; there was no melodrama, no sensationalism, no extreme violence or suffering. Conclusions were not drawn, explicit comments not made. The compression and understatement yielded powerful effects.

In *The Archipelago*, Solzhenitsyn moves freely into all the areas which

---

[2] He alludes himself to his repetitiveness and justifies it by blaming reality for it: "Repetition? No, this was Perebory, in the year 1937, Loschilin's story. It is not I who is repeating himself, it is Gulag [The Chief Prison Administration] which is repeating itself" (p. 570; part 2, chap. 3).

he chose to deny himself in *Ivan Denisovich*: he comments, explains, draws conclusions, exhorts, deplores, makes connections, pontificates.

Alternating with whatever the dominant tone of a given section may be are the styles of high rhetoric, or at other times, folksy proverbs, homely similes, vernacular phrases. Solzhenitsyn does not merely use figures of speech taken from folk speech and dialect; he also refers to the fact that he does so. For example, he begins his account (although the word "account" is inadequate to describe the rich mixture of varied styles and ways of approaching his topic) of Stalin's prosecution in 1931 of the Workers Peasant Party: "The White Sea folk speak this way about the tide: the water '*zadumalas*' bethought itself. That is before it begins to ebb. Well, it is not fitting to compare the troubled soul of Stalin with the water of the White Sea. But it is possible that he did not at all bethink himself. And there was no ebbing, either." (P. 61; part 1, chap. 2)

The peculiarities of Solzhenitsyn's manner of writing emerge strikingly when one alternates reading *The Archipelago* with some of the other books about the same subject. Boris Yakovlev's *The Concentration Camps of the USSR [Kontsentratsionnye lageri SSSR]* (Munich: 1955) an early account of prison camps, and George Fischer's *Soviet Opposition to Stalin* (Harvard University Press, 1952), largely the story of the Vlasov movement, provide information similar to Solzhenitsyn's. Yakovlev reviews the history of the camps since 1918, the organization of the penal system, the various prisons, and even has some of the same subdivisions (for example, "Methods of Questioning"). Sometimes he supplies more general information than Solzhenitsyn. Yakovlev lists 165 camps, each with a paragraph or more of description (climatic conditions, agriculture, geography, special characteristics of the camp). There are maps and texts of governmental decrees concerning camps. Fischer gives more space to the biography of General Vlasov than does Solzhenitsyn, and has three divergent accounts of how he fell into Soviet hands in 1945. He not only compiles material, but gives analyses and conclusions. However, both he and Yakovlev remain on the expository level.

Solzhenitsyn, on the other hand, complicates his narration. As we have seen, he steps outside the conventions of detached, descriptive, historical or legal reports of research results. There are passages of meditation, dramatization, dialogue. He refers frequently and explicitly to himself and to the "we" who are seeking to unravel the yarns of evidence. (For example: "However, we shall not reach the essence of the matter" [p. 321; part 1, chap. 8].) He makes of his prose an instrument to generate a collective effort in which "we" the readers move together with the author through heterogeneous materials and are engaged in the common quest to find out the "Truth," and also an instrument to guide us to the proper interpretation of the matters before us.

Solzhenitsyn strives for rhetorical effects; he switches sides. He may tell the story from the point of view, ironically assumed (and deliberately unconvincing) and with the pretended excitement of the Soviet police officials and their supporters: "Such an unmasking will stain the heavenly garments of the Cheka! Is the chairman of the Moscow Revolutionary Tribunal in his senses? Is he taking care of his business?" (p. 322; part 1, chap. 8). And on the next page: "What witnesses came before the Tribunal of their own free will!" There are exclamations: "Oh how many plots! Oh where is Shakespeare!" (*ibid.*, n. 41). When Solzhenitsyn writes neutral expository prose, the reader knows it will last only for a short time. Dramatic materials (mini-plays) and authorial comments will follow quickly.

A partisan chorus is always present to comment, often in colorful language. Prose turns into drama in direct addresses to the reader, rhetorical questions, melodramatic exclamations ("Terrible days!"). Movement is generated by switching tenses from future to past: "Are we ever going to read the old archives from Lubyanka? No, they will burn them. They have already burned them" (p. 327; part 1, chap. 8).

Historical narratives modulate imperceptibly into autobiographical illustrations which in turn metamorphose into fragments of memoirs reminiscent of bits of Solzhenitsyn's novels. During a brief period of travel by train, when Solzhenitsyn was still a prisoner, he mingled with free men, was mistaken for one of them, and offered beer by a fellow passenger: "Beer?? Beer! For three years I had not drunk one swallow of it! Tomorrow in the cell I will boast: I drank beer" (p. 585; part 2, chap. 4). There is a perpetual drive to dramatize, to fictionalize. Even in this trivial incident, Solzhenitsyn is creating a mini-fiction, a mini-drama, recalling how things were, and how they will be the next day when he is in his cell again; he invents what he will say to his audience of prisoners about the events of the present moment in the train.

There is perpetual awareness of an audience, a drawing in of the listeners into the circle listening to the story. There is always tension between human beings, between past, present, future, between levels of tone, modes of discourse.

The multifarious events are set in motion by multifarious rhetorical modes and styles of language. They drive home the conclusion that not only since Stalin took power, not merely since 1937 or 1938, not through some aberration of the system, but from the beginning of the Soviet state in 1917, and basically, from root to crown, the Soviet Union has been a perversion of a true human community.

We can regard Solzhenitsyn's achievement also in the light of what we might call "Berthoff's Law." In a recent article Warner Berthoff attributes Walter Scott's revolutionary force in European literature to his compositional decision "to describe manners minutely," as Scott phrased it. In Berthoff's view, Scott introduced into the novel,

> through his concrete allegiance to the data of Scottish history, folklore, balladry, social habituation and linguistic usage, and through the sheer pedantry of his respect for the ways of speaking by which all these things lived in ordinary consciousness—a plenary treatment of available materials that has, in the performance, the very character of the mythic.[3]

Berthoff moves from an assessment of Scott's structural innovations to the formulation of a sweeping criterion:

> That work of fiction will have an extraordinary interest and importance, a grander capacity to persuade, in which the author has put into combination a greater rather than lesser multiplicity of familiar ways of speaking—more precisely, of the familiar substances of human speech and discourse, the "things that are said," in love, school, politics, the market, gossip, superstition and fantasy, law, philosophy, standard literature, work, games, ritual, prayer. It must of course be a new combination, though every element in it traces to a traditional and recognizable source. And it must be carried through in a way that substantially respects the locutionary character of each of its components, and that at the same time can take quick and regular advantage of the opportunities thus created for illuminating any one of these components by putting it in relation with another or others having special appropriateness. The tonal blend resulting will vary, like the choice of formal genre, according to the governing rhetorical intention. . . . it is this element of combinative resourcefulness in a great work of fiction, rather than lexical fanciness or ingenuities in story arrangement, that permanently arrests interest and makes changes in the history of literate consciousness.[4]

Solzhenitsyn's first wife, Natal'ya Reshetovskaya, said in a newspaper interview that *The Archipelago* reports not camp conditions, but the

---

[3] Warner Berthoff, "Fiction, History, Myth," in *The Interpretation of Narrative: Theory and Practice*, ed. Morton W. Bloomfield, *Harvard English Studies*, Vol. 1 (Cambridge, Mass.: Harvard University Press, 1970), pp. 284–85.

[4] *Ibid.*

folklore of the camps. She could have said, more accurately, that it also incorporates, in addition to the folklore of the camps, the language of legal analysis, drama, philosophy, theodicy, comments, conclusions, *mea culpa, j'accuse,* meditation, research, and belles-lettres, in a mixture which stands both in clear relation to today's Soviet literature and to nineteenth-century Russian classics, and at the same time, delivers an all-out barrage against Soviet ideology and reality.

On Reading
The Gulag Archipeligo

by Victor Erlich

In his excellent review of *The Gulag Archipelago*—by far the most effective American response to date—George Kennan called it "the greatest and most powerful single indictment of a political regime ever to be leveled in modern times." [1] Intrepid Lidiya Chukovskaya spoke of Solzhenitsyn's mammoth endeavor as an "enormous event," comparable in its repercussions to Stalin's death. Roy Medvedev, a man who has serious philosophical and political disagreements with Solzhenitsyn, maintains that no one who has read *The Gulag Archipelago* can remain the same person he or she was before reading it.

To approach such a momentous moral-political act in primarily literary terms may appear as fatuous as "reading the Bible for its prose." Yet we could do worse, I submit, than begin our effort to pin down the nature and import of this harrowing montage—an unorthodox and potent blend of history, political commentary, personal reminiscence, and composite eyewitness testimony—by focussing on some aspects of its texture and genre. Solzhenitsyn seems to have legitimized such a procedure by providing a curious subtitle "An Experiment in Literary [literally "Artistic"] Investigation." While I am not entirely clear about the precise implications of this phrase, I sense here something akin to the intent behind the title of Dostoevsky's publicistic miscellany *A Writer's Diary*—notably a suggestion that the body of nonfictional writing thus labeled has been shaped in part by the exigencies and the resources of literary. craft.

As one immerses oneself in the Solzhenitsyn text, the ramifications of the subtitle gradually emerge. First, there is the presence of pervasive images or clusters of images which dominate the description and the history of the Soviet penal and forced labor camp systems. The quality of the Gulag world and its monstrous expansion are

"On Reading *The Gulag Archipelago*" by Victor Erlich. From *Dissent*, Fall 1974. Copyright © 1974 by Victor Erlich. Reprinted by permission of *Dissent*.

[1] See *The New York Review of Books*, March 21, 1974.

captured in the graphic phrase "the sewage disposal system" and concomitantly, the "murky, stinking pipes" into which successive "torrents" of prisoners—democratic socialists, churchmen, alleged industrial saboteurs, dispossessed *kulaks* and others—are channeled. By the same token, the title metaphor, "archipelago," triggers, in sections dealing with the Gulag topography and modes of transportation, such terms as "islands," "ships" and "boats."

More importantly, this, Solzhenitsyn's first major work of nonfiction, has all the evocativeness, all the vividness of individual scenes, episodes and encounters that has long been recognized as his major literary trademark. The cumulative power and the overwhelming credibility of the indictment are due in no small measure to the fact that the statistics and the typologies are repeatedly anchored in, and authenticated by, the wealth of physical and human detail, either remembered by the author or conveyed to him by other former denizens of the Archipelago, in the identifiable, and often identified, human ordeal. Thus, it is no reflection necessarily on the historical portion of the book to say that it is most effective in such sections as the autobiographical chapter "That Spring"—a masterly evocation of the fervent hopes of amnesty which pervaded the camps in the wake of the victory over the Nazis, hopes which were brutally dashed as one inmate after the other was casually and callously consigned to additional 5, 10, or 15 years of the forced labor camp inferno.

The adeptness of Solzhenitsyn the novelist at dramatizing the wanton arbitrariness of the Soviet penal system and the unrelieved wretchedness of its victims is demonstrated here in countless episodes ranging from the grotesquely anecdotal to the almost unbearably poignant. Let me quote a few salient instances.

Here is a vignette of a district party conference in the Moscow province, held at the peak of the "personality cult":

> It [the conference] was presided over by a new Secretary of the District Party Committee, replacing one recently arrested. At the conclusion of the conference a tribute to Comrade Stalin was called for. Of course, everyone stood up. The small hall echoed with stormy applause, rising to an ovation. For three minutes, four minutes, five minutes the stormy applause rising to an ovation continued. But palms were getting sore, and raised arms were already aching. . . . However, who would dare to be the first to stop? The Secretary of the District Party Committee could have done so. He was standing on the platform and it was he who had just called for the ovation. But he was a newcomer. He had taken the place of a man who had been arrested. . . . He was afraid. . . . The director of the local paper factory, an independent and strong-minded man stood with the presidium. Aware of all the falsity and impossibility

of the situation, he still kept applauding. Nine minutes, ten! . . . After
eleven minutes the director of the paper factory assumed a business-like
expression and sat down in his seat. . . . And oh, what a miracle took
place! . . . To a man everyone else stopped dead and sat down. . . .
That same night the factory director was arrested. . . .[2]

By the time such scenes were occurring all over the Soviet Union
"the sewage disposal system" had acquired a momentum of its own.
The greedy machine had to be fed, the swollen policy corps had to
justify its existence and demonstrate its vigilance by dumping down
the "stinking pipes" ever-increasing numbers of random victims.
Hence this remarkable admission made a few years later: "At the
Novosibirsk Transit Prison in 1945 they greeted the prisoners with a
roll call based on cases. "So and so! Article 51 and 58–1A, twenty-five
years." "The chief of the convoy guard was curious 'What did you get
it for?' 'For nothing at all.' 'You are lying. The sentence for nothing at
all is ten years.' " [3]

Finally, in the chapter "The Ships of the Archipelago," a chance
encounter in a prison van. Riding in the infamous "Black Maria"
from the Butyrkij Prison to the railroad station, the author overhears a
whispered conversation between his fellow inmate, lieutenant-colonel
I. and a woman prisoner next to whom the officer finds himself and
who turns out to have shared for five fateful months a prison cell with
his wife.

> "Where is she now?" he inquires anxiously. "All that time she lived
> only for you! Her fears weren't for herself but were all for you!" . . .
> "But what has happened to her now?" "She blamed herself for your
> arrest. Things were so hard for her!" "Where is she now?" "Just don't
> be frightened"—and Repina put her hands on his chest as if he were
> her own kin. "She simply couldn't endure the strain. They took her
> away from us. She became, you know, well, a little confused. You
> understand?"
>   And that tiny storm boxed in sheets of steel rolled along so peacefully
> in the six-lane automobile traffic, stopped at traffic lights and signaled
> for a turn.[4]

But all this is only part of what "literary investigation" may properly
imply: for the adjective "artistic" can connote not only a command of
characteristically literary techniques, an ability to embody a tragedy

[2] *The Gulag Archipelago, 1918–1956, An Experiment in Literary Investigation*, I–II.
Translated from the Russian by Thomas P. Whitney. (New York: Harper and Row,
1974), pp. 69–70.
[3] *Ibid.*, p. 293.
[4] *Ibid.*, p. 531.

of millions in sharply etched individual images, but also the writer's recognizable signature, the imprint of his personal vision, a moral emphasis that is unmistakably his own. This brings me to a theme which bulks large in *The Gulag Archipelago*—that of the soul-destroying potential of *any* exercise of authority within the Soviet system, a theme which had been sounded memorably in *The First Circle*.

Let us recall the seeming moral paradox which lies at the heart of that novel: only in prison can one be really free. Only those who like Nerzhin, Bobynin, Khorobrov have nothing to lose, since they have already lost everything—all their material possessions and often their loved ones—can maintain their basic humanity and their personal dignity, can act upon the dictates of their conscience. That is why, in contradistinction to his brilliant and equally intransigent fellow inmate Sologdin, Nerzhin chooses to forego the relative comforts of the elite prison and the glimmer of freedom as a possible reward for collaboration and opt for one of the circles of the inferno. He does so, Edmund Wilson notwithstanding,[5] not because he craves suffering, but because he knows only too well the moral cost of playing the game, and the system's capacity to degrade anyone who does its bidding.

In *The Gulag Archipelago* this moral vulnerability of the average Soviet citizen or inmate becomes an insidious and ubiquitous threat. Hence the "dreadful question" which Solzhenitsyn raises as his discussion of the KGB mentality ("The Bluecaps") shades off into autobiography: "If my life had turned out differently, might I myself not have become just such an executioner?" It seems that at a certain point in his career as a student Solzhenitsyn was urged to enter a secret police academy. Some of his colleagues "were recruited at the time." Solzhenitsyn himself at the last moment refused to apply out of some "vague sense of revulsion" which he traces to an earlier, less "relativistic" morality. He now claims that this was a narrow escape: "if they had really put the pressure on, they could have broken everybody's resistance."[6] But, clearly, what was involved was not merely "pressure"; in a society where the alternative to authority, however limited, is either total misery or total insignificance, temptations of power are extremely difficult to resist. By the same token where "higher"—moral or religious—constraints are effectively removed, abuse of power is virtually inevitable: "Power is a poison well known for thousands of years. . . . For those, however who are

---

[5] See "Solzhenitsyn" in *A Window on Russia*. (New York: Farrar, Straus and Giroux, 1972.)

[6] Solzhenitsyn, *op. cit.*, pp. 160–61.

unaware of any higher spheres it is deadly poison." [7] In passages of remarkable effectiveness and characteristic candor Solzhenitsyn recalls ruefully that during the few months of his army career, abruptly terminated by imprisonment, he proved far from immune to this poison: when an army captain, he was not above throwing his weight around, taking inordinate pride in his rank and uniform, treating ordinary soldiers and prisoners of war in a high-handed and arrogant manner. For Solzhenitsyn's purposes Lord Acton's famous dictum "power tends to corrupt and absolute power corrupts absolutely" might be amended to read: "in an absolutist (i.e. totalitarian) state even limited power can corrupt absolutely."

Let us take one step further: in the nightmarish world of the Gulag Archipelago the source of corruption lies not in the power *per se,* but in its being legitimized and sanctioned by an all-embracing ideology: "Ideology—that is what gives evildoing its long sought justification and gives the evildoer the necessary steadfastness and determination. . . . That was how the agents of the Inquisition fortified their wills: by invoking Christianity; . . . the Nazis, by race; and the Jacobins (early and late), by equality, brotherhood and the happiness of future generations." [8]

What is the name of the latter-day Jacobin ideology that served as an alibi for the atrocities recorded here? Is it Marxism that is deemed responsible for what happened to Russian society? Though Solzhenitsyn's hostility to Marxism as a fallacious and "alien" doctrine is by now part of the public record, on the evidence of the first four parts of *The Gulag Archipelago* it would be more accurate to say that he places the blame at the door of the Bolshevik variant of Marxism, specifically, of Vladimir Ilyich Lenin.

Solzhenitsyn's insistence on tracing the story of the Soviet police state back to the halcyon days of the October Revolution is precisely what makes *The Gulag Archipelago* so thoroughly subversive a document. It is also an emphasis which has been queried by a number of Western reviewers, including those who on the face of it do not seem to have any stake in the early phase of the Soviet regime. In a thoughtful review of *The Gulag Archipelago* Stephen F. Cohen found Solzhenitsyn's strictures somewhat unfair. Where legitimizing terror is concerned Lenin's legacy is "ambiguous," he opined.[9]

Let us concede as a general proposition that modulated political analysis is not Solzhenitsyn's forte. Thus, in his salutary challenge to

---

[7] *Ibid.,* p. 147.

[8] *Ibid.,* p. 174.

[9] *New York Times Book Review,* June 16, 1974.

the Khrushchevite notion that the "abuses of socialist legality" had not begun until the mid-30s and that the Great Terror was due to the tyrant's paranoia and blood lust, he can on occasions understate the differences between the Stalin and the pre-Stalin periods. (Since the monstrous distinctiveness of Stalin's contribution emerges unmistakably from the massive documentation adduced here, no major distortions can be said to have occurred.) By the same token, he feels too vindictive—and again not without reason—toward all the major architects of the Soviet system to be able to accord the old Bolsheviks arraigned in the public purge trials, *e.g.* N. Bukharin, as sensitive and compassionate a treatment as he offers millions of ordinary Russians, including the half-starved and misguided prisoners of war sucked into General Vlasov's ill-fated "Russian Liberation Army." [10]

Yet none of this diminishes the force of Solzhenitsyn's most explosive thesis, notably that the foundations of Stalinist arbitrariness and lawlessness, of the use of terror as the "mode of persuasion" were laid in the formative years of the Soviet regime. The evidence marshaled in behalf of this proposition is as ample as it is difficult to refute. There is the indiscriminate savagery of the War Communism terror, the succession of revolutionary kangaroo courts held in the early 20s, the raving and ranting of Lenin's protégé, the chief prosecutor Krylenko, bluntly deriding the concept of personal guilt as a bourgeois survival and enthroning the principle of "class expediency" as the cornerstone of the Soviet judicial system. Last but not least there are *ipsissima verba magistri,* the ominously explicit quotations from Lenin's writings and edicts, his call to "purge the Russian land of all kinds of harmful insects," his flat assertion in the 1919 letter to M. Gorky that the intelligentsia "are not the nation's brain but shit," his directive to the People's Commissar of Justice "to extend the use of execution by shooting to all activities of the Mensheviks, SR's etc.," finally and most relevantly, his laying down only two months after the October Revolution of the "guiding principle of the Gulag Archipelago." In December 1917 Lenin drew up the following list of penalties for violation of a recently promulgated law: "confiscation of all property, incarceration . . . and *forced labor*" (my italics—V.E.).[11]

[10] Soviet official slander and some Western obfuscation notwithstanding, Solzhenitsyn never comes anywhere close to justifying Gen. Vlasov's precarious collaboration with the Germans. His main interest is in probing Stalin's responsibility for this large-scale defection, in pressing the question: how could it happen that "several hundred thousand young men, aged twenty to thirty, took up arms against their Fatherland as allies of its most evil enemy?"

[11] Solzhenitsyn, *op. cit.,* pp. 308, 328, 357; *ARKHIPELAG GULag,* 1918–1956, III–IV (Paris: YMCA Press, 1974), p. 10.

That on the eve of his death Lenin should have had second thoughts about the authoritarian drift of the Bolshevik regime is a matter of some psychological and historic interest. The dying leader's alleged last-minute shudder may well be interpreted as a belated tribute to the humanistic tradition of the Russian intelligentsia to which his successor owed scant allegiance. But it is hardly enough to absolve Lenin from a major share of responsibility for the establishment of the Soviet penal system.

Some Western students of Russia should have little quarrel with Solzhenitsyn's position. In fact they can properly argue that ruthlessness and lack of scruple in dealing with "class enemies" had been a trademark of Bolshevism well before its advent to power. Yet ultimately what is at issue here is not just the nature of the Bolshevik doctrine or, as George Kennan correctly puts it, "not so much the actual content of the [dominant] ideology as . . . the absolute value attached to it." [12] For only an intoxication with one's historical rightness could provide what Norman Cohn has called in another connection "a warrant for genocide." [13] Only the terrible righteousness of self-appointed saviors of mankind could induce otherwise honorable men and women to proscribe entire segments of society, to waive all legal and moral constraints with regard to those branded "socially alien" and stigmatized as "harmful insects" to be exterminated without mercy or discrimination.

One of the most repellent aspects of the Gulag universe recorded previously in such forced labor camp memoirs as Evgeniya Ginsburg's *Journey into the Whirlwind* and fully borne out by Solzhenitsyn's account, is the complete impunity with which hardened criminals harass and humiliate their "political" fellow inmates. The privileged status enjoyed by bandits and thieves in the Archipelago can be said to epitomize the wantonness and brutality of "l'univers concentrationnaire" (David Rousset).[14] But it is also a measure not so much of the regime's tenderness toward the criminals—though it was these *Lumpenproletariet* gone astray who are dubbed "socially akin" and thus capable of reeducation—as of its utter scorn for the "politicals." (How different in this respect, Solzhenitsyn never tires of reminding us, were the Tsarist jails!) In this seedy ideocracy a thief, or for that matter a murderer is simply a Soviet citizen who has run afoul of the law and

---

[12] See above, note 1.

[13] *Warrant for Genocide.* The Myth of the Jewish World-Conspiracy and the Protocols of the Elders of Zion. (New York: Harper and Row, 1967.)

[14] [The reference is to an early and notable account of Nazi concentration camps; for the English translation see David Rousset, *The Other Kingdom* (New York: Reynal and Hitchcock, 1947).—ED.]

who during his prison interlude is encouraged to use his not inconsiderable resources to act as a scourge of the allegedly unredeemable "enemies of the people." The "political" offender or anyone who could be remotely—or fraudulently—construed as one[15] is a pariah, an outcast; he has truly been placed beyond the pale.

At one of the least convincing moments in Maksim Gorky's famous play "The Lower Depths" a protagonist exclaims: "Man! This has a proud ring!" This humanistic cliché—singularly unpersuasive in the squalid circumstances under which it was uttered—has since been quoted *ad nauseam* by official Soviet publicists and critics. Nor is it particularly surprising. Abstract enthusiasm for Man, faith in his unlimited potential and his glorious future, has never prevented inhuman treatment of the believer's notoriously imperfect contemporaries, in fact, it has often legitimized it. Ironically, it is to the accompaniment of such ringing celebrations of Man that millions of actual men and women were marched into the lower depths of degradation in the land which Alexander Solzhenitsyn, to his everlasting credit, has dared to chart.

Whatever its flaws or inconsistencies *The Gulag Archipelago* is indeed, as Chukovskaya put it, an "enormous event." Whether the "repercussions," the overall impact, of Solzhenitsyn's act will match its inherent significance is quite another matter. Few of his Russian readers—and it is to them that *The Gulag Archipelago* is principally addressed—will fail to respond to this book without a shock of either recognition or discovery. But how many of them will be reached? The Soviet authorities can be relied upon to make access to Solzhenitsyn's bombshell difficult and hazardous. In the West where the availability of the book is not at issue the barriers are of a different order. One of them has to do with the harrowing nature of Solzhenitsyn's material. This unsparing account of arrests, tortures, executions and of grinding day-to-day brutalities and indignities, the spectacle of the millions of innocent people frozen, starved, beaten to death would be literally unbearable, were it not for Solzhenitsyn's remarkable narrative gifts

[15] One of the salient findings of Solzhenitsyn's "literary investigation" is that since the early 30s only an infinitesimal fraction of those convicted on ideological charges under the catch-all article 58 have been principled opponents or even critics of the regime. During the Stalin years one could be sentenced to anywhere from five to twenty-five years under this article for such crimes as hanging one's jacket on Lenin's bust, wrapping a herring in a newspaper which featured Stalin's photo, or asking at a Party meeting why Trotsky was allowed to leave the country. (The sentiment was thoroughly orthodox, but questioning the Party's wisdom was an intolerable offense.) No wonder the chief of the convoy guard in Novosibirsk could calmly state: "The sentence for nothing at all is ten years."

and for the flashes of humanity and spiritual fortitude that occasionally light up the inferno. As it is, the journey is a long and arduous one, and not a few Westerners who admire Solzhenitsyn and trust him implicitly will balk at these hardships. (Recently a lady neighbor told me with feeling: "I believe every word he says, but I'm not going to *read* this book!") Some of those who will take the plunge are liable to be occasionally "turned off." If readers naturally attuned to Solzhenitsyn's towering rage will marvel at its sustained power, others may find his unmodulated anger, his heavy sarcasm which punctures the text and keeps spilling into the footnotes obtrusive, if not counterproductive. More substantively, many an otherwise sympathetic Westerner is apt to be irked by the parallels drawn between the Soviet police state and other systems of organized repression, including the Nazi terror, parallels which may appear to minimize the horrors of the latter. I am saying "appear" since at no point does Solzhenitsyn view Nazism as anything else but the epitome of modern Western evil. Yet his passionate and to an extent legitimate insistence on the uniqueness of Soviet experience—in its utter arbitrariness and its grotesque size the Stalinist police apparatus has no equals in modern history!—and may at times clash head on with one's awareness of an equally unique, and unsurpassable grisly modern atrocity—the Nazi "final solution."

Yet it is one thing to note the pitfalls of Solzhenitsyn's Russia-centered cosmology (nothing less than candor can do justice to his own fearless honesty); it is quite another to use his blind spots or rhetorical excesses as a pretext for distancing ourselves from a great and an immensely important book. In a *New Yorker* review George Steiner deems it necessary to warn his readers: "But let us not fool ourselves. Even where it moves and instructs us most *The Gulag Archipelago* is violently at odds with the Western style of feeling and argument. It is filled with Slavophile, liturgical rhetoric. Citing those broken under torture Solzhenitsyn exclaims: "Brother mine! Do not condemn those who finding themselves in such a situation turned out to be weak and confessed to more than they should have. . . . Do not be the first to cast a stone at them!" [16]

The characteristically Russian "liturgical" tonality of the above is undeniable: Dostoevsky's Father Zossima could have spoken thus. But is not the "style of *feeling*" which shapes this passage, especially its richly resonant last phrase, part of the patrimony which many a Western reader will readily recognize as his own?

Let me conclude: we have before us a triumph of relentless, heroic memory, a staggering recreation of a man-made hell, of an institu-

[16] *The New Yorker*, August 5, 1974.

tionalized horror perpetrated in our own time and still extending, albeit in a significantly truncated and modified form, over one sixth of the globe, a horror whose very existence was for a number of years strenuously denied by some of the more "advanced" minds of our era out of misguided loyalty to a besmirched and degraded utopian project. Solzhenitsyn has written a book which, in his own words, "cries out" not only to the "two hundred million" Russians but to us all. Is it too much to hope that a significant number of those vouchsafed the opportunity to hear his message, will bestir themselves to do so?

Solzhenitsyn in English:
An Evaluation

by Alexis Klimoff

Some hold translations not unlike to be
The wrong side of a Turkey tapistry.

James Howell (1594?–1666)

To any reader of Solzhenitsyn's works in the original, the writer's concern with language is as obvious as the moral and social thrust of his narrative. More consistently and more imaginatively than any other contemporary Soviet writer, Solzhenitsyn has attempted to eschew the ubiquitous clichés that have long ago spilled over from the pages of *Pravda* and *Izvestiia* and inundated Soviet writing. Solzhenitsyn's fiction represents a conscious endeavor to offer an alternative. For this purpose he has mobilized the full resources of the Russian language; especially bold use has been made of what the grammar books call "popular" or "substandard" speech *[prostorech'e]*. His syntax is dense, elliptical, and will appear innovative and thorny to those accustomed to urbane commonplaces. The vocabulary range is so great that a recent seventeen-volume dictionary of the Russian language is of no help for many hundreds of items. With few concessions to his readers, Solzhenitsyn makes use of technical terminology, prison-camp slang, rare words culled from Vladimir Dal's famous glossary, as well as large numbers of neologisms.

These qualities alone make the task of Solzhenitsyn's translators extremely difficult. But the caliber of the translations has also been

"Solzhenitsyn in English: An Evaluation" by Alexis Klimoff. From John B. Dunlop, Richard Haugh, and Alexis Klimoff, eds., *Aleksandr Solzhenitsyn: Critical Essays and Documentary Materials*, (Belmont, Mass.: Nordland Publishing Company, 1973), pp. 533–57. Copyright © 1973 by Nordland Publishing Company. Reprinted by permission of the publisher and the author. The article has been slightly revised by the author for this collection.

affected by two external factors. To begin with, there is the problem of textual uncertainty. The manuscripts of many of Solzhenitsyn's works (including *Cancer Ward* and *The First Circle*) came to the West by indirect channels, and there are significant differences between the various Russian-language editions of his works. Certain of these variants can be attributed to revisions made by the author; others seem to be corruptions resulting from what has been called the "neo-scribal" process of *samizdat* distribution. Translators and publishers have been forced to make choices and compromises, some of them unfortunate.

But much greater damage has been wrought by the unseemly haste with which many of the translations were produced. Before Solzhenitsyn retained a Swiss attorney, Dr. Fritz Heeb, to defend his interests in the West (1970), each new work by the author was liable to set off a race—not to say a free-for-all—between competing translations. Considerations of quality were all too obviously subordinated to the single-minded aim of "cornering the market" by appearing on the bookshelves before a rival edition. The publishing history of *One Day in the Life of Ivan Denisovich* gives an inkling of the tempos involved. The novel appeared in the Soviet Union in mid-November of 1962, and the first reviews of *two* different English translations had already been published by the second half of January, 1963. If one subtracts the time needed for the technical production of the book, it is evident that the translators were accorded no more than a few weeks to render a text of enormous stylistic subtlety and complexity. Such deadlines are as unrealistic as they are intolerable: the publishers who impose them should bear a large share of the responsibility for the inevitable flaws of the end product.

In this review essay I offer an evaluation of the major English translations of Solzhenitsyn's fiction. My list does not aspire to bibliographic completeness: the principal aim has been to examine critically those translations which have had the greatest impact on the English-speaking world in the course of the past decade. For this reason all translations of Solzhenitsyn published in periodicals and in various literary anthologies have been excluded from consideration; my review is limited to books or book-length collections consisting entirely of works by Solzhenitsyn. Even this more manageable list has had to be restricted to the author's best-known works. The present survey does not include a discussion of the English renditions of "For the Good of the Cause" (separate edition, trans. by David Floyd and Max Hayward, 1964) or of the plays (*The Love-Girl and the Innocent*, trans. by Nicholas Bethell and David Burg, 1969; *Candle in the Wind*, trans. by Keith Armes, 1973).[1]

In each case I have examined a recent edition of the translation in question, generally a paperback. The analysis is concerned solely and exclusively with the quality of the translation per se. No mention is made of the various introductions, appendices, or afterwords which enhance the value of several of the editions reviewed. I have also avoided all consideration of the legality or propriety of the various editions, some of which have provoked sharp controversy and even litigation.

The criterion in my evaluation has at all times been accuracy: the degree to which the translation communicates the content, spirit, and manner of the original. Defined in this way, accuracy goes far beyond "basic meaning" to include stylistic level, imagery, tone, and "flavor." I shall note further that I have assumed at all times that these translations are addressed to non-readers of Russian. This excludes considering their worth as a crutch or "pony" to help the reader who is partially familiar with the language of the original. Literal, word-by-word translations have their proper place and function but they can never be appropriate for a general audience. As Pushkin observed about Chateaubriand's earnest but misguided attempt to reproduce Milton in French with absolute literal fidelity:

> There can be no doubt that in his endeavor to render Milton *word for word*, Chateaubriand was, at the same time, unable to maintain a faithfulness to meaning and expression. An interlinear translation can never be accurate. (*A.S. Pushkin o literature* [M., 1962], p. 474).

I should add, finally, that I do not claim to have checked every word of the translations discussed against the original. My judgment is based primarily on a close scrutiny of selected chapters or passages in each of the works reviewed. At least ten percent of the translated text has been checked against the Russian in the case of the major novels; a considerably greater proportion was examined in each of the shorter works.

A. *One Day in the Life of Ivan Denisovich*

All presently existing translations of *One Day* were rendered obsolete upon the publication of the authorized and unexpurgated Russian

---

[1] This article was completed before the appearance of *The Gulag Archipelago* in English. See note 7 on p. 155.

version in Paris in May of 1973. (Aleksandr Solzhenitsyn, *Odin den' Ivana Denisovicha. Matrenin dvor* [Paris: YMCA Press, 1973]. The book is prefaced by a note, signed by Solzhenitsyn, in which he declares this edition to be "the authentic and final version.") The translations reviewed here are all based on the censored text which was published in *Novyi mir* in 1962. Five different English translations of this novel have appeared in print up to 1974:

1. *One Day in the Life of Ivan Denisovich.* Translated by Max Hayward and Ronald Hingley. New York: Frederick A. Praeger, 1963. [My references are to the Bantam paperback edition, 1972.] [2]

2. *One Day in the Life of Ivan Denisovich.* Translated by Ralph Parker. New York: Dutton; London: Gollancz, 1963. [My references are to the Signet paperback edition, 1971.]

3. *One Day in the Life of Ivan Denisovich.* Translated by Thomas P. Whitney. New York: Fawcett [Crest paperback], 1963.

4. *One Day in the Life of Ivan Denisovich.* Translated by Bela Von Block. New York: Lancer, 1963. [My references are to the Lodestone paperback, 1973.]

5. *One Day in the Life of Ivan Denisovich.* Translated by Gillon Aitken. Revised Edition. New York: Farrar, Straus and Giroux, 1971.

One Day presents a formidable challenge to the translator. The greater part of this short novel is expressed in the idiom of the protagonist, a man of peasant origin and no formal education. To achieve this effect, Solzhenitsyn has made use of a narrative style far removed from standard literary Russian. Folksy colloquialisms are combined with vivid slang and prison-camp jargon into a pungent and original but nevertheless entirely credible mixture. In addition, the dialogue contains some of the earthiest language ever to appear in print in the Soviet Union.

Only Hayward and Hingley (No. 1) have faced up to this challenge in a systematic fashion. As they state in a prefatory note, the translators have attempted to capture the stylistic flavor of the original by turning to the speech forms of uneducated American English. While this is not the only possible solution (surely Cockney English is at least as rich), it is certainly a legitimate one. The translators have evidently found this approach productive and they have been able to render many difficult passages with imagination and striking success.

---

[2] The paperback editions listed in this article are the latest printings available to me. Among the many printings of each edition, I have found some instances of a change in prefatory materials but no instance of differences in pagination or in the text itself.

But they have not always followed their own prescription, especially in the second half of the novel. All too many colorful phrases have been pruned to bare and unremarkable English prose. I will cite only a few typical examples. *Ocheredi ne bylo . . . Zakhodi* is translated with the almost neutral: "there wasn't a big crowd lined up . . . So he went straight in" (p. 15). If American slang is to be used, several expressions come easily to mind for *zakhodi* in this context, including "in you go" or perhaps even "waltz right in." *Ekh, da i povalili zh! Povalili zeki s kryl'tsa!* is toned down to "They were all pouring out down the steps now" (p. 191). The visual immediacy of the original is almost entirely erased in the process. A more accurate rendering—once again in accordance with the translators' own program—might be: "Just look at 'em pour out! The zeks are just pouring down the steps." *Zagnat' v dereviannyi bushlat* means literally "to drive into a wooden jacket" and is a jocose euphemism for causing death. Hayward and Hingley have chosen the conventional "to finish off" (p. 50), while there are numerous expressive possibilities in American slang which would reproduce the tone if not the image of the original (e.g. "to put to bed with a shovel").

Many of the abusive epithets have also been unnecessarily reduced in variety and expressiveness. *Obaldui, spina elovaia,* "numskull, clumsy ox" is clipped to "dope" (p. 15); *fitil',* a term for a weakling or someone on his last legs, becomes simply "old bastard" (p. 5). In general, "bastard" serves with monotonous regularity for a whole series of epithets, including *padlo, gad, svoloch', chert, chuma,* and *sterva.* Alternative translations can easily be found for at least some of these. At other times, Hayward and Hingley have added abusive terms where none, not even "disguised forms" of obscenities, are to be found in the original (e.g. p. 191).[3]

Apart from such stylistic inadequacies, the Hayward-Hingley version of *One Day* is not entirely free of "ordinary" mistranslations. *Kum* is prison slang for "chief security officer," and *kumu stuchat'* is therefore much more specific than "to squeal to the screws" (p. 2). *Grazhdanin nachal'nik* is decidedly not "Comrade Warder" (p. 13) but

---

[3] Hayward and Hingley indicate in their "Translators' Note" that they have decided to spell out the obscenities that appear in the Russian text in an altered but recognizable form. Their assumption is that these euphemistic veils exist in the Russian text only due to "the prudish conventions of Soviet publishing," and may therefore be ignored. However the authorized Paris edition of 1973 differs only marginally from the Soviet editions in this respect, thereby making the translators' decision debatable. (The Soviet book edition of *One Day,* published by "Sovetskii pisatel'" in 1963, restored many of the cuts of the *Novyi mir* version, but retained almost intact Solzhenitsyn's ingeniously disguised system of obscenities.)

"Citizen Warder" (prisoners were forbidden to use the term "comrade"). *Serzhant prikladom karabin povorachivaet* does not mean the sergeant "was twisting the butt of his rifle" (p. 136) but rather that the sergeant was turning his rifle over in order to strike butt-first. Several more errors of this type were noted, most of them quite minor. Apart from the regrettable tendency toward stylistic reduction noted earlier, this translation rates quite high for general accuracy.

Parker's translation (No. 2) appeared simultaneously with the Hayward-Hingley version. (It is of interest that Parker's text as printed in *Soviet Literature* [February, 1963] differs considerably from the text published by Dutton.) Parker has frequently followed the syntactic structure of Solzhenitsyn's Russian more closely than Hayward and Hingley. But this is a questionable virtue, especially when combined with Parker's lack of regard for stylistic levels. Thus *Fetiukov, shakal, podsosalsia* is rendered by "Fetiukov, that jackal, had come up closer" (p. 40). At least two things are wrong here. First of all, a strongly marked slang term with derisive overtones, *podsosat'sia*, has been transformed into the neutral paraphrase "to come closer." Second, though *shakal* does indeed literally mean "jackal," the figurative sense of this word does not coincide in the two languages. In Russian, it implies primarily a greedy person, someone on the prowl; in prison-camp usage it means "scrounger, scavenger." In English, according to both OED and Webster, "jackal" is used primarily to describe a person who does base work for his superiors. Parker's quasi-literal approach is conducive to such questionable renderings and examples can be cited from practically every page. In some cases this method has been carried to unacceptable extremes. In an apparent attempt to retain the sound of the Russian interjection *ukh*, Parker translates *Ukh, kak litso brigadirovo perekosilo* by "Ugh, what a face Tiurin made" (p. 99). (The Hayward-Hingley version is clearly preferable here: "God, the way the boss's face twitched all over.")

There are a number of other translation problems. To name but a few, *Volkovomu ustupka* means "a concession to Volkovoi," not "thanks to Volkovoi" (p. 130). *Balanda*, a derisive term for the watery gruel fed to prisoners—the use of this word was a punishable offense in some camps—is euphemistically christened "stew" (p. 28). Even less plausibly, *magara*, the grass-like mush which they receive, is labelled "oatmeal" (p. 27). *Zona* [compound] is translated as "zone" (p. 29), a term which would be puzzling to most readers. Another minor, but irritating point: the Gospel passages quoted by Aleshka are given in Parker's own and definitely uninspired translation from the Russian (pp. 36, 155). The first of these, besides, contains an error: *zlodei*, a common word rendered as "wrongdoer" or "evildoer" in the standard translations of this passage (I Peter 4:15), is unaccountably construed as "[one guilty of] sorcery."

To be fair, Parker's version is not without all merit. On a few occasions it is somewhat preferable to the Hayward-Hingley rendition, especially towards the end of the novel where the dual translators have engaged in excessive paraphrase.

Thomas Whitney's version (No. 3) tends to be still more literal than Parker's. Where other translators have used paraphrase, Whitney has attempted—and frequently succeeded—to reproduce the Russian syntactic structure in a meaningful English sentence. Thus he translates *shu-shu—sredi rebiat* as "buzz buzz among the men" (p. 82). But this method entails obvious risks and on numerous occasions it leads Whitney into awkward or misleading renditions. The camp artist who paints numbers on the prisoners' caps is described at work: *pomaliuet, pomaliuet i v perchatku dyshit* [he'd paint for a little while and then he'd breathe into his glove]. Whitney follows the Russian "surface structure" at the expense of meaning: "he painted away and painted away and breathed into his glove" (p. 41). When Der threatens to report Tiurin to the authorities, the gang leader reacts menacingly: *I k Deru—shag!* [And he takes a step toward Der!]. Whitney reproduces the Russian syntax exactly, even though the ellipsis of the verb is highly misleading: "And right toward Der—one step" (p. 94).

The faults of this mechanical approach are especially evident in Whitney's treatment of abusive terminology. Sacrificing all stylistic suitability to the thankless idol of literalness, Whitney offers "carrion" for *padlo* (p. 28), "plague" for *chuma* (p. 107), etc. It is simply not credible English to have a crowd of angry prisoners curse a man in the following manner: "Scum! Vomit! Putrefaction!" (p. 107).

At other times, strangely, Whitney has not been literal enough. It is especially disquieting to discover unnecessary departures from the original alternating with an excessive adherence to the Russian syntax. A passage from the end of the novel may serve as an illustration: *A sam kolbasy kusochek—v rot! Zubami ee! Zubami! Dukh miasnoi! I sok miasnoi, nastoiashchii. Tuda, v zhivot, poshel. I—netu kolbasy.* Whitney translates: "Shukhov shoved a little piece of sausage into his mouth. Bite with his teeth. Bite again. Meat fragrance. And real meat juice. It flowed down to his stomach. No more sausage" (p. 148). The basic meaning has been preserved, but there are serious stylistic discrepancies. On the one hand Whitney renders *Zubami ee!* by the literal but very labored "Bite with his teeth," and *Dukh miasnoi!* by the equally literal but inadequate "Meat fragrance." (The latter phrase surely needs to begin with an interjection like "ah.") On the other hand, Whitney has summarily—and unwisely—removed Solzhenitsyn's exclamation marks, thereby significantly dampening the tone of the utterances. Even more damaging for this passage, the second-last sentence, *Tuda, v zhivot, poshel* [There it goes, down to the stomach] is needlessly restructured and thus deprived of its immediacy: "It flowed down to his stomach." The net result of these operations is to rob Shukhov of his one pitifully brief moment of physical enjoyment.

The general impression produced by this rendition is a mixed one. Although there are relatively few mistakes in basic meaning (but some omissions were noted, e.g. on p. 40), Whitney's translation, like Parker's, suffers from stylistic incongruities and from a lack of consistent methodology.

Bela Von Block in her version of *One Day* (No. 4) has not felt constrained by considerations of literal accuracy. In fact she has gone to the opposite extreme, and the unsuspecting reader is in for some surprises. For example, we witness one Soviet prison-camp guard "flipping his wig" (p. 31), a singular translation of *metat'sia* [to rush about frantically]. And Ivan Denisovich, we learn at another point, had "a pain running from his shoulders to his can" (p. 46). The original speaks of "the small of his back and all the way up to his shoulders" [*poiasnitsu i spinu vsiu do plechei*]. These examples are typical of Von Block's apparent wish to spice up Solzhenitsyn's prose. Consistent with this policy, four-letter words have been used with great abandon, often quite gratuitously.

But the most reprehensible aspect of this translation is Von Block's apparent readiness to tamper with the text in fundamental ways. A guard turning his rifle butt-first is transformed into one "fingering the trigger" (p. 115). Since Von Block has translated *priklad* correctly as "rifle butt" a few lines earlier, one is led to suspect that she has deliberately altered a text that seemed too "tame."

This is by no means an isolated example. A far more serious instance occurs early in the novel where we are shown a young prisoner crossing himself before his meal. The original continues: *Znachit, ukrainets zapadnyi, i to novichok*, translated correctly by Hayward and Hingley as "Must have been a Western Ukrainian and new to the place." Von Block expands this to read "Must be from the Western Ukraine, we didn't liberate it 'til '39, so they've still got the old habits. A new prisoner, too, by the looks of things" (p. 20). Since the narrative voice here is Shukhov's, this inexcusable addition makes him mouth a Soviet cliché about "liberation." Nothing could have been further

from the author's intention. Several other "improvements" of Solzhenitsyn were noted.

Gillon Aitken's translation (No. 5) was first published in Great
Britain in 1970. Apart from introducing unmistakably British slang
("that was a mug's game" for *durakov, mol, net* [p. 163]; "old sod with a
mustache" for *bat'ka usatyi* [p. 152], etc.) this rendition breaks very
little fresh ground. It is frequently similar to the Parker or the
Hayward-Hingley versions—to the point of repeating their mistakes
and inaccuracies—or else it tends to be a cut below either of these two
earlier translations. The passage below, one of many possible examples, illustrates each of these points (P stands for Parker, HH for
Hayward and Hingley; the emphasis has been added by me throughout):

AITKEN	*COLLATION OF HH AND P*
Inside it was as steamy	It was like a steam bath
as in THE bath-house—	inside—
what with the frosty air	what with the frosty air
coming through the	coming in through the
doors and the steam	doors and the steam
from the gruel.	from the thin camp gruel.
MEMBERS OF THE GANGS	The men
were sitting at tables	were sitting at tables
or crowding in the	or crowding in the
areas between them,	spaces between them,
waiting for places.	waiting for places (HH, 15) . . .
Yelling to each other	*Shouting to each other*
across the crush,	*across the crush,*
two or three workers	two or three men (P, 27) . . .
from each gang were	from each gang were
carrying bowls of	carrying bowls of
gruel and porridge on	gruel and mush on
wooden trays and	wooden trays and
trying to find places	looking for a place
for them on the tables.	for them on the tables.
And even so, *they don't*	And even so, *they don't*
hear you, the dolts,	*hear you, the dopes,*
and UPSET your tray	they bump into your tray (HH) . . .
—and splash, splash! IF	Splash, splash!
you have a free hand	You've a hand free (P) . . .
—then give it to *them*	let *them* have it
in the neck! That's	in the neck (HH) . . . That's
the way! Don't stand	the way. Don't stand
there in the way,	there (P) . . . in the way (HH) . . .

looking for something
to LICK UP (p. 16).

looking for something
to swipe! (P)

The capitals indicate significant words and phrases in Aitken's text that do not have any analogous constructions in earlier translations. Of the five instances so designated in this passage, only "to lick up" (for *podlizat'*) is an improvement over both HH and P. "Members of the gangs" is an indifferent alternative translation for *brigady*. The three other instances are less than satisfactory. The definite article in the opening sentence implies—without any supporting evidence in Solzhenitsyn's text—that the camp had a steam-bath; "to upset" is a poor rendering of *tolknut'* [to bump; to shove]; there is no "if" in the phrase where Aitken has placed it.

The italics point to constructions which are inaccurate in both Aitken and an earlier version. *Proklikat'sia* is a neologism formed by analogy to a verb such as *prodirat'sia* [to fight one's way through a crowd]. Both Aitken and Parker have misread it as *pereklikat'sia*. (Hayward and Hingley have it right: "Shouting their way through the mob . . .") "They don't hear, the dolts" closely resembles the HH version. But this is an altered and incomplete translation of *[on] ne slyshit, obaldui, spina elovaia* [(he) doesn't hear, the blockhead, the clumsy ox].

This is not to maintain, of course, that Aitken's entire text could be dealt with in this fashion. Nor is the resemblance noted here meant to imply any impropriety whatever. After all, there are only so many ways to translate any given passage. The point is rather that Aitken brings few improvements to "the state of the art": he has learned little from the mistakes of his predecessors. Since the text chosen here is not unique, it seems safe to say that Aitken's translation does not represent an important addition to the literature.

If one were to grade the relative merits of the five translations, Hayward and Hingley would unquestionably take first place. Parker and Whitney each have their strong points but are frequently marred by stylistic dissonance. The two others are not recommended.

B. Collections of Short Works

There have been two English collections of short prose works by Solzhenitsyn. They are:

6. *"We Never Make Mistakes": Two Short Novels.* Translated by Paul W. Blackstock. Columbia, S.C.: U. of South Carolina Press, 1963.[4] [I refer to the Norton paperbound edition, 1971].

[4] A "second edition" was produced by the University of South Carolina Press in

7. *Stories and Prose Poems.* Translated by Michael Glenny. New York: Farrar, Straus & Giroux, 1971. [References are to the Bantam paperback, 1972].[5]

The Blackstock collection (No. 6) contains "Incident at Krechetovka Station" and "Matrena's Home." Two excellent short stories are here presented in a blurred and barely recognizable form. The following is a sample of the kind of errors which fill this book. *Beloemigrant* [White Russian émigré] is stood on its head to become "White Russian immigrant" (p. 77); *goluboi, belyi i zheltyi* [blue, white and yellow] is recolored "deep white and yellow" (p. 114); trains are said to have "slowed their march" (p. 89), a curious rendition of *zamedliali svoi khod* [slowed down]; *dobraia ulybka* [kindly smile] becomes "pleased smile" (p. 101); *za god do togo* [a year earlier] is translated "for a year afterward" (p. 89); *dazhe elektrikom na poriadochnoe stroitel'stvo menia by ne vziali* [they would not even have hired me as an electrician on a decent construction job] turns into "already after considerable construction work has been completed, they had turned me down as an electrician" (p. 90). In Solzhenitsyn's "An Incident at Krechetovka Station," a blundering demolitions specialist panics and blows up the station's water tower at the first sight of a stray German soldier [*uspel rvanut' vodokachku zalozhennym ranee tolom*]. In Blackstock's version of this episode, no damage of any sort occurs; the demolitions man even acquires praiseworthy efficiency, since he "succeeded in pulling away the water-tank car which had been loaded with TNT" (p. 18). It is then impossible to understand why repairs should take several days, as is clearly stated one sentence later. Needless to say, errors of this type do tremendous damage to Solzhenitsyn's carefully constructed narrative. For example, Matrena's account of her fateful decision concerning the missing Faddei is completely misrepresented. *Poshel on na voinu—propal* [He went off to the war—and disappeared] has been twisted into "He went off to war—and fell" (p. 114). The reader is left to puzzle out the best he can why then Matrena should have waited for Faddei for three years thereafter (as Blackstock has correctly translated in the very next sentence). Nearly every page of this collection yields several mistakes of this type.

Under the circumstances, there is no point in discussing Blackstock's success at rendering stylistic levels. I might note only that he has

---

1971. It differs from the 1963 edition only by the addition of a preachy "Afterword." The translation has not been revised.

[5] Nineteen seventy-four saw the additional publication of a Noonday paperback edition of this collection. Glenny's translation is reprinted here without changes.

attempted to provide "local color" by popping Russian words into the narrative (e.g. "Da, Comrade Sergeant" [p. 14]).

Some sentences are missing (e.g. on p. 101). Total chaos reigns in the transcription of Russian names and words. Russian *kh* appears in at least four guises: "*Kh*arkhov" (p. 18), "M*X*AT" (p. 70), "Dyachi-*ch*in" (p. 13), and "Ber*h*ova" (p. 18). (The last of these, incidentally, is Blackstock's version of "Verkhov'e.") Russian *ch* and *ts* appear either in this form (Kre*ch*etovka," "Lipe*ts*k" [p. 13]) or else acquire a quasi-Germanic look ("Vasili*tch*" [p. 36], "gorni*tza*" [p. 93]). It is "Varnako*ff*" on p. 13, but "Varnakov" on p. 14. Other unlikely transcriptions include "Rtistchev" for Rtishchev (p. 25) and "nanya," an aberrant variation on *niania* [nanny] (pp. 10, 129).

This woeful inability to cope with Russian sounds leads directly to the most spectacular blunder of all. Blackstock's title for his collection, *"We Never Make Mistakes,"* is drawn from the ending of Solzhenitsyn's "Incident at Krechetovka Station." The phrase is part of the curt answer given by an NKVD officer to Zotov's inquiry about the fate of Tveritinov. In his translation of this passage, Blackstock has missed the key point. The NKVD man in his response to Zotov garbles Tveritinov's name, pronouncing it "Tverikin": *Raz-berutsia i s vashim Tverikinym. U nas braka ne byvaet* [They'll sort out your Tverikin all right. We never make mistakes]. Blackstock, confused by all those Russian names, substitutes the correct "Tveritinov" in this sentence, with one stroke depriving the story of its grimly ironic punchline. No mistakes, indeed.

The Glenny collection (No. 7) contains all of Solzhenitsyn's short works published in *Novyi mir* with the exception of *One Day in the Life of Ivan Denisovich*. This includes "Incident at Krechetovka Station," "Matrena's Home," "For the Good of the Cause," and "Zakhar-Kal-ita." In addition, the book contains several works not published in the USSR like "The Right Hand," "The Easter Procession," and sixteen "prose poems" or "sketches."

Although it is on the whole less helpless than Blackstock's transla-tion in rendering the basic meaning of the original, Glenny's translation is also unacceptably marred by serious errors. At the beginning of "Matrena's Home" the narrator, who has just returned from the hot wastelands of Central Asia, speaks with deep feeling about his love for the Russian heartland. To him this is tied directly to language and he is moved by the sing-song speech of a woman who sells milk in the market: *slova ee byli te samye, za kotorymi potianula menia toska iz Azii* [her words were the very ones which nostalgia had drawn me out of Asia to hear]. Glenny has reversed the meaning, introducing a jarring discord with all that comes before: "her words made me feel nostalgic for Asia" (p. 3).

Glenny disregards context in this fashion on a number of other occasions; I give two examples from "Matrena's Home." To the narrator's chagrin, Matrena disapproves of Fedor Shaliapin's singing: *Chudnó poiut* [It's a strange way of singing]. In spite of the accent (provided in the original) and in the teeth of context, Glenny translates: "He sings beautifully" (p. 18). A little earlier in the story, Solzhenitsyn tells us that Matrena had gone to church for the blessing of water *[vodosviatie]*. We are told, furthermore, that this is a holiday in December or January. *Kreschen'e,* therefore, could only be "Epiphany," a holiday that falls on January 6 (O.S.) and at which the Christian East commemorates the Baptism of Jesus. Undeterred by such considerations, Glenny translates *kreschen'e* as "christening party" (p. 17). (It must have been at this fancied occasion, incidentally, that Glenny re-baptized Faddei, Matrena's ex-fiancé and one of the major characters in the story, into "Ilya" [p. 22 ff]. No explanation is offered for this strange decision.)

A depressingly long catalogue of other mistakes could be listed, and I shall give only a sample. *V poltysiachi let* [in the course of five hundred years] becomes "for fifteen hundred years" (p. 107); *khorosho dogadalis' my v loshchinke u kolodtsa napit'sia* [we had the good sense to drink our fill at the well in the valley] turns into "we guessed rightly that we would be able to quench our thirst . . . at the well in the valley" (pp. 107–108); *izbu Matreny do vesny zabili* [Matrena's house was boarded up till spring] is given as "Matrena's cottage was handed over before winter was out" (pp. 40–41); *v ogorode—slepoi saraichik* [in the garden there is a small windowless shed] is translated as "outside is a little fenced-in yard" (p. 209); an allegorical sculpture of Victory *[Pobeda]* is transformed into one of "History" (p. 205). An especially farfetched translation occurs in "Matrena's Home." In a halfhearted effort to get her illness diagnosed, Matrena agreed to undergo some tests. The results were sent to the district hospital for analysis, *da tak i zaglokhlo. Byla tut vina i Matreny samoi* [but nothing more was heard of it. Matrena was herself partly to blame here]. The point is that Matrena should have tried again. In his translation of this passage, Glenny would have us believe that Matrena was sent to the district hospital, "where the illness just subsided. Matrena, of course, was blamed for wasting their time" (p. 15).

At other points Glenny's rendition is unintelligible rather than merely wrong. In the sketch which describes a visit to a desecrated monastery where the poet Polonskii had been buried, the narrator is told the following bit of local tradition: *Monastyr'tut byl, v mire vtoroi.*

Pervyi v Rime, kazhetsia, a v Moskve—uzhe tretii [There was a monastery here, the second biggest in the world. The largest is in Rome, I think, and the one in Moscow is already third]. Glenny's translation is completely opaque: "There was a monastery here, in the second world. They say the first world was Rome, and Moscow is the third" (p. 201).

There are omissions: several were noted in "Matrena's Home" alone. An entire paragraph which relates the narrator's first impression of Matrena is absent (p. 5), a sentence in the description of her struggle to get a pension has been left out (p. 10), and one of the geographic units (*selo* [village]) which make up Solzhenitsyn's credo-like ending of the story has been cut (p. 42).

Solzhenitsyn's stories have undergone much stylistic leveling. *Mnogopudovaia tsarstvennaia svin'ia* [an enormous and majestic pig] is refashioned into simply "pig" (p. 209); *sapozhnik-dezertir* [the deserter-shoemaker] becomes plain "shoemaker" (p. 40); *rychali vokrug ekskavatory na bolotakh* [excavators roared around us in the bogs] is typically—and needlessly—changed into "excavators were digging peat out of the bogs all around us" (p. 11). The narrator's faintly amused comment about the custom of singing the hymn "Eternal Memory" just before eating *kisel'* at a wake is deprived of its light touch of irony: *tak i ob"iasnili mne, chto poiut ee—pered kiselem obiazatel'no* [that's just how they explained it to me: it had to be sung before the *kisel'* without fail]. This comes out as "they explained to me that traditionally this had to be sung before the *kisel'* " (p. 39).

It is clear that neither the Glenny nor the Blackstock collection can be safely recommended. To get a more reliable idea of the quality of Solzhenitsyn's short fiction, the English reader is directed to a competent translation of "Matrena's Home" by Harry T. Willets, which appeared first in *Encounter*, May, 1963. (It has been reprinted in *Halfway to the Moon: New Writings from Russia*, ed. Patricia Blake and Max Hayward [New York: Holt, 1964] and in *Fifty Years of Russian Prose: From Pasternak to Solzhenitsyn*, ed. K. Pomorska [Cambridge: MIT, 1971], vol. 2.)

C. The First Circle

As in the case of *One Day*, the existing translations of *The First Circle* are based on an incomplete text. Unlike *One Day*, however, the full and authorized text has not yet appeared anywhere. Furthermore, there are certain differences between the Russian versions of *The First*

Circle published so far in the West. In an interview with Western
newsmen on March 30, 1972, Solzhenitsyn stated: "I worked for many
years on that novel. I started it while I was in exile. There are indeed
different versions (. . .) I continued to work on that novel after it
was published in the West, and the latest version is the one I prefer."
(See *The New York Times*, April 3, 1972, p. 10.) In the fall of 1973,
Solzhenitsyn announced that he would begin *samizdat* distribution of
two additional chapters belonging to a "rewritten version" of his
novel. These are Chapters 44 and 88, entitled, respectively, "In the
Open" and "Dialectical Materialism." (See *NYT*, September 22,
1973, p. 2.) [6]

In the remarks that follow, I have systematically eliminated all
references to passages which were not identical in the principal
Western Russian-language editions of *The First Circle* (I have checked
those published by Flegon, Harper and Row, Posev, and YMCA
Press).

The two extant translations are:

8. *The First Circle.* Translated by Thomas P. Whitney. New York:
Harper and Row, 1968. [I refer to the Bantam paperback, 1973].

9. *The First Circle.* Translated by Michael Guybon [pseud.]. London:
Collins and Harvill, 1968. [References are to the Fontana paperback,
1972].

Whitney's translation (No. 8) has a consistent tendency to simplify
Solzhenitsyn. Modifiers and sometimes whole subordinate clauses
have been simply cut. For example, *nezatumanennye dvoinye stekla vysokogo
okna, nachinaiushchegosia ot samogo pola* which means, "The mist-free
double panes of a tall window which reached to the floor" has been
"streamlined" by Whitney to read: "the double panes of the tall
window" (p. 1). *Nerzhin rezko pokachal rukoi i golovoi* [Nerzhin shook his
head and hand sharply] is abridged to "Nerzhin shook his head"
(page 39); *tomishche* [huge tome] is demoted to just plain "volume" (p.
76); *golova kak budto eshche molodogo, no uzhe lyseiushchego Poskrebysheva* [a
head belonging to a still seemingly young but already balding
Poskrebyshev] is shorn of its qualifiers to become "the young balding
head of Poskrebyshev" (p. 104). Dozens of other examples were noted.
In some cases an image is destroyed, as when Rubin describes
Nerzhin's philosophical eclecticism in the following terms: *ty vydiraesh'
otovsiudu po tsvetnomy peru i vse vpletaesh' v svoi khvost* [you pluck out

---

[6] Chapter 44 appeared in *Vestnik RSKhD*, No. 111 (1974); Chapter 88 in *Kontinent*,
No. 1 (1974). Two further chapters were published in *Vestnik RKhD*, Nos. 112/113 and
114. The final form of the novel contains 96 chapters.

colorful feathers everywhere you go and add them all to your own tail plumage]. This has been stripped of the peacock image to read, "You pluck bright feathers from everywhere" (p. 39). More damaging still is the transformation of *kriterii praktiki v gnoseologii* [practicality as a criterion in epistemology] into simply "gnoseology" (p. 443). This renders part of the argument between Rubin and Sologdin incomprehensible. Although the majority of cases do not involve such serious injury to the meaning, at the very least these reductions impoverish Solzhenitsyn's style.

Whitney also has some difficulty with prison and underworld slang. His most serious blunder in this regard is the translation of *Pakhan*, an epithet used repeatedly for Stalin, by the puzzling "Plowman" (p. 26, etc.). The Russian word means "head of a gang of thieves," and might be rendered for an American audience by "the Boss." Other instances noted include *rvite kogti* [get lost] rendered as "you're wasting time" (p. 17); *kurochit'* [to steal blind; to rob] translated by "to fool around" (p. 9), and *shalashovka* [camp prostitute], by "female prisoner" (p. 36). *Na tsyrlakh*, an expression which Solzhenitsyn has defined elsewhere as "simultaneously on tip-toe, at great speed, and with the greatest diligence," is left out entirely (p. 7).

A substantial number of other mistakes could be cited. To quote only a few of the more serious ones, *[trubka] plavilas' v ruke* means the receiver "was melting in his hand," not "swimming" in it (pp. 5–6). *Poslushnik* is "novice" in the religious sense, not "obedient pupil" (p. 132). *Na pomin dushi* is not "for the good of one's soul" (p. 132) but "for the remembrance of [their] souls." Abakumov, in his fit of rage at the "troika of liars" is said in Whitney's version to have "stamped on their feet" (p. 137), a misreading of *nastupal na nikh*, which in the given context means rather that he threatened or menaced them.

There are irritating errors in the verse citations. In Chapter 2, Rubin recites several lines from Dante interspersed with comments. Quotations from Canto IV of the *Inferno* are given in the following order: lines 106, 107, 110, 112–113, 84, 71–72, 74–75. Whitney, who quotes Dante in John Ciardi's translation, has managed to scramble this sequence completely. Line 108 is substituted for 110, making Rubin's subsequent remark incomprehensible. Instead of lines 112–113, he cites line 83; lines 71–72 are not translated at all. A similar fate befalls the hackneyed war correspondents' songs quoted in Chapter 59; in two of the four examples cited by Solzhenitsyn, the essential meaning has been completely altered in the translation (p. 435).

Michael Guybon's translation (No. 9) appeared in print a short time after Whitney's. It suffers from a different set of problems.

Although Guybon has not engaged in the stylistic "streamlining" so evident in Whitney's version, he has by no means refrained from cutting deeply into the text. In fact, Guybon's omissions are if anything more irresponsible and damaging. A particularly serious instance is his exclusion of all chapter titles. This represents a wanton excision of information that is important for a proper understanding of the text (e.g. such headings as "Abandon Hope, All Ye Who Enter Here" which is the only explicit connection to the Dante theme in the chapter describing Volodin's arrest).

The majority of the quotations of poetry have been simply dropped by Guybon. In some cases they have been transformed into a brief paraphrase, frequently without any indication that verse has been cited. For example, Chapters 53 and 54 contain a total of six poetic passages, each of which is closely integrated into the narrative. Four of these have disappeared without a trace in Guybon's translation, one is given in paraphrase, and only one has survived as a recognizable verse citation (p. 392). This proportion is not untypical. Other types of cuts involve entire sentences. Thus when Potapov prepares to tell the story entitled "Buddha's Smile" he takes a dig at Rubin by asserting with mock earnestness that no literary work can be understood without knowing the social conditions that determined it. Potapov is complimented for this observation by Nerzhin in the same mock-serious tone: *Vy delaete uspekhi, Andreich* [You're making progress, Andreich]. For inscrutable reasons, this line has been replaced by three dots in Guybon's translation (p. 398). Later on the same page, at the very end of Ch. 53, Guybon has left out four entire lines of the original. Several other instances of this type were noted.

Mistranslations abound as well. One occurs in the very first line of the novel, where *piat' minut piatogo* [five past four] is translated as "five to five" (p. 11). Some mistakes are hard to explain, as in the case of *zhir* [fat] rendered by "milk" (p. 48). Others are grotesque, as when *lobok* [pubic region] has been misconstrued as the diminutive of *lob* [forehead] and is repeatedly translated by "head" (pp. 403, 411). Guybon has not fared much better than Whitney with prison slang; most of the errors and omissions cited in my comments on Whitney's translation are repeated in Guybon's version. (*Pakhan*, however, is translated more or less correctly as "Big Chief" [p. 36].) And Guybon, like Whitney, has scrambled the quotations from Dante. But he adds a characteristic twist: since one of Rubin's interpolated comments no longer fits the disarrayed sequence, it is simply cut (p. 20).

But perhaps the most disastrous aspect of this rendition is Guybon's apparent inability to cope with irony and parody. Chapter 54

("Buddha's Smile") is a case in point. In a manner that seems almost perversely methodical, phrase after phrase of Potapov's brilliant improvisation is stripped of its irony and reshaped into doggedly neutral style. *Opekuny Butyrskogo sanatoriia* [the legal guardians of the Butyrki health resort] becomes "the men in charge of Butyrki Prison" (p. 399). *Vragi naroda* [enemies of the people], a Soviet cliché deliberately employed for ironic effect, appears simply as "prisoners" (p. 400). *Tartar* [Tartarus], a mock-heroic metaphor used to describe the sterilization room *[prozharka]*, is transformed humorlessly (and inaccurately) into "fumigation chamber" (p. 402). When Mrs. R. wonders whether the prisoners might be hungry, her reasonable question is reported with the following scandalized comment by the narrator: *vyskazala nelepoe predpolozhenie vstrevozhennaia gost'ia* [the alarmed lady guest made the absurd suggestion]. Guybon translates this as "suggested the anxious lady guest" (p. 410), thereby neutralizing the narrator's voice. The list goes on. One is tempted to conclude that Guybon has either consciously tried to edit Solzhenitsyn or else that he simply does not understand irony.

In spite of all my strictures it should be said that both translations are "readable." On the whole, Whitney has a better style and transmits the spirit of Solzhenitsyn's novel more effectively than Guybon. (Among other things, Whitney has captured the irony very well.) But it is clear that both versions would benefit from revision.

D. Cancer Ward

This novel shares the fate of *The First Circle* in that no authorized Russian text has been published to date. In compiling the remarks that follow, I have checked two Russian editions (YMCA Press, and Posev) and have refrained from commenting on translations of passages where variant readings exist.

Several independent English translations of the novel were planned in 1968. In view of Solzhenitsyn's vigorous protests against foreign publication of *Cancer Ward*, two of the publishers involved withdrew from the project. The two English translations that were brought to completion are:

10. *Cancer Ward.* Translated by Nicholas Bethell and David Burg. 2 vols. London: Bodley Head, 1968 and 1969. Published as one volume, New York: Farrar, Straus and Giroux, 1969. [My references are to the Bantam paperback, 1972].

11. *The Cancer Ward.* Translated by Rebecca Frank [pseud.]. New York:

Dial Press, 1968. [My references are to the Dell paperback, 1973, which has the same pagination].

The Bethell-Burg version of *Cancer Ward* (No. 10) is uneven in quality. The translators have made a genuine effort to make their English style rich and full-blooded. Unfortunately, their imagination has on more than one occasion exceeded their discipline in this regard. To give a relatively harmless example, Solzhenitsyn writes that Efrem Podduev *ostanovilsia kak byk* [stopped like a bull]. Bethell and Burg write "stopped dead like a thwarted bull" (p. 12). While this may sound like "good English," one is left wondering whether "thwarted" does not impose an unwanted dimension on this image. It is generally true that adding gratuitously to a translation is more damaging than suppressing an equal amount of information: new variables with potentially significant relationships are superimposed on the original text, often with far-reaching implications. An example of this in the Bethell-Burg translation is the rendition of Kostoglotov's appellation for Zoia, *pchelka s chelkoi*, by "Teddy bear with the golden hair" (p. 36). The Russian means literally "honeybee with bangs," with *pchelka* being an affectionate term for a girl. The word falls somewhere mid-range in terms of emotional weight, and carries connotations of praiseworthy industriousness. Since no exact equivalent seems to exist in English, the translators have evidently decided to imitate the rhymed-jingle quality of the Russian phrase. It was this consideration ("bear": "hair") that has presumably led to their decision to use "teddy bear." But their choice injects strong "cuddly" associations into the text which are simply absent in the original. The fact that subsequent developments in the novel confirm this "cuddly" image is precisely proof of the highly misleading nature of such a rendition. A conscientious reader of the novel in the Bethell-Burg translation would naturally assume that Solzhenitsyn has meant Zoia's appellation to be prophetic or otherwise symbolic in a way not intended by the author. (It should be pointed out that the word *pchelka* gets more than passing mention. Among others things, it is the title of Chapter 3).

The translation has its share of more conventional errors. I give only a representative sample here. When Nellia announces she will catch up on her sleep on the sofa *v zasedaniiakh*, this is merely her way of saying "in the conference room" (*Komnata vrachebnykh zasedanii* is mentioned two lines later). Bethell and Burg have translated this as a joke, "[I shall be] in session" (p. 27). Kostoglotov's blunt accusation, *v blokade vinovat kto-to drugoi* [someone else is to blame for the (Leningrad) blockade], has been softened to read "there was someone else responsible for the blockade too" (p. 30). *V karuseli zhe bylo i spasenie ot karuseli* [the merry-go-round was in itself a means of salvation from the merry-go-round] is completely misinterpreted as "a merry-go-round that didn't even protect him from other merry-go-rounds" (p. 328). *Zhuravl' dolgonogii* [long-legged stork] is rendered "long-nosed stork" (p. 323), possibly due to a misprint in the Russian; an ordinary brown bear *[buryi medved']* is transformed into a "grizzly" (p. 505). A particularly unfortunate mistranslation occurs in Chapter 24. In the course of Kostoglotov's blood transfusion, just after he has flung his accusations at Vega, she makes a desperate attempt to communicate her beliefs to him: *Golosom izlomivshimsia, sverkh sily, ona peretiagivalas' cherez rov* [With a broken voice, she was making a supreme effort to reach across the chasm]. Bethell and Burg have not understood this image: "Her voice was shattered. She was trying to pull herself up out of the ditch, but it was beyond her strength" (p. 333). A few lines later, when Solzhenitsyn tells us that Vega has indeed succeeded in reaching across the gulf that separates her from Kostoglotov *[peretianuvshis']*, she is shown instead by Bethell and Burg to be clambering out of the ditch into which they so unfairly placed her: "she had pulled herself up and over the edge." Another significant error of this type was noted in the novel's last chapter. Kostoglotov is riding an unbelievably jampacked streetcar and thinking: *Tak stiskivalo, byvalo, tol'ko v voronkakh* [Only in the Black Marias had there ever been a crush like this]. Bethell and Burg write: "Only in the shell holes had he ever been as close to people as this" (p. 521). The translators have implausibly interpreted *v voronkakh* as the locative plural form of *vorónka* [shell hole], whereas the context of all that comes before makes clear that the reference is to *voronók* [Black Maria; paddy wagon]. It is in fact an important point which emphasizes how Kostoglotov's mind continues to operate in images determined by his prison experience (cf. his manner of viewing the animals in the zoo in the preceding Chapter 35).

The Bantam edition of *Cancer Ward* also contains a substantial number of misprints, certainly more than any of the other translations of Solzhenitsyn reviewed. Some occur in sensitive spots; for example, the date of the letter that begins Part II is given as March 3, 1956; the correct year should have been 1955. The date as printed would (among other incongruities) place the action after the Twentieth Congress of the CPSU.

No embroidering on Solzhenitsyn's style was noted in the much more sober Rebecca Frank translation (No. 11). This rendition suffers, instead, from the more usual sin of flattening and impoverishing the original. The first sentence is typical. *Rakovyi korpus nosil i nomer trinadtsat'*, translated correctly by Bethell and Burg as "On top of everything, the cancer wing was Number 13," is reduced by Frank to "The cancer wing was Ward No. 13" (p. 1). Needless to say, this is not a unique instance. But perhaps more serious is the high number of mistranslations uncovered; I shall cite only a few here. In the first paragraph of the novel, Rusanov continues to object to the numeration of the cancer ward: *Vot uzhe takta ne khvatilo nazvat' trinadtsatym kakoi-nibud' proteznyi ili kishechnyi* [They might have had the tact to assign number thirteen to some prosthetic or intestinal ward]. Frank twists this into "they should have had the tact to call it something like 'prosthetic' or 'intestinal,' not '13' " (p. 1). When Kostoglotov says to Efrem: *nadoel bol'no, skulish'*, he means something like "I'm sick and tired of your whining" and not Frank's strange "you're sick and tired of things, you go around whining" (p. 15). Many errors concern simple words or constructions. *Kaznit'* is "to execute," not "to jail" (p. 501). *Ves' vek ia proboialsia* [I've lived my entire life in fear] is unaccountably rendered "All my life I lived in fear of your fate" (p. 504). *Stolik dlia pisem* means "table for writing letters" not a "mailbox" (p. 609). *Vy razreshili mne prikosnut'sia gubami—k zhizni nastoiashchei*, an important phrase from Kostoglotov's letter to Zoia, which means "you have permitted me to touch my lips—to genuine life," is deprived of much of its meaning and virtually all of its force: "[you] let me come close to your lips, to real life" (p. 610). The most amusing gaffe noted concerns the description of two Uzbek girls whom Kostoglotov presents with the flowers originally intended for Vega. They had their hair done in the same manner: *s odinakovymi chernymi kosichkami, zakruchennymi tuzhe elektricheskikh shnurov* [with identical little black braids, twisted more tightly than electric cords]. Frank translates: "with identical black braids, tied tightly at the ends with bits of electric-wire cord" (p. 595).

There are also omissions. For example one of the obscene ditties quoted by Chalyi to Rusanov has been censored out by the straight-laced Ms. Frank. We are left with: "He recited a bawdy verse and slapped Rusanov on the knee" (p. 371).

As in the case of *The First Circle,* neither of the two English translations of *Cancer Ward* can be recommended without certain reservations. In terms of relative merit, the Bethell-Burg version is written in a more attractive style than Frank's; it also seems to have somewhat fewer errors. But this advantage is offset by the more serious nature of the mistakes noted.

E. *August 1914*

There is one English version of this novel:

12. *August 1914*. Translated by Michael Glenny. London: Bodley Head, 1972; New York: Farrar, Straus and Giroux, 1972. [My references are to the Bantam paperback edition, 1974].

The story of this translation is particularly disheartening. Solzhenitsyn had taken special pains to see this novel into print properly: he had not released the text "for reading and copying" and his newly-acquired Western agent successfully prevented the appearance of a pirated Western edition. With an authorized Russian text available and under Solzhenitsyn's full legal control, the stage seemed to be set for a careful and unrushed translation of what is undoubtedly his most complex and difficult work.

But things went wrong from the beginning. During the negotiations among the several publishers who were undertaking translations into the major European languages, a singularly shortsighted proposal was made and adopted. It was decided that "because of the title [of Solzhenitsyn's novel] . . . it would be nice to publish in August [1972]." To meet this arbitrary deadline, Michael Glenny was cajoled and pressured into producing an English translation in an unreasonably short period. (See Glenny's embittered interview, as reported in Roger Jellinek's *"August 1914:* The Last Word," *The New York Times Book Review*, September 24, 1972, p. 63). Not surprisingly, the translation shows every sign of haste.

But even more distressing is the attitude of the translator toward the work entrusted to him. With a total lack of sympathy for Solzhenitsyn's linguistic goals, Glenny has characterized *August 1914* (in the interview cited above) as a book written in "pseudo-vernacular" and "would-be-conversational" style. The novel exhibits, he contends, "insecure verbal control" and is stylistically "very regressive in Solzhenitsyn's development"; in short, "no one has yet dared to say how badly written the book is." Glenny's conclusion follows naturally. In order to make the novel acceptable to readers of English, "the whole tone had to be altered and much had to be smoothed out." Only one thing is indisputable in this harangue: Glenny is defending his role as an actively hostile editor of Solzhenitsyn.

Since a detailed and reliable account of Glenny's attempts to "smooth out" Solzhenitsyn's prose has already appeared in print—I refer to Simon Karlinsky's perceptive review of *August 1914* in *The New York Times Book Review*, September 10, 1972, esp. pp. 49–51—there is no need to go over the same ground here; I shall cite just one typical

example. Among Solzhenitsyn's favorite devices in *August 1914* (as well
as in all his preceding works) is the technique of shifting back and
forth between third-person narrative and a direct transcription of the
unuttered thoughts of his protagonists. The following example is
drawn from Chapter 3. Irina Tomchak has just woken up: *Raspakhnula
stavni v park—a utro kakoe! a vozdukh s tenevym kholodkom!* [She flung open
the shutters facing the park—what a morning! what air with its touch
of shady coolness!]. Glenny has changed the narrative structure and
the tone in his translation of this passage: "She threw open the
shutters giving onto the park. It was a wonderful morning, with just a
touch of coolness in the air from the shade . . ." (p. 23). Perhaps the
most annoying aspect of this revision (which stands for scores of similar
cases) is its needlessness. Modern readers would hardly have been
confused by the more accurate rendering, let alone devotees of Joyce
or Faulkner. Glenny's fastidiousness is at least half a century out of
date.

Other stylistic tampering includes omissions (e.g. on p. 499) and the
reduction of complex sentences to their simplest components. One can
only agree with Simon Karlinsky's severe conclusion in his review of
the book: "In fairness to the reader, the English version of the novel
should have been labeled by the publishers 'adapted' or 'paraphrased'
by Michael Glenny, rather than translated by him."

With the manner and form of Solzhenitsyn's novel betrayed, one
has the right to expect at least the content to have been grasped
properly. Not so. Numerous mistakes in basic meaning were found in
every chapter checked; the following list is but a brief selection. When
med is blessed after the Transfiguration service, this is "honey," not
"mead" (p. 23); *inoi god* means "in some years" or "in other years," not
"one year" (p. 70); *bumaga okazalas' ser'eznaia* should be "the document
turned out to be important," not "the paper appeared to be
important" (p. 87); *tut i nemtsy podzhigali* means "the Germans set fires
here as well" not "it was set on fire by the Germans" (p. 168). *Bral
gorod. Ne vzial* is a classic example of Russian aspect usage that should
read "He tried to take a town. He didn't succeed," not Glenny's
"Took a town, but lost it again" (p. 173). When Samsonov contem-
plates his lack of rapport with the rest of the top command he puts it
in the following terms: *i Rennenkampf i Zhilinskii byli luidi kakoi-to chuzhoi
dushi* [both Rennenkampf and Zhilinskii were men of an alien cast of
soul]. It is clear that they are alien *to Samsonov*, not to each other as
Glenny would have it: "Rennenkampf and Zhilinsky were tempera-
mentally ill-matched" (p. 91). In the course of the remarkable burial
service for Kabanov, Blagodarev chants a supplication that the soul of
the departed be granted refuge in "a place of light and of peace."

Solzhenitsyn continues: *otchasti uzhe sbyvalas' molitva* [the prayer was already being answered in part]. Glenny's translation of this phrase is unrelated to the correct meaning: "the prayers for the man's soul were almost over" (p. 567). A number of errors bespeak carelessness and haste, as when *nevestka* [daughter-in-law] is mistaken for *nevesta* and is translated as "fiancée" (p. 71).

To summarize: Glenny's translation of *August 1914* is exceedingly mediocre, and Solzhenitsyn's novel must not be judged by it.

The reader who has stayed with this cheerless survey to the end is entitled to wonder whether it is even worth the effort to read Solzhenitsyn in English. The answer must be yes, for in spite of the countless infelicities, mistakes, revisions, and "corrections," the prose of this verbal master still produces a powerful and sometimes overwhelming effect. This is not because a poor translation does little damage—the opposite is surely true—but because Solzhenitsyn's work is so rich in thought, imagery, and texture, that even an imperfect or partial rendering retains abundant literary worth. But that Solzhenitsyn deserves better treatment than he has received—of this there can be little doubt.[7]

[7] The first volume of Solzhenitsyn's massive study of the Soviet prison-camp system, *The Gulag Archipelago*, was rendered into English by Thomas P. Whitney in 1974. This translation is unfortunately less than successful; especially serious is the translator's apparent lack of sensitivity for Solzhenitsyn's esthetic goals. For a detailed analysis, see my article, "Translating Solzhenitsyn (contd): *The Gulag Archipelago*," in John B. Dunlop, Richard Haugh, Alexis Klimoff, eds., *Aleksandr Solzhenitsyn: Critical Essays and Documentary Materials*, 2nd ed. (New York: Collier-Macmillan, 1975), pp. 636–649.

Solzhenitsyn and Autonomy

by Walter Kaufmann

Decidophobia provides a revealing perspective for a look at Solzhenitsyn. What I mean by decidophobia is fear of the fateful decisions that mold our future. In *Without Guilt and Justice: From Decidophobia to Autonomy* (1973)—a book dedicated to Alexander Solzhenitsyn—I have argued at length that humanity craves but dreads autonomy. Autonomy consists of making the decisions that give shape to one's life with one's eyes open to objections and alternatives. Most people are afraid of getting dizzy if they keep their eyes open at such moments, without anything to lean on, and have recourse to various strategies to avoid this frightening experience.

Some lean on religion to tell them what to do, or at least to determine what is right and wrong. Others drift along either in the *status quo,* as many middle-aged people do, or by living a life governed by caprice, like the hero, or antihero, of Camus's novel, *The Stranger.* Two further strategies consist in allegiance to a movement or a school of thought; a fifth, in exegetical thinking, which assumes that the text or tradition one interprets is right, so that one can read one's own ideas into it and get them back endowed with authority. Yet another strategy is Manichaeism, which makes much of the need for fateful decisions but stacks the cards. In effect, we are asked to choose between an evil-tasting, poisonous dish and one that tastes good and is good for our health: all good is on one side, all evil on the other, and the choice makes itself. A seventh strategy might be called moral rationalism. It claims that purely rational procedures can show us

Author's Note: This article is based on my *Without Guilt and Justice: From Decidophobia to Autonomy* (New York: Peter H. Wyden, 1973). The definition of *autonomy,* the claims about its relation to intellectual integrity, and all the philosophical points in this article are developed much more fully in the book. The publisher's permission is acknowledged gratefully. The book has also been issued in paperback, as a Delta Book, by the Dell Publishing Company.

what is right and good. Another strategy is pedantry. As long as one is absorbed in microscopic choices, one is safe from fateful decisions. Obviously, these eight strategies can be combined in various ways. The ninth strategy is the faith that one is riding the wave of the future which dictates what is to be done. And the tenth, which like religion and drifting sometimes spells total relief, is marriage. One can be married or religious without becoming a decidophobe. The point is merely that marriage can be used as a strategy for avoiding ultimate responsibility for fateful decisions.

One can play all sorts of games with these ten strategies—for example, by arranging them in groups—even before adding to their number. Some of them are ways of avoiding fateful decisions; others are ways of loading the choices to make one option clearly the right one, thus eliminating all risk; while still others are ways of declining responsibility.

Another game one can play is to give people points for each strategy they use. This can be done with oneself, which is a very good idea; with people one knows; and with famous people. At some point one is apt to wonder whether it is at all possible to score zero. What is at stake, however, is no mere game. The question is whether a human being is capable of autonomy.

I think it can be shown that a few people here and there have achieved it; for example, to mention two utterly different types, Nietzsche and Eleanor Roosevelt. Both are dead. Among the living I cannot think of a finer example than Solzhenitsyn.

We do not have to read biographies of the man, nor need we pry into his personal affairs, to make a case for this claim. A large part of his life is, as it were, on the record; and anyone who wants to see the man and not merely the author can hardly do better than read *Solzhenitsyn: A Documentary Record*, edited by Leopold Labedz. Anyone familiar with this record will find it pathetic when students in Western countries plead that "in our society" autonomy is simply impossible. Was it any easier in the USSR, and especially in Stalin's camps? Or is it easier in China? or in India? or in Africa? in Poland? in East Germany? Was it easier in the European Middle Ages, in the face of the Inquisition? One feels like saying with Hillel: If not now, when?

Rarely has it been more difficult for anyone to stand alone, utterly alone, without any prop of any kind, than it was for Solzhenitsyn. Yet his life has been autonomy in action. For that alone he would deserve our gratitude and admiration even if he had not written several momentous books. In an age that has produced Stalin, Hitler, and their henchmen, as well as legions of essentially mediocre men who come close to destroying one's faith in humanity, he has shown us what man can be.

Has he also shown us by his own example how to achieve autonomy? Can we follow the path he chose? The last question seems almost absurd; but one can learn to become a good mountain climber and to overcome dizziness by initially climbing with a guide and imitating him. What one can learn from Solzhenitsyn's example, however, is that autonomy is in some ways different from climbing. The goal is not that clear at the outset, and the path to it is even less straight. Solzhenitsyn spent three and a half years in the Russian army, during World War II; then eight years in concentration camps; and then lived in exile, interrupted by two spells in a cancer ward. One could hardly prescribe that route to others.

What is exemplary, however, is his keen sense that he is a survivor—and the way in which he has dealt with it. Being a survivor generally breeds guilt feelings. Of course, we are all survivors, but most people do not think of themselves that way until someone very close to them dies. When such deaths are especially horrible or violent, and even more so when it is not only one person who dies but large numbers, and one witnesses their deaths at close range, the guilt feelings that issue from such an experience can be crippling. Solzhenitsyn had this archetypical experience three times over, each time for several years; first as an army officer at the front, then in the camps, and then in the cancer ward. Instead of being crippled by the sense that he did not deserve to live when so many had died, or trying to repress and forget as best he could his memories, he made a fateful decision that is exemplary. He decided to do with his life what nobody who had not had these horrible experiences could do. And he became a writer.

All of his writing is informed by his sense that he is a survivor—by a sense of solidarity with the dead. But his writing is never guilt-ridden or morbid. Instead of being overwhelmed by his cruel fate, he dominates his fate and makes it serve his purposes. He uses his experiences to do for humanity what, but for that fate, he could not have accomplished. This central dedication to humanity and humaneness can scarcely be missed in his books. Hence *The First Circle* and *Cancer Ward* are not depressing as, given the subject matter, one might expect. Chapter upon chapter bears the imprint of a strong mind with a purpose—not to moralize but to expand and sensitize the conscience of humanity. There is something here of the ethos of Sophocles and Euripides who also piled suffering upon suffering to make men and women more humane. The comparison is doubly appropriate because Solzhenitsyn shares with them the fierce intellectuality, the intense delight in language and ideas, and the mordant wit that survives disaster.

What has here been said of Solzhenitsyn's solution of the problem of being a survivor is, of course, by no means unique with him. Other great writers have done the same thing. Nor does the point apply only to being a survivor. Few people see that guilt feelings are incompatible with autonomy; fewer still would opt for autonomy after seeing this. Just as most people dread autonomy, they are most reluctant to give up guilt feelings and try to persuade themselves and others that the alternative to guilt feelings is total amorality if not sheer wickedness, brutality, and brutishness. If you have done wrong, they feel, you ought to feel remorse. You ought to feel that you deserve punishment, suffering, retribution. But if "guilty" is defined as "deserving punishment," and "guilt feelings" as "the feeling that one deserves punishment," then it is not at all true that one cannot be humane after ceasing to think in terms of guilt, or that guilt feelings are a prerequisite of humanity. This is not the place to recapitulate long arguments against the notions of desert, justice, and guilt. Suffice it to say that the case of the survivor is paradigmatic. When a surgeon has done wrong, and it was his fault, and the harm he did someone else was avoidable, and he is responsible, it does not follow that he should feel guilty in the sense described here. On the contrary, his ability to serve humanity depends on his self-confidence. Guilt-ridden surgeons can be a menace. Far better, if a surgeon gives himself a clear account of what he did and why, and then—like the survivor—goes on to do what but for that experience he might never have been able to do. Thus he might now teach others how to avoid certain pitfalls, and he might become wiser, more humane, more sensitive. This, too, is merely a paradigm. The point applies to everything that is widely held to call for guilt feelings.

Being afraid of autonomy, which involves the resolve to consider objections and alternatives, some people question the obvious point that an autonomous person could not have followed Hitler or Stalin. If only one could taint autonomy by associating it with amoral brutes—perhaps even with Stalin and Hitler themselves—one would have a wonderful excuse for not being autonomous. In *The First Circle* and *Cancer Ward* Solzhenitsyn has shown convincingly how an autonomous person could live under Stalin only in a camp or by keeping silent, how silence usually corrupts, and how this corruption spread like a disease through the whole society. The chapter on "Idols of the Market Place" in *Cancer Ward* makes this point expressly and at length.

In the West so many people are so ignorant of totalitarianism that they take it for granted that one could swallow Stalinism or Hitlerism the way one swallows any other world view. And anyone who believes that American society is just as repressive as was Hitler's Germany or Stalin's Soviet Union obviously does not have the habit of examining objections and alternatives and might indeed have swallowed Nazism or Stalinism.

Of course, one could be sincere and a Nazi or a Stalinist. But nobody who made it a rule to consider objections and alternatives could have accepted Hitler's or Stalin's irrational views; and teaching students to develop an intellectual conscience and to make major decisions about their beliefs and conduct only after carefully exploring what speaks for and against various alternatives without any appeal to authority, would have been a recipe for death. One did not have to be a teacher; simply to ask such questions openly or to encourage others to become autonomous instead of simply accepting what the leader had said, was enough to become a martyr.

Few people have ever been autonomous or had the keen intellectual conscience that autonomy requires. Only those who fail to see this could possibly suppose that some of Hitler's or Stalin's followers were autonomous. The party line kept changing, and followers were required to change their views overnight, again and again and again. If they believed that whatever the leader did was best, that he knew better than anyone else, and that whatever the latest edition of the Great Encyclopaedia said was true, they could escape terrible qualms, but in that case they were decidophobes and not autonomous.

It might be objected that we cannot reasonably expect people to say, like Job: "Till I die I will not part from my integrity." In *La Force des Choses* (1963) Simone de Beauvoir, though merciless in her self-accusations, said of those who followed Stalin: "They had to live; they lived." She repudiated anyone's right to judge them. But whatever one may think about that, the point here is not to pass judgment. The point is that anyone who gave up intellectual integrity to save his life—if only to preserve himself for the sake of his family—did give it up. After all, that is one of the differences between Solzhenitsyn and millions of others: they did, and he did not. He was autonomous, and they were not.

An autonomous person decides for himself—not capriciously but by considering with his eyes open what speaks for and against alternatives. Now it might still be asked whether a person might not decide after weighing the pros and cons to join "the Party." He might; just as a person might decide to go to a surgeon and ask him: Please—I can't take it any more—give me a frontal lobotomy! Those who decide to commit themselves in such a way that henceforth they will never have to face fateful decisions any more are decidophobes and not autonomous. And those who abandon or sacrifice their intellectual integrity cannot be said to have retained it.

The Nazis and Stalin, of course, understood this very well and realized that there was no place in their societies for autonomous human beings. The Germans had a name for their principle; they called it the *Führerprinzip*, the leadership principle. Rudolf Hoess, the commanding officer of Auschwitz gave a good account of it in his autobiography. His definition: "Every German had to submit unconditionally and uncritically to the leadership of the state"; and this involved "surrender of one's own will." In the same vein he spoke of Himmler, "whose orders, whose utterances had been gospel for me," and called him "the most extreme representative of the *Führerprinzip*." Another revealing remark is this: "After such talks with Eichmann humane feelings almost seemed to me treason against the *Führer*."

Hitler himself, of course, was not autonomous either. He was not only singularly dishonest but also quite lacked the habit of subjecting his irrational convictions to critical examination. He was the type Sartre has described in his portrait of the anti-Semite (English in my *Existentialism from Dostoevsky to Sartre*), and Eric Hoffer in *The True Believer*. He could not tolerate disagreement and in the end became more and more interested in astrology.

As for Stalin, the classical portrait of the man is Solzhenitsyn's in *The First Circle*. Plato had argued long ago in his *Republic* that the despot was not a free man but at heart a slave, and he had argued elsewhere that Socrates was a free man even in prison. Solzhenitsyn has developed both points at length and lent substance to the claim about the despot. Some have called his portrait of Stalin a caricature. I am in no position to judge its historical accuracy, but the portrait rings true. It is a *tour de force* of genius and should not be dissociated altogether from its context. What Solzhenitsyn shows compellingly— and what is surely true—is that at each echelon in a totalitarian state one looks up to someone higher in the system who has one's own fate in his hands and looks autonomous; but in fact they are all unfree, all in terror, all, depending on one's point of view, either pathetic or contemptible, and in the last analysis both.

The wretched film based on *The First Circle* caught at least a little of this point but quite missed its counterpart. In the film only one prisoner stood up to the authorities with defiant autonomy, suggesting that it takes an almost superhuman hero to do that. In the book the scenes that were merged in the film are distributed over several men, and there is no suggestion whatsoever that they are superhuman heroes. Solzhenitsyn suggests forcibly that simple people can have and sometimes do have the requisite integrity.

This does not mean that it is easy to be autonomous, but Solzhenitsyn sometimes suggests that it was easier in the camps than outside. This looks paradoxical, but basically the reason is the same why it was easier for Jews than Gentiles to be autonomous in Nazi Germany. What was needed was a thoroughgoing rejection of the authority of those in power, an uncompromising refusal to accept their views uncritically, a raw independence of judgment. To maintain that stance as long as one had a job somewhere in the system was more difficult by far than it was for those who were, beyond doubt, outsiders.

One of Solzhenitsyn's major novels, *August 1914*, may seem to bear little or no relation to our theme, but in fact those who have written about this novel have missed much of its thrust, and our perspective may make possible a better understanding of it. I began by listing ten strategies of decidophobia, and one was the belief that one rides the wave of the future. In 1940 Anne Morrow Lindbergh published a short book called *The Wave of the Future*, defending an isolationist position. "The wave of the future is coming and there is no fighting it," she said (p. 37). But those who claim to discern the future are often wrong; and an autonomous person might well say: even if this should be the wave of the future, I choose to go down fighting it.

Sartre among many others has called Marxism "the philosophy of our time" and evidently felt that this endowed it with some special authority.[1] If any particular world view were "the philosophy of our time" many people would feel that it was no longer necessary to examine alternatives and what speaks for and against each. For similar reasons, people turn to astrology, oracles, the Chinese *I Ching*, to help them decide what to do—or to find out what will happen anyway, regardless of what we do. Millions find it frightening to face up to the lack of necessity in human affairs.

For the Soviet Writers' Secretariat, which considered Solzhenitsyn's *Cancer Ward* unpublishable as written—they were generous with offers to help him rewrite it!—one of the major provocations was the concluding image of the novel: "An evil man threw tobacco in the Macaque Rhesus's eyes. Just like that. . . ." The provocation was not merely that Stalin was likened to an evil man, but that the author

---

[1] In the opening pages of his *Critique*; i.e., at the beginning of *Search for a Method*. In context, this is a plea for exegetical thinking, as defined in the second paragraph of this essay.

implicitly denied the Marxist philosophy of history and insisted on the element of caprice in human affairs. One does not have to be a member of the Soviet Writers' Secretariat to be dizzied by the thought that what some individual decides "just like that" might determine the misery and death of millions. To avoid this dizziness, people have always found it tempting to believe in a divine government, the stars, or "History."

Solzhenitsyn's opposition to all forms of historical determinism is central in his *August 1914*. Here he develops a view of history that stands squarely opposed to Marxism and to that "Tolstoyan philosophy, with its 'worship of passive sanctity and meekness of simple, ordinary people' " which one of his Soviet detractors had found in his early work. For obvious reasons, the polemic against Marxism is not formulated explicitly, but Tolstoy's ideas about history are rejected expressly. The subtlety and richness of this novel cannot be discussed here, but the points that bear on autonomy can be stated succinctly.

In the first part of *August 1914* the author shows how decrepit, obsolete, and hopeless the Tsar's army was. Soon one feels that there is no need to go on in this vein; the disastrous Russian defeat at Tannenberg was overdetermined, and any one or two of the endless reasons mentioned would have been enough. The reader is led to feel that it did not require the superlative efficiency and technological superiority of the German army to defeat such a wretched force. But then Solzhenitsyn tries to show that if the celebrated German victors, Hindenburg and Ludendorff, had been obeyed, the Russian army would *not* have been encircled and destroyed: the shattering Russian defeat was accomplished by two German generals who disobeyed orders. And the Russian officers who defied *their* stupid orders and fought courageously inflicted serious defeats on the Germans and broke through the encirclement. Solzhenitsyn calls upon his readers to reject the false faith in the wave of the future and to make decisions for themselves, fearlessly.[2]

Yet Solzhenitsyn is far from feeling contempt for those who lack the rare qualities required for successful insubordination and autonomy. His compassion for the sufferings of the less gifted sears the heart. In *August 1914* his sympathetic portrayal of General Samsonov, the commander of the encircled Russian army, becomes one of the glories of world literature precisely when we are shown how a severely limited man dies from the inside out, how despair and death permeate his

---

[2] Even if Solzhenitsyn is mistaken about the date when Hindenburg and Ludendorff took charge, and the orders in question were actually given by their predecessors, the philosophical point remains untouched.

body. Had Samsonov been more independent, defying his orders, he might have avoided defeat and failure; but he had some sense of decency, courage enough to wish to die with his troops and, when that proved impossible, to commit suicide—and he did not tell lies.

Solzhenitsyn's hatred of dishonesty is a physical thing and finds superlative expression in the overwhelming final scene of the book, in which a colonel simply cannot keep quiet even though his explosion may not do any good and is almost certain to ruin him. Nothing in Solzhenitsyn's works is more obviously autobiographical than the description of the feelings of this man. But the same passion for honesty finds succinct expression in an aside in the early story, "Matryona's House": "There was nothing evil about either the mice or the cockroaches, they told no lies."

Autonomy does not entail any "elitist" scorn for simple folk. But it does require courage and high standards of honesty. And it precludes any deference to the wave of the future.

Autonomy is not enough, and there is much more to Solzhenitsyn than autonomy. I have here confined myself to a single theme. But in conclusion I should like to cite one passage from *Cancer Ward* that may lend a little more depth to this all too brief discussion by suggesting another dimension. The passage points to a central motive in Solzhenitsyn's work.

It comes in a discussion between Kostoglotov and a poor woman. It is tempting to quote much of it, but I shall confine myself to the main point. She says:

> School children write compositions: On the Unhappy, Tragic . . . Life of Anna Karenina. But was Anna really unhappy? She chose passion—and paid for passion, that's happiness! She was free and proud! But what if, in peacetime, men in caps and overcoats come into the house where you were born, where you've lived all your life, and order the whole family to leave the house and the city in twenty-four hours, taking only what your weak hands can carry? . . . and your little daughter in a hair-ribbon sits down to play Mozart for the last time, but bursts out crying and runs away,—why should I re-read *Anna Karenina*? Maybe I've suffered enough? Where can I read about *us, about us?*
>
> And although she had almost begun to shout, still her training by many years of terror did not desert her: she was not shouting; it was not a real shout. Indeed, it was only Kostoglotov who heard her.[3]

[3] Aleksandr Solzhenitsyn, *Cancer Ward*, chap. 34, translated by the editor. The corresponding passage may be found on p. 479 of the translation of the novel by Nicholas Bethell and David Burg (New York: Bantam Books, 1969).

It is easy to imagine that someone really spoke this way to Solzhenitsyn. In any case, that is a large part of the burden of his authorship—to write about millions of people whose suffering has remained mute and not reached the ears of the world—millions who have suffered and died under Stalin and Hitler and elsewhere, legions who are still suffering.

In the early fifties Sartre and many others in France were arguing about two seemingly unrelated questions: whether it was permissible to admit that there were camps in the Soviet Union, and whether the novel was dead. At one blow, Solzhenitsyn made these debates ridiculous. Instead of inquiring what might be the artistic form of our time or the wave of the future, he found people crying out to be heard; but as in a nightmare "it wasn't a real shout" and the only one who heard was he. He gave their suffering a voice. That was what mattered, the humanity of it. But to do that required courage, independence, taking his own counsel, pitting his autonomous self against a vast and all but omnipotent system. Being autonomous, he did not simply use old forms; he made innovations; but all that was incidental, and to concentrate mainly on that would have been vanity. What was crucial was that he should no longer be the only one who heard the voice.

Perhaps one must really understand that woman, as one cannot understand her simply on the basis of a brief quotation, to love Solzhenitsyn and to understand his work.

Chronology of Important Dates

1918   December 11: Solzhenitsyn born at Kislovodsk in the North Caucasus. His father, an army officer, had died six months earlier.

1924   Solzhenitsyn and his mother move to Rostov-on-Don, where she supports them by working as a typist and they live in poverty.

1936   Graduation from high school; enrolment at Rostov University (where, in 1937, he submitted an essay on "The Samsonov Disaster" of 1914).

1940   Marriage to Natal'ya Reshetovskaya, a chemist.

1941   Graduation from the University, with a double degree in mathematics and physics. Winner of a "Stalin Scholarship."

1941   Completion of a correspondence course, begun in 1939, at the Moscow Institute of Philosophy, Literature, and History.

1941   October 18: Inducted into the army; ill-health; service as driver of horse-drawn vehicles.

1942   Graduation from Artillery Officers' School. Active service on three fighting fronts until 1945.

1945   Having been already twice decorated, promoted to rank of Captain.

1945   February: Arrest (for criticism of Stalin in intercepted private letters to a friend).

1945   July 7: Sentenced (under Article 58, Sections 10 and 11) to eight years in a hard labor prison camp plus three years' exile.

1950   Writes the *poema*, *Prussian Nights*.

1953   February–March: Release; sent to "perpetual exile" after time in several prisons including a special scientific prison institute *(sharashka)* near Moscow, and three years in the Karlag labor camp in Dzhezkazgan, Karaganda Region. Exile to Kok-Terek in Dzhambul, Southern Kazakhstan.

1954   Spring: Treatment for cancer in Tashkent hospital (an operation having been performed in a camp hospital in 1952).

1954   Writes *The Lovegirl and the Innocent.*

1955   Begins work on *The First Circle*—finished December 1958.

1956   Release from exile, moves to Ryazan, teaches physics and mathematics in a local school—until end of 1962.

1957   February 6: Official rehabilitation by decree of the Supreme Court.

1959   Writes *One Day in the Life of Ivan Denisovich.*

1960   Writes *Candle in the Wind.*

1962   November: Publication of *One Day in the Life of Ivan Denisovich* in *Novyi Mir.*

1963   Publication of "Matryona's Home," "An Incident at Krechetovka Station," and "For the Good of the Cause."

1963   March: Public praise by Khrushchev, in *Literaturnaya Gazeta,* March 12. March 19, public attacks on Solzhenitsyn begin to appear in the press; attacks and defenses continue into 1965, after which the defenders can no longer publish their views, although many defenses appear in *samizdat.*

1963   December: *One Day in the Life of Ivan Denisovich* nominated for a Lenin Prize. In April, the work was removed from the list of nominees.

1963   Begins *Cancer Ward*—finished in 1966.

1964–65   Prohibition of publication of *The First Circle, Candle in the Wind, The Lovegirl and the Innocent.*

1965   November 4: Publication in *Literaturnaya Gazeta* of Solzhenitsyn's article on the Russian language, "You Don't Use Tar to Whiten Cabbage Soup; for That There is Sour Cream."

1966   January: Publication of "Zachary-the-Pouch," last work to appear in the Soviet Union (except in *samizdat*).

1966   November 17: Special Meeting of the Writers' Union to discuss the proposed publication of *Cancer Ward* in *Novyi Mir*; permission refused.

1967   May 16: Open Letter to the Fourth Congress of the Union of Soviet Writers, followed by a second letter to the Union Secretariat, September 12.

1967   September 22: Meeting between Solzhenitsyn and the Secretariat of the Union, followed by an ultimatum to Solzhenitsyn to stop writing letters, followed by more letters from Solzhenitsyn.

1968   Publication in the West, unauthorized by Solzhenitsyn, of Russian and translated editions of *The First Circle* and *Cancer Ward.*

1969   November 4: Expulsion from the Russian Writers' Union; "ratification" by the Union of Soviet Writers. November 12: Public announcement of the expulsion and, on the same day, Solzhenitsyn's letter of protest to the Union.

1969   Begins *August 1914*—finished in 1970.

1970   March 5: Solzhenitsyn engages Dr. Fritz Heeb of Zurich as his only authorized literary agent and legal representative. Confirmed September 18, 1971.

1970   June 15: Letter in defense of Dr. Zhores Medvedev, eminent geneticist, forcibly confined in a mental hospital for political reasons.

1970   August: Solzhenitsyn protests KGB spying on him and persecution of his friends.

1970   October 8: Announcement of award of the Nobel Prize for Literature to Solzhenitsyn; his reply that he will accept the prize in Stockholm.

1970   November 27: Solzhenitsyn writes that he will not go to Stockholm for fear of not being allowed to return home; asks to receive the prize in the Swedish Embassy in Moscow; the Embassy refuses to award the prize on its premises.

1971   June: Publication in Paris, by YMCA Press, of *August 1914*, with authorization by Solzhenitsyn and accompanied by an "Afterword" dated May 1971, explaining why he has for the first time decided to publish abroad.

1971   December 18: Death of Alexander Tvardovsky, poet and editor of *Novyi Mir*; Solzhenitsyn's eulogy, which he could not deliver at the funeral, released in *samizdat*, dated December 27.

1971   Publication of the Autobiography submitted by Solzhenitsyn to the Nobel Foundation in 1970.

1972   March 12–18(?): Lenten Letter to Pimen, Patriarch of the Russian Orthodox Church, pleading that the Church concern itself with the plight of Christians within the USSR.

1972   March 30: Interview with Western correspondents; announces that he is working on the Second "Knot" of *August 1914*, to be titled *October 1916*.

1972   August: Publication of the Nobel Lecture.

1973   April: Divorce from Natal'ya Reshetovskaya; marriage to Natal'ya Svetlova.

1973   August 23: Solzhenitsyn is barred from living in Moscow and denounces Soviet residence curbs as "serfdom."

1973   August 28: Solzhenitsyn tells Western newsmen of threats to his life, which he blames on the KGB. "And since I have not suffered from serious diseases for a long time and since I do not drive a car and since because of my convictions under no circumstances of life will I commit suicide, then if I am declared killed or suddenly mysteriously dead, you can infallibly conclude, with one hundred percent certainty that I have been killed with the approval of the KGB or by it." (*New York Times*, August 29, 1973, p. 8.)

1973   August 30: *Izvestiya*, commenting on the trial of Pyotr Yakir and Viktor Krasin, links Solzhenitsyn's name to the illegal publication, *The Chronicle of Current Events*.

1973   September 6: Solzhenitsyn announces the suicide of a friend, Elizaveta Voronyanskaya, who, after five days of police questioning, had revealed the whereabouts of a copy of *The Gulag Archipelago*.

1973   September: Solzhenitsyn nominates Andrey Sakharov for the 1973 Nobel Peace Prize.

1973   December 20: Publication of *The Gulag Archipelago* I–II. "With a reluctant heart I have withheld this completed book from publication for many years; my duty to those still alive outweighed my duty to the dead. But now that the State Security has nonetheless seized the book, I have no alternative but to publish it immediately."

1974   January: Threatening attacks on Solzhenitsyn mount in the Soviet press.

1974   February 8–13: Solzhenitsyn twice refuses summons to the State Prosecutor's office; he is forcibly arrested by seven policemen, taken to Lefortovo prison, stripped, put into prisoner's uniform, interrogated and charged with treason. Next day he is placed on a plane with security guards; only when it lands does he learn that he has been exiled and is in Frankfurt. He goes as a guest to his friend (and fellow Nobel Prize winner) Heinrich Böll.

1974   March 3: Publication of the *Letter to the Leaders of the Soviet Union*, a somewhat revised version of a fifty-page letter, dated September 5, 1973, and sent by Solzhenitsyn at that time.

1974   March 29: Solzhenitsyn's second wife (the former Natal'ya Svetlova), their three sons and stepson, and his wife's mother arrive in Zurich, where the family is now settled.

1974   May 27: Solzhenitsyn publishes in *Time Magazine* documentation of KGB forgeries of his handwriting, probably designed to serve as evidence at a future trial.

1974   June: Publication of *The Gulag Archipelago* III–IV.

1974   Russian language publication (in Paris) of *Prussian Nights*.

1974   September 1: In an Introduction to *The Current of the Quiet Don* by "D." (an unnamed Soviet scholar) Solzhenitsyn appeals to Western literary scholars to investigate the authenticity of Mikhail Sholokhov's authorship of *Quiet Don*, for which Sholokhov won the Nobel Prize for Literature in 1965. (See *Times Literary Supplement*, October 4, 1974, pp. 1056–57.)

1974   Besides work on *October 1916* and other projects, Solzhenitsyn is writing a film script, tentatively titled "The Tanks Know the Truth," about mutinies in several Soviet camps in the years 1954–59. Announcement is also made of a new quarterly, *Kontinent*, to be published in five languages, including English. The journal will be devoted to works of resident and émigré writers of the Soviet Union and Eastern Europe; its first issue will include greetings from Solzhenitsyn and a previously unpublished excerpt from *The First Circle*.

1974   October: Passage of a bill by the United States Senate conferring honorary citizenship on Solzhenitsyn (an award made only twice in the past, the other recipients being the Marquis de Lafayette and Winston Churchill).

1974   November: Publication in Russian by YMCA Press in Paris of *From Under the Ruins*, a collection of eleven essays on the future of Russia, three of them by Solzhenitsyn himself. In connection with this publication, he holds his first full-scale press conference outside the USSR. For a summarized translation, see A. I. Solzhenitsyn, *On the Future of Russia*, edited and translated by D. Pospielovsky (London, Ont.: Zaria, 1975).

1974   December 10: Solzhenitsyn belatedly receives his Nobel Prize in Stockholm.

1975   February 10: Publication by the YMCA Press of *When the Calf Horns the Oak*, Solzhenitsyn's account of the time from 1961, when he was released from exile within the Soviet Union, through his expulsion from the USSR in 1974. The book reveals that Solzhenitsyn has already completed several screen plays, tales, and a work called *Decembrists without December*. Solzhenitsyn also discusses the sequels to *August 1914*, probably to include *October 1916* and *March 1917* and *R*[evolution?] *1917*, in which Lenin will receive major treatment. The English translation of *When the Calf Horns the Oak* will be published by Harper & Row.

1975   May–September: Visit to Canada and the United States. Attendance at Russian Orthodox Easter services in Montreal; meetings with Dukhobors in Western Canada; award of honorary membership in The Hoover Institution, Stanford, California (where he conducts research on Lenin and the Russian Revolution); major addresses to the AFL-CIO in Washington, D.C. (June 30) and New York City (July 9).The speeches have been published under the title *The Voice of Freedom* (Washington, D.C.: AFL-CIO, 1975).
        A White House official announces that President Gerald Ford has refused to meet with Solzhenitsyn, on advice of the National Security Council that such a meeting would be inconsistent with the policy of détente. After much adverse comment President Ford says that Solzhenitsyn will be welcome at the White House; Solzhenitsyn replies that no useful purpose could be served by a visit, since he sees no hope of dissuading President Ford from going to Helsinki to sign agreements which will "legitimize" the annexation by or subjection to the USSR of formerly independent Baltic, East and Central European states. Solzenitsyn's summer in the United States also includes a visit to the Tolstoy Farm in New York, a center for assisting Russian émigrés and for perpetuating Tolstoyan ideas, under the direction of Tolstoy's only living child, Alexandra L'vovna Tolstaya. Solzhenitsyn visits Vermont, is sighted driving around the state alone, with a Swiss driver's license, in a car bearing Quebec plates; he manages to find Russian-speaking Vermonters of whom to ask directions. He praises the Russian School at Norwich University (Northfield, Vt.) "for your efforts to preserve Russian Culture without the Soviet imprint." While there he fulfills a "lifetime dream" and plays tennis for the first time. Asked if he might make his home in

North America, Solzhenitsyn replies: "I would like some day to make my home in Russia."

1975   October: Publication in Russian by the YMCA Press (Paris) of a nonfictional work *Lenin in Zurich.* (English translation to be published by Farrar, Straus & Giroux.)

1975   October 9: Announcement of the award of the 1975 Nobel Peace Prize to Andrey Sakharov. (See the entry for Sept. 1973.)

Notes on the Editor and Contributors

MICHEL AUCOUTURIER is a professor at the Sorbonne. His published works include *Pasternak par lui-même* and articles on Pasternak, Tolstoy, Akhmatova and Soviet literature. He has also been a cotranslator, into French, of works by Pasternak and Solzhenitsyn.

PATRICIA BLAKE has written widely on Soviet literature. She has edited *Antiworlds: Poetry by Andrei Voznesensky, The Bedbug and Selected Poetry* by Vladimir Mayakovsky, and coedited with Max Hayward *Dissonant Voices in Soviet Literature* and *Halfway to the Moon.*

ROBERT CONQUEST is a specialist on Soviet internal political affairs who has published a score of books on the subject; among them *The Great Terror, The Nation Killers: the Soviet Deportation of Nationalities* and *Courage of Genius: the Pasternak Affair.* He is also a poet: *Between Mars and Venus* (a collection of his own work) and *Back to Life: Poems from Beyond the Iron Curtain.*

VICTOR ERLICH is Professor of Slavic Languages and Literatures at Yale University. He is the author of many articles on Russian literature and of *Russian Formalism, Gogol,* and *The Double Image.*

KATHRYN FEUER is Professor of Slavic Languages and Literatures at the University of Toronto. Her published works include fiction and articles on Tolstoy and Solzhenitsyn, on relationships between the Russian and West European novel, and on Soviet literature.

GEORGE GIBIAN is Professor of Russian Literature at Cornell University. He is the author of many articles on Russian and Czech literature and his books include: *Russia's Lost Literature of the Absurd, The Interval of Freedom: Russian Literature During the Thaw,* and *Tolstoy and Shakespeare.* He is also the editor of critical editions of *Crime and Punishment, War and Peace,* and *Anna Karenina.*

ROBERT LOUIS JACKSON is Professor of Slavic Languages and Literatures at Yale University. Besides his many articles on Turgenev, Tolstoy, and other major writers, he is the author of *Dostoevsky's Quest for Form* and *Dostoevsky's Underground Man in Russian Literature* and has edited *Chekhov: a Collection of Critical Essays* and *Twentieth Century Interpretations of "Crime and Punishment."*

WOLFGANG KASACK is Professor of Slavic Literatures at the University of Cologne. Besides articles on Tolstoy, Pasternak, Chekhov, Rozov and on Russian-German literary relationships, he is the author of several books including studies of Gogol and Paustovsky.

WALTER KAUFMANN is Professor of Philosophy at Princeton University. He has translated much of the major work of Friedrich Nietzsche. Among his many books are *Tragedy and Philosophy* and *Religion in Four Dimensions: Existential and Aesthetic, Historical and Comparative*, to be published in 1975, a work which will include 245 photographs taken by Professor Kaufmann.

ALEXIS KLIMOFF is Assistant Professor of Russian at Vassar College. A coeditor of *Aleksandr Solzhenitsyn: Critical Essays and Documentary Materials*, he has written on Vyacheslav Ivanov and has published translations from Russian into English and from English into Russian.

ROY MEDVEDEV is a Soviet historian, who in 1971 was dismissed from his position as Senior Scholar at the Institute of Professional Education in Moscow. He is coauthor, with his brother Zhores Medvedev, of *A Question of Madness*, and author of *Let History Judge*, a political analysis of Stalinism and *On Socialist Democracy*.

GEORGES NIVAT is Professor of Russian Language and Literature at the University of Geneva in Switzerland. His publications have been chiefly devoted to Gogol, Solzhenitsyn, and Russian Symbolism. He has translated into French *Cancer Ward* and *August 1914* and is now preparing a book, *Solzhenitsyn's Literary Craftsmanship*.

NIKITA STRUVE is Professor of Russian at the University of Paris and the editor of the invaluable periodical *Vestnik RSKhD* (Messenger of the Russian Student Christian Movement). His numerous publications include *Anthologie de la poésie russe* and *Christians in Contemporary Russia*.

Selected Bibliography

Note: This list might be better titled "Supplementary Bibliography" since the many critical works cited in the Introduction to this volume and in footnotes to the articles are not mentioned again here. Nor are the many excellent essays in the Dunlop, Haugh, Klimoff collection listed separately. Only works in English are included.

Belinkov, A. V. "Defense of Solzhenitsyn's *The Cancer Ward*." *Russian Review*, October 1969, pp. 453–58.

Blake, Patricia. *Solzhenitsyn: A Historical Biography*. Forthcoming. Harcourt, Brace, Jovanovich.

Bradley, Thompson. "Alexander Isaevich Solzhenitsyn." In *Soviet Leaders*, ed. George W. Simmonds, pp. 329–39. New York: Crowell, 1967.

Brown, Deming. Review Article: "*Cancer Ward* and *The First Circle*." *Slavic Review*, June 1969, pp. 304–13.

Brown, Edward J. "Solzhenitsyn's Cast of Characters." *Slavic and East European Journal*, Spring 1971, pp. 153–66. Reprinted in Edward J. Brown, ed., *Major Soviet Writers*, pp. 351–66. New York: Galaxy, 1973.

Clardy, J. V. "Alexander Solzhenitsyn's Concept of the Artist's Relationship to Society." *Slavonic and East European Review*, January 1974, pp. 1–9.

Dunlop, John B.; Haugh, Richard; and Klimoff, Alexis, eds., *Aleksandr Solzhenitsyn: Critical Essays and Documentary Materials*. Belmont, Mass.: Nordland, 1973.

Fiene, Donald M. *Alexander Solzhenitsyn: An International Bibliography of Writings by and about Him*. Ann Arbor, Mich.: Ardis, 1973.

Friedberg, Maurice. Review Article: "Solzhenitsyn and Russia's Jews." *Midstream*, August–September 1974, pp. 76–81.

Garrard, John. "The 'Inner Freedom' of Alexander Solzhenitsyn." *Books Abroad*, Winter 1971, pp. 7–18.

Heller, Michael. "The Gulag Archipelago." *Survey*, Spring–Summer 1974, pp. 211–27.

————. "The Gulag Archipelago, Volume 2." *Survey*, Autumn 1974, pp. 152–66.

Kennan, George F. "Between Earth and Hell" [Review of *The Gulag Archipelago*]. *The New York Review of Books*, March 21, 1974, pp. 3–7.

Kern, Gary. "Solzhenitsyn's Portrait of Stalin." *Slavic Review*, March 1974, pp. 1–22.

Labedz, Leopold, ed. *Solzhenitsyn: A Documentary Record*. First published in 1970, the most recent editions of this invaluable work have been published by Penguin Books, 1974, and by Indiana University Press, Bloomington, 1973.

Lourie, Richard. "The Prophet and the Marrano: Two Ways of Religious Being in the Soviet Union." *Social Research*, Summer 1974, pp. 328–39.

Mathewson, Rufus W., Jr. *The Positive Hero in Russian Literature* (Stanford, California: Stanford University Press, 1975). A revised and expanded version, containing three valuable chapters on Solzhenitsyn.

Medvedev, Zhores. *Ten Years After Ivan Denisovich*. New York: Alfred A. Knopf, 1973.

Moody, Christopher. *Solzhenitsyn*. New York: Barnes and Noble Books, 1973.

Muchnic, Helen. *Russian Writers: Notes and Essays*. New York: Random House, 1971. (Chapter on Solzhenitsyn, pp. 400–450.)

Schapiro, Leonard. "Some Afterthoughts on Solzhenitsyn." *The Russian Review*, October 1974, pp. 416–21.

Solzhenitsyn: A Pictorial Autobiography. New York: Farrar, Straus & Giroux, 1974.

Williams, Raymond. "On Solzhenitsyn." *Tri-Quarterly*, Winter–Spring 1972, pp. 318–34. (This volume was also published in a hardbound edition by Holt, Rinehart and Winston.)

Zekulin, Gleb. "Solzhenitsyn's Four Stories." *Soviet Studies* 16, no. 1 (1964): 45–62.